CW00370201

Café Crème Guide
to the
Cafés of Europe

ACKNOWLEDGEMENTS

Thanks are due firstly to our team of researchers who have travelled the length and breath of Europe in search of the finest examples of European café culture.

Thanks also to our editorial team, Alan Greene and Frank Ainscough at Compendium, Peter Long and Nicole Keogan in the office and Adam Baines, Jake Exelby and Paul Cope, for all their input and insight in the writing and design of this year's guide.

For his continuing skill with the camera, thanks go to Leigh Simpson, who has provided the photography that adorns this guide for the fifth consecutive year.

Thanks to you, the reader, for buying this edition of the guide and to those of you who have written to us about your own favourite cafés.

Finally, I would like to thank to our six award winning cafés this year, particularly our European Café of the year, Majestic Café in Oporto, for providing the best in class in food, drink, service and atmosphere.

Roy Ackerman

Published by Compendium
43 Frith Street, London, W1A 4SA, UK

© 2002
Tadema Studios
35 Tadema Road
London SW10 0PZ

A CIP Catalogue record for this book is available
from the British Library

ISBN 1-902579-63-1

Designed by Frank Ainscough
Photography by Leigh Simpson unless otherwise credited
Printed and Bound in Hong Kong through Printworks International Ltd

Contents

Defining the Finest

Your at-a-glance guide to finding the café that's right for you, right now

In the best of all possible worlds, every café would offer mouth-watering food, world-class coffee, jaw-dropping decor and breath-taking views. In fact, as we all know, many cafés build a reputation on excelling in one of the above. And finding the café that's right for you, right now, can be tricky.

Unless, of course, you've got your *Café Crème Guide to the Cafés of Europe 2003* handy. Listing the classic café ingredients under two headings (Food and Mood) we've created an at-a-glance guide to the cream of Europe's establishments.

Look at these pages, or turn to the city section of the country you're visiting, and you'll find the outstanding view, best cup of coffee, finest wine (and many more) highlighted for you with an icon. Pleasure has never been easier.

Enjoy!

FOOD

BEER (**B**) If you class yourself a 'beer hunter', track down these cafés – and bag a trophy or two.

WINE (**W**) In a continent blessed with some of the world's finest wines, these cafés have more than their fair share of them.

PATISSERIE (**P**) Looking for the 'king of croissants'? Visit these cafés for some of the best patisserie in Europe.

COFFEE (**C**) Reviewers who've drunk coffee in over 500 European cafés rate these as some of the best cups available.

FOOD (**F**) Whether it's fine food or elaborate bar snacks – the chefs in these cafés know what they're doing.

MOOD

LIVE MUSIC (**M**) If you like your music live, you'll love these cafés. Phone for details of the best nights/times.

VIEWS (**V**) We rate the views from these cafés as some of the best around.

CHILLED OUT (**Ch**) Looking for a soothing, tranquil café? Relax. You've found it.

UPBEAT (**U**) On the right night, with the right crowd, these places rock. Phone for details of the best nights/times.

DECOR (**D**) Whether ancient or modern, these cafés boast some of the best interiors you'll see.

AUSTRIA
Vienna
Café Diglas **P**
Im Kunst Haus **M**
Café Landtmann **C**
Café Sperl **D**
Valena **Ch**

Salzburg
Niemetz **P**
Winkeler Café **V**

BELGIUM
Brussels
Café Amadeus **F**
Le Corbeau **U**
Poechenellekelder **B**

Antwerp
De Groote Witte Arend **B**
De Muze **M**

Bruges
't Hof van Rembrandt **B**

Ghent
Waterhuis **B**

Liege
Bruit Qui Court **Ch**
L'Elysée **C**

CZECH REPUBLIC
Prague
Café Milena **V**
Kavárna Obecní Dum **D**
Café Patio **U**
La Provence **M**

FRANCE
Paris
La Coupole **D**
Les Deux Magots **V**
Café Marly **D**
Pause Café **U**
Les Pipos **W**

Bordeaux
Chez Ducou **M**
Café La Concorde **Ch**
Café Gourmand **F**

Lyons
Café Chantecler **B**

Nice
Le Grand Café de Lyon **F**
Les Ponchettes **U**

Tolouse
Le Café Bibent **D**
Au Père Louis **W**

GERMANY
Berlin
Café Einstein **D**
Café Leysieffer **P**
Wintergarten im
Literaturhaus **Ch**

Cologne
Café Fleur **C**
Café Reichard **F**

Frankfurt
Café Extrablatt **C**
Café Karin **U**

Hamburg
Brasserie Gröninger **B**

Munich
Arzmiller Konditorei-Café **P**
Café am Beethoven **M**
Faun **F**
Luigi Tambosi am
Hofgarten **Ch**

HUNGARY
Budapest
Café Angelika **V**

ITALY
Rome
Babington's **V**
Antico Caffè Greco **D**
Caffè Palombini **C**
Café de Paris **P**
Il Trimani Wine Bar **W**

Florence
Enoteca Baldovino **U**
Enoteca de Giraldi **M**

Milan
Taverna Moriggi **F**
Le Trottoir **M**

Naples
Bilancione **V**
Mario Daniele **Ch**

Venice
Trattoria Antica Mola **V**
Il Caffè **C**
Cantina Do Mori **W**
Caffè Florian **D**

NETHERLANDS
Amsterdam
Café Ebeling **C**
Inter-Continental Hotel,
American Bar **D**
Café Luxembourg **F**
De Tuin **U**
Twee Prinsen **Ch**

Eindhoven
Trocadero **F**

Maastricht
Grand Café 'in de
Moriaan' **D**

Rotterdam
Café 't Bolwerk **V**

Utrecht
De Morgenster **Ch**

PORTUGAL
Lisbon
A Brasileira **D**
Gambrinus **F**
Martinho da Arcada **C**

Oporto
Majestic Café **F**

SCANDINAVIA
Copenhagen
Drop Inn **M**
Los Flamencos **F**
Langelinie Pavillonen **V**
Opera Caféen **U**
Victor Café/Brasserie **D**

Helsinki
Café Ekberg **P**
Robert's Coffee House **C**
Café Ursula **V**

Oslo
Café Hemingway **B**
Theatercaféen **V**

Stockholm
Engelen/Kolingen **M**
Operabaren **U**
Sundbergs Konditori **P**

SPAIN
Madrid
Café Comercial **D**
Café Gijón **F**
Nuevo Café Barbieri **P**
Café de Oriente **D**

Barcelona
Café de l'Opera **D**
Els Quatre Gats **C**

Bilbao
Serantes **F**
La Viña **W**

Seville
Bar Belmonte **U**
Meson 5J **F**

Valencia
Cafeteria Noel **C**

UK & IRELAND
London
The Arches **W**
Konditor & Cook **P**
Le Metro **F**
Picasso **U**
The Troubadour **D**

Brighton
Browns **F**

Bristol
Tantric Jazz Café Bar **M**
Taverna dell' Artista **F**
The Vintner Wine Bar **W**

Leeds
Café In Seine **C**
Quid Pro Quo **V**

Manchester
Barça **U**
Via Fossa **U**

York
Café Concerto **F**

Edinburgh
The Elephant House **Ch**
Plaisir du Chocolat **P**

Glasgow
Café Rogano **F**

Belfast
McHugh's **M**
Monico Bars **B**
Vincents **C**

Dublin
Kaffé Moka **U**
Oliver St John Gogarty **M**
Thomas Read **C**

In the 300 or so years that the café has been part of human life, there's never been a time when more people enjoyed more cafés in as many countries as now. As a planet, we've decided that the café fits into modern life like a hand into a glove. And we want more of them.

As a result, old cafés are being lovingly restored and stylish new ones are being launched every day. It's a great era for the café-goer.

Except, of course, that the booming number of cafés and our collective passion for travel mean that finding the perfect café (to suit your mood and in the city you happen to be in) is becoming a little harder.

Unless you've got your copy of the *Café Crème Guide to the Cafés of Europe* handy.

Written by café-goers for café-goers, the fifth edition of *Café Crème Guide to the Cafés of Europe* goes further than ever to steer you towards the café that's right for you. Starting out by visiting 50 European cities, we hand-picked the very best cafés in each (and yes, we drank an awful lot of coffee, not to mention the occasional beer and glass of wine). If it's in here, we've been there – and we liked it.

And that's just the start. Among the elite of Europe's cafés, we also steer you towards the places that have a particular area of excellence. It might be the decor, the menu, live music, beer, wine, coffee, the view, or the atmosphere. Check the 'menu' on page 7, and you'll find the cream of Europe's cafés laid out for you on a plate.

So, when you're in Paris and looking for a café with outstanding patisserie – or in Amsterdam and looking for somewhere to party – you're just seconds away from finding the address. And the best way to get there.

As long as you've got your copy of the *Café Crème Guide to the Cafés of Europe* handy.

How to use this Guide

Aims and Ethics
The Guide does not try to be comprehensive in any of the towns and cities included. Every one of the 550 or so cafés featured has been visited at least once by our researchers, but there are inevitably many more which could be worthy of inclusion. We would always like to hear from owners who think their cafés deserve an entry in future editions and from readers telling us about their favourite cafés (see the 'Write Your Own Review' section for a chance to win a great prize).

Information by Country
Countries are listed alphabetically. Each begins with a title page showing the international dialling code from the UK. The country's capital city heads the entries, followed by other towns and cities in alphabetical order. In the UK & Ireland the order is England, Scotland, Northern Ireland and the Republic of Ireland.

Entries
Recommended establishments are listed alphabetically in each town or city. Prefixes such as Bar, Café, The and La are usually ignored; thus Café Bellecour appears under 'B' and Le Cintra under 'C'.

Write your own review

...and win a sumptuous long weekend for two in Oporto, Portugal

In an ideal world we'd all spend our time doing precisely what we wanted, while somebody else picked up the bill. Well, if you win this fabulous prize from the *Café Crème Guide to the Cafés of Europe 2003* you'll be doing just that.

That's right, we're giving away three nights in a four star hotel (bed and breakfast), plus flights, a meal at Majestic Café and £250 spending money.

How to Win
All you need to do is write a review of your favourite café in no more than 100 words. The café can be anywhere in Europe but should not be featured in this edition of the Guide. Please include all the key details of the establishment (address, telephone number and opening hours) as well as your own address and telephone number.

Isn't it time that somebody else started paying for your pleasure? Send us that review!

For the Overall Winner (one prize)
A published review with acknowledgement in the next edition of the *Café Crème Guide to the Cafés of Europe* and a free copy of the Guide. Plus a three night weekend break for two in Oporto, Portugal (including flights, transfers and bed and breakfast in a four star hotel), a meal in Majestic Café – our Grand Award winner – and £250 spending money.

For the runners-up (five prizes)
A published review with acknowledgement in the next edition of the *Café Crème Guide to the Cafés of Europe* and a free copy of the Guide. Please send your review to:

Write Your Own Review Competition
Café Crème Guide
35 Tadema Road
London SW10 0PZ
or fax to: 020 7352 2041
or email to: tadstudios@ukgateway.net

Café Crème Awards

The Café Crème Café of the Year Awards were initiated to recognise and honour the outstanding contributions that the winning cafés have made to their own environments and to society in general by providing the best in ambience, service and style – places to relax with a drink and a snack and reflect on the good things in life.

The Café Crème Café Awards were created to recognise cafés that are outstanding in every aspect of their business: quality of food and drink, welcome, service and decor. *The Café Crème Special Awards*, meanwhile, acknowledge all of the above and also recognise individuality, personality, history and tradition – attributes that can turn a good café into a very special one.

The Café Crème Café Awards are recognised throughout Europe as the supreme awards for café-owners, adding greatly to the prestige and standing of their establishments. Top of the Awards is the *Grand Award European Café of the Year*, this year awarded to Majestic Café in Oporto, Portugal (see page 131 for a full review).

Whether you've come to Austria to ski the world-class pistes in St Anton, wander the museums and parks of Vienna, listen to a star-studded classical concert in Salzburg or take a gentle drive through the vineyards above the Danube, there's one experience that's guaranteed to happen to you in this country – and that's the Austrian café. The façade might take the shape of a magnificent Habsburg building beside Vienna's imperial summer palace; it might be a rustic café in the winelands of Wachau. Whichever you choose, the place will tell you everything you need to know about Austria. The atmosphere will be dignified, but relaxed (you don't run the Holy Empire from 1440 to 1806 without a bit of dignity). The coffee will be sensational (thanks to regular Turkish invasions) and the pastries will be out of this world (only an Austrian winter could have inspired the Sachertorte and apple strudel). Finally, the genteel ambience will be sealed with a discreet soundtrack – the classical genius of Mozart, Haydn, Strauss, Schubert or Beethoven – all of whom lived and worked in Austria, and whose work is performed across the country today. If you ever find yourself hungering for elegance, comfort and calm… head for an Austrian café.

Vienna

As water is to Venice, so coffee is to Vienna. The blest liquid is everywhere, and it keeps the city afloat. With a café tradition dating back to 1683 (when Georg Franz Kolschitzky helped repel a Turkish attack, found some abandoned Turkish beans, and won the right to open the first coffeehouse) Vienna has always fancied itself as coffee capital of the world. Pull up a seat in any of the capital's fragrant cafés, and you'll agree. In the past, the local café scene helped infuse the genius of Schiele and Klimt (their work hangs in the Leopold Museum) as well as 'Waltz King' Johann Strauss. Today, it's the same caffeine buzz that inspires the Danube Island Festival – Europe's biggest youth party in Europe with 2.5 million visitors – as well as the Jazz Festival, Music Film Festival and countless other local shindigs. So just how good are Vienna's cafés? You'll have to come here to find out.

Kaffee Alt Wien
Bäckerstrasse 9 *U-Bahn: U3 Stubentor*
Tel: 1 512 5222
Open: 10.00-02.00 (Fri & Sat till 04.00)
A homely, traditional café tucked away in narrow Baker Street, popular as a local rendezvous during the day. Kaffee Alt Wien is a 'brown' café in many ways: the walls are covered in posters, there are lots of newspapers, and the nicotine-stained paintwork may well have been cream once, but now it's certainly brown. The atmosphere is the main draw to this typical old Viennese café dimly lit with globe lighting. At night it comes to life with a sociable younger crowd. Great goulash.

Bränerhof
Stallburggasse 2 *U-Bahn: U3 Herrengasse*
Tel: 1 5 12 38 93
Open: 07.30-20.30 (Sat till 18.30, Sun 10.00-18.30)
Bränerhof is located close to many of Vienna's important sights: the Imperial Palace, the Treasury, and the famous Spanish Riding School are all nearby, and the Dorotheum auction house, which began operating almost 300 years ago, is around the corner in the company of a number of antique shops. It offers a relaxed coffee house atmosphere, with excellent waiter service and fine cakes and pastries, and on Saturday and Sunday between 15.00 and 18.00 a trio of violin, piano and cello plays gentle music. The cream interior and globe lighting are classic. Inside the tables are marble-topped, while the flowery terrace is a favourite warm-weather spot for enjoying an excellent apple strudel and coffee while browsing through the newspapers.

Café Central
Herrengasse 14 *U-Bahn: U3 Herrengasse*
Tel: 1 533 37 63 26
Open: 08.00-20.00 (Sun 10.00-18.00)
Massive pillars and decorated arches distinguish Café Central, which is situated in the very centre of Vienna in the Ferstel Palace. This was a meeting place for the city's intelligentsia and literary figures at the end of the 19th century and was apparently a favourite haunt of Leon Trotsky. Occupying a point on the fork with Strachgasse, the café has terrace tables secluded from the pavement by potted shrubs. A concert café, with live music every weekday, this is a very smart place, equally popular with locals and tourists.

Demel
Kohlmarkt 14, 1010 *U-Bahn: U3 Herrengasse*
Tel: 1 535 17 17-0
Open: 10.00-19.00
Demel has taken its place in history as the great imperial patisserie, and the setting of rococo mirrors, ornate plasterwork, glittering chandeliers and marble-topped tables is as grand as ever. In 1786, Ludwig Dehne opened his patisserie in St Michael's Square and in 1857 his eldest son passed it on to his chef-patissier Christoph Demel, in whose honour it was later renamed. Meanwhile it acquired the patronage of Emperor Franz Josef I. Demel prides itself on its excellent hand-made delights and the old-fashioned courtesy of the staff. On the list are hors d'œuvre, soup, snacks, sandwiches and pastries, among which *Demeltorte*, filled with glacé fruit, is a speciality; the savoury buffet is an equal delight to eyes and palate. Wines

by the glass, and a very good coffee with cream. At the back of this venerable, much photographed institution is an elegant winter garden.

Café Diglas

Wollzeile 10, 1010 *U-Bahn: U1, U3 Stephansplat*
Tel: 1 512 57 65
Open: 07.00-23.30 (Thur-Sat till 01.00)

The Diglas family have been associated with gastronomy since 1875, when Franz Diglas senior opened restaurants and a casino in Vienna. It was in 1918 that he persuaded his sons Hans and Franz back from America, and in 1923 they opened this café. It's located right behind the wonderful St Stephen's Cathedral in the centre of the city. After the Second World War, artisans, composers and cabaret artists were frequent guests; it then lost its way for a while, and it was not until the fifth-generation Hans renovated the café in 1988 that the original concept and the original look were restored. This famous and much-loved place attracts tourists, the young crowd and the many devoted regulars who sit under the chandeliers and enjoy the superior cakes and pastries, the speciality coffees and the wide selection of teas served in outsize cups. The tinkling of cups and the gentle chat are accompanied by waltz melodies on Fridays and Saturdays. In the same ownership is Kaffe Konditorei Diglas at Fleischmarkt 16, A -1010.

Café Dommayer

Auhofstrasse 2, 1130 *U-Bahn: U4 Hietzing*
Tel: 1 877 54 65
Open: 07.00-24.00

Vienna is cafés, waltzes and Johann Strauss, and it was at Dommayer, then a concert hall, that Strauss made his debut as a conductor in 1844. Here in the 13th district close by the Schönbrunn summer palace, visitors sit on the pretty terrace at the front, in the elegant interior, or in the even prettier garden at the back, where Saturday afternoons in summer bring small classical or waltz concerts. The speciality is five kinds of sausage with sauté potatoes and the highly esteemed sauerkraut, and the café serves a vast selection of coffees.

Café Drechsler

Linke Wienzeile 22, 1060 *U-Bahn: U4 Kelten-Brückengasse*
Tel: 1 5 87 85 80
Open: 03.00-20.00

A long-time favourite with locals, students and market traders, Café Drechsler is located in the lively and popular foodie district of the Naschmarkt, where fruit, vegetables, meat and fish are sold in great variety. The food is fresh and wholesome, and good value for money: soups, main dishes, apple strudel. There are two billiards tables in the lower room.

Frauenhuber

Himmelfortgasse 6 *U-Bahn: U1, U3 Stephansplatz*
Tel: 1 512 8383
Open: 08.00-23.30
Closed: Sun

With a history going back to 1824, Frauenhuber has claims to being the oldest restaurant in Vienna, and it soon became a favourite retreat of civil servants and retired colonels. It's just off the main pedestrian shopping street, but the granite-topped tables with burgundy velvet upholstered armchairs, the oak parquet flooring, and the general air of peace and

relaxation will transport you miles away from its more up-to-date and much less genteel neighbours, and the homeliness and the aroma of coffee are delightfully welcoming.

Café Gloriette
Schönbrunner Schlosspark *U-Bahn: U4 Schloss Schönbrunn*
Tel: 1 879 13 11
Open: 08.00-17.00
Café Gloriette enjoys a most distinguished setting in the park of the Schönbrunn Palace, the summer residence of the Hapsburgs with its 1,401 rooms, and Vienna's equivalent of Versailles. Originally the gatehouse of an even grander palace that was never actually built, it existed only as a folly until 1996, when it opened as Gloriette to acclaim for its impressively ornate plasterwork and huge arched windows. It also won instant praise for its patisserie, all baked on the premises, which can be enjoyed at their smart tables and armchairs inside, or looking at the wonderful gardens from the terrace.

Hawelka
Dorotheerstrasse 6 *U-Bahn: U1, U3 Stephansplatz*
Tel: 1 512 82 30
Open: 08.00-02.00 (Sun from 16.00)
Closed: Tue
An archetypal Viennese art-conscious coffee-house, indeed a rendezvous for artists, and steeped in legend. It still has the feel of the 1950s and 1960s, when it was a haunt of the bohemian set, and the walls are adorned with arty posters and the occasional actual painting. The speciality is the Bucheln, a square brioche-like bun, served hot either with a vanilla custard, or filled with jam, and available from 22.00. A splendidly sociable and evocative place that buzzes with life, Hawelka is café to visit again and again.

Korb
Brandstätte 9/corner of Tuchlauben *U-Bahn: U3 Herrengasse U1, U3 Stephansplatz*
Tel: 1 5 33 72 15
Open: 08.00-24.00 (Sun 12.00-21.00)
On a corner site close to St Stephen's Cathedral and St Peter's Church, this elegant café has down the years been a favourite rendezvous of many of Vienna's famous literary figures. Korb, which means basket, has a 1960s interior, loads of newspapers, and a cabinet of cakes, including their excellent apple strudel. Inside there's a hushed atmosphere, away from the skittle alley, but for noise and bustle there are the terrace tables outside. Live classical music plays from 20.00 to 22.00.

Im Kunst Haus
Weissgerberlände 14
Tel: 1 712 0497
Open: 10.00-24.00 *U-Bahn: U3 Rochusgasse or Landstr.(Wein Mitte)*
Located on the banks of the Danube to the east of the city centre, Im Kunst Haus is in the same building as the Friedensreich Hundertwasser Art Gallery. Cloth-covered tables on a black and white tiled floor look out through tall french windows on to a pretty terrace and a wonderful garden, and even inside there are plants everywhere. The typical coffee-house fare is delightfully enhanced by creative and imaginative cuisine, with a wide

selection of drinks to wash it down. Live classical music is played between 19.00 and 22.00.

Café Landtmann
Dr Karl-Lueger-Ring 4 *U-Bahn: U2 Schottentor*
Tel: 1 532 0621
Open: 08.00-24.00

Entertaining customers since 1873, when it was opened by Franz Landtmann, this has from the start been one the most elegant places to go to in its time, always at the social centre of city life. The café has a very grand and seductive look, with chandeliers, bas reliefs and marble-topped tables. It lies opposite the City Hall, with the National Theatre to one side and the University across the road, so it regularly plays host to politicians, civil servants and students, theatre audiences and their stars. It's well-known for its traditional fare and excellent coffee and pastries, particularly the *marmorgugelhupf* – a circular yeast cake with a hole in the middle dusted liberally with vanilla sugar, and with a marbled appearance from the chocolate flavouring added before baking. Live classical music is played here every Wednesday and Sunday from 14.30 to 17.30.

Café Mozart
Albertinaplatz 2 *U-Bahn: U1, U2, U4 Karlsplatz*
Tel: 1 513 0881
Open: 08.00-24.00

This elegant café has been going for some 200 years, but it came to real fame in the 1940s when it was used as a location in the Orson Welles film *The Third Man*. It's right behind the Vienna State Opera, as any tourist will tell you, and is renowned for its in-house pastries, and its traditional and international cuisine. It's comfortable and spacious inside, but the best spot of all is a table under the awning along the terrace. Classical waltz melodies are played here regularly on Wednesdays and Sundays from 14.30 to 17.30. What no zither?

Café Museum
Friedrichstrasse 6 *U-Bahn: U1, U2, U4 Karlsplatz*
Tel: 1 586 5202
Open: 08.00-24.00

On the corner of Karlsplatz, the café was designed by the Austrian architect Adolf Loos is typical of the plain austere style of his middle years, owing nothing at all to the art nouveau movement that was all the rage at the time. The minimalist interior, with its half-panelled walls, is lit with bright globe lights, and some of the original furnishings are still in place. The terrace tables under their permanent awning are a popular alternative. The look did not appeal to everyone – some called it 'Café Nihilist' – but such notables as Egon Schiele and Gustav Klimt were big fans and spent much of their time here. It's a haunt of regulars, a rendezvous for poets and intellectuals who come to read the piles of newspapers and magazines and set the world to rights. The L-shaped room wraps around the kitchen, which produces the excellent cakes that are the speciality of the house. Espresso and more exotic coffees.

Café Prückel
Stubenring 24 *U-Bahn: U3 Stubentor*
Tel: 1 512 6115
Open: 09.00-22.00
This is a large classic Viennese café with the look and feel of the 1950s. It stands on a corner of the ring road opposite the Museum of Applied Arts and Vienna's City Park. It is also just two shakes from the heart of old Vienna. Prückel serves super home-made cakes and good snacks, and the international newspapers attract a cosmopolitan crowd. For anyone staying or living nearby and feeling lazy, it's a great place to spend a Sunday afternoon (the popular long terrace is in the quiet side street). Card playing is popular, and on Mondays, Wednesdays and Fridays there's live classical music from 19.00 to 22.00.

Café Sacher
Philharmonikerstrasse 4 *U-Bahn: U1, U4 Karlsplatz*
Tel: 1 51 4560
Open: 06.30-23.30
The café of the renowned Sacher Hotel has long been one of Vienna's most fashionable meeting places. It is also the home of the world-famous sachertorte, which was created in the absence of the head pastry chef by the 16-year-old second-year apprentice Franz Sacher for Prince Metternich in 1832. Franz Sacher completed his apprenticeship in Pressburg (now Bratislava) and used the success of his recipe to become a wealthy businessman. He returned to Vienna, opened a delicatessen behind St Stephen's Cathedral and raised a family of three sons and a daughter. In 1876 the middle son, Eduard, bought a new building on the site of an old theatre, took up residence and turned three floors into guest rooms. Thus was the Hotel Sacher born. Today's Sacher pastry chefs use more than 800,000 eggs, 50 tons of chocolate and 40 tons of sugar each year in making the sachertorten, which are exported all over the world. The café's beautifully preserved 19th-century decor, with rich red velvet, brocade curtains, chandeliers, antiques and portraits of the royal family, cannot fail to impress the visitor, who is pampered by the smartly dressed waitresses in their frilly aprons. Classical music is played from 17.00 till closing time in the hall and the red bar. In fine weather the terrace is a popular spot.

Sailer's Gulaschmuseum
Schulerstrasse 20 *U-Bahn: U1, U3 Stephansplatz*
Tel: 1 512 1018
Open: 09.00-24.00 (Sat & Sun from 10.00)
The clue is in the name. It's goulash almost all the way at this splendid little place tucked away in a narrow street not far from St Stephen's Cathedral. Proprietor Herbert Svatunek, with his distinctive moustache and grey ponytail, offers many versions of this tasty, satisfying dish – at least seven of them are always available! At the marble bar counter, with matching tiled floor, you can enjoy a range of five red wines to go with it, or on their own.

Savoy (Café Linke Wienzeile)
Linke Wienzeile 36 *U-Bahn: U4 Kelten-Brückengasse*
Tel: 1 586 7348
Open: 17.00-02.00 (Sat 09.00-18.00 & 21.00-02.00)
Closed: Sun
Behind the ornate facade and finely glazed windows, the Savoy has an elaborate interior of huge mirrors, trompe l'œil ceiling, marble table-tops

and imperial style decor. It stands opposite the Naschmarkt, a vegetable and meat market in the week, but increasingly a flea market especially at the weekend, and its grand appointments seems incongruous with the area. But the Savoy has a soul and drive of its own and down the years many a star has glittered in the sumptuous imperial-style surroundings, including Leonard Bernstein, Rudolf Nureyev and Elizabeth Taylor. Savoy is also called Linke Wienzeile Café, which is embossed over the revolving door on the corner of Köstlergasse; the ivy growing up the front gives it a timeless appeal.

Café Sperl

Grumpendorferstrasse 11, 1060 *U-Bahn: U2 Babenbergergasse*
Tel: 1 586 41 58
Open: 07.00-23.00 (Sun from 15.00)
The charm and character of old Vienna are alive and well in Café Sperl, which triumphantly maintains the appeal of its 1880s origins: old oak parquet floor; to the right, billiard tables made by the court billiard maker; marble-topped tables in all the windows, with the better light to read the papers by; brass chandeliers; a mouthwatering display of cakes; outside tables under a mature leafy oak. This is old Vienna, but is much appreciated by modern Viennese and a much further flung clientele. Herr Staub, third generation of the current owners, keeps a careful watch on proceedings from behind his desk. Coffees, wine, snacks and main meals are served; among the specialities is wiener schnitzel, a dish that originated in Milan before being introduced to Vienna by Field Marshal Radetzky and perfected by Viennese chefs.

Valena

Zirkusgasse 36 *U-Bahn: U1 Nestroyplatz*
Tel: 1 214 5577
Open: 06.00-18.30 (Sat till 13.00)
Closed: Sun
Kurt Valena and his wife are the charming hosts at this friendly little café, which was founded in 1860 as an Imperial Court patisserie. It still has Hapsburg blue walls and floor tiles and in the cellar, still working away hard, is a steam baking oven of 1924 – practically the last of its kind in Vienna. This is a very unusual little café and bakery, complete with armchairs to sit in while you're waiting to be served in the shop. It's a real treat to choose from the vast array of pastries, cakes and bread and then settle snugly into an armchair to enjoy a pot of coffee and one or two tasty delights.

Café Weimar

Währingerstrasse 68/corner of Wilhelm Exnergasse
Tel: 1 317 12 06 *U-Bahn: U6 Währingerstr.- Volksoper*
Open: 08.00-24.00 (Fri & Sat till 04.00, Sun from 10.00)
A grand café dating from 1900, close to the Volksoper, the Vienna State Opera House, and a very popular rendezvous for artists and audiences alike. A shiny black Bösendorfer upright piano has pride of place in the centre of the café, because, on Wednesday and Saturday from 19.30 to 22.30 and on Sunday at 16.30 it's concert time. A visit here makes it clear why Danish pastry is called Viennoiserie everywhere else (even in Denmark!) – it's absolutely delicious! Equally in demand are the splendid breakfasts and the imaginative lunchtime menu.

Salzburg

You have to wait for Christmas for a sip of Samichlaus, the world's strongest lager, brewed once a year near Salzburg. But at any time of year it's a treat to while away the day in this confection of a city, famously the home of Mozart (born here in 1756 and remembered in a small museum) and the scene for much of The Sound of Music (there's a guided tour with taped sound-track). When you've had your fill of Mozartkugeln – the chocolate sweets featuring Mozart's face that adorn every café counter – take the funicular railway to the Hohensalzburg Fortress to hear the notes of its mighty organ, Der Stier (The Bull), bring the hills alive.

Zum Fidelen Affen
Priesterhausgasse 8 *Area: Right bank, north of Mozart Wohnhaus*
Open: 17.00-24.00
Closed: Sun
Tel: 662 877361
Close to the River Salzach, the Mirabell Palace and Gardens, Mozart's House and Holy Trinity Church, this is one of the very best evening places in Salzburg for food and atmosphere. 'Fidelen Affen' means 'The Jolly Monkey', and the walls of this jolly place close to the Salzach River are covered with cartoon pictures and carvings of monkeys up to their monkey tricks. Locals of all ages gather to enjoy an excellent beer or two, either at terrace tables in the pedestrianised street or inside, where there are wooden tables and chairs, solid stone pillars, a brick-paved floor and a circular copper-topped bar under a vaulted ceiling, all adding up to a very Austrian feel in an old building that was once the main post office. Business is particularly brisk on music nights, when customers slake their thirsts and discuss the entertainment. Staff dressed all in blue rush cheerfully about their business, serving drinks and good wholesome food at reasonable prices. The pastries and the goulash with dumplings are particularly good.

Glockenspiel Café
Mozartplatz *Area: Left bank nr tourist information*
Tel: 662 841403
Open: 09.00-23.00 (winter till 19.00)
Closed: last 3 weeks Jan
The Platz and the café are both popular spots on the Mozart tourist trail, located in 'his' square, where an imposing statue of the great man, created by Ludwig von Schwanthaler in 1842, stands facing the café. The café takes its name from the 17th century musical clock that strikes twice a day and never fails to attract tourists. After a hard stint of sightseeing, what better than a glorious ice cream or perhaps a cake and a drink. The interior has something of an art deco look, and *the* place to be is sitting on the first-floor veranda watching the world go by and hearing it as well when there's a live music performance. A full restaurant menu is also available.

Hagenauerstube
Universitatsplatz 14 *Area: Left bank of Salzach by Kollegienkirche*
Tel: 662 842657
Open: 09.00-24.00 (Sun in summer from 15.00)
Closed: Sun in winter
A splendid bierstube/café in University Square, with tables and chairs set out under parasols among the market stalls. Five steps lead down to the bar, where a pils and an excellent fraziskaner weiss beer are on draught and four wines are available by the glass. Visitors can make a wish at the wishing well and set their watches by the sundial, whose steel gnomon (bar) above the

water casts its shadow on to brass Roman numerals on the pavement. Close by is the Collegiate Church, one of the most important sacred buildings in Europe. In the same ownership is Bazillus, a little place with some tables out on the banks of the broad Salzach River that divides the old city.

Humboldt Stuben
Anton Neumayerplatz 4, A-5202 *Area: Left bank nr Blasiurkirche*
Tel: 662 843171
Open: 16.30-02.00 (Fri, Sat & Sun from 11.00)
The name gives no clue that this is actually a tapas bar, with around 40 little dishes displayed on the white marble bar counter and a good range of alcoholic and non-alcoholic beverages to accompany them. Bigger dishes, also with a Spanish flavour, cater for more serious appetites, including a very good paella. Outside, on the sloping square, are five planked levels of folding tables and chairs, Spanish pottery ashtrays and a statue of the Madonna and Child dated 1692. The bar is located close to the Museums of Art History and Natural History.

Café Konditorei Fürst
Brodgasse 13, A-5020 *Area: Left bank nr Residenz*
Tel: 662 843759
Open: 08.00-20.00 (Sun & Bank Holidays from 09.00)
The place for the sweet of tooth, and the birthplace of Salzburg's very own *Mozartkügel*, aka Mozart Balls, a harmonious trio of pistachio marzipan, nougat cream and dark bittersweet chocolate. Apple strudel and the renowned *Salzburger Nockerl*, a soufflé-like sweetmeat of eggs, sugar and raspberries, baked and heaped in three mounds to resemble the three hills of the city, are other specialities, and the goodies are accompanied by an excellent range of teas and coffees, and even a few wines. Fürst stands opposite the renowned Tomaselli (*qv*) in the Cathedral District; the historic Goldsmith's Workshop is close by.

Niemetz
Herbert-von Karajan-Platz 11, A-5020
Tel: 662 843367 *Area: Left bank nr Spielzeugmuseum*
Open: 09.30-18.00 (later during the Music Festival)
Closed: Sun (except during the Music Festival)
Edmund Niemetz, growing up in the tradition that gave Viennese pastries and chocolates their worldwide reputation, opened a pastry shop here in 1890, and in 1930 his son Walter founded the now famous chocolate factory, where the *Schwedenbombe*, known worldwide as Vienna Delights, was developed. This smart, chintzy little patisserie palace is a favourite place of refreshment for singers from the modern Festspielhaus, one of the main venues for the prestigious Salzburg Music Festival, which has been running since 1920. Niemetz was formerly an archbishop's home; it has pink marble floor tiles, marbled pillars supporting the low ceiling, and at the end a small set of organ pipes. Outside, a row of terrace tables stands in a decoratively cobbled courtyard away from the bustle of the square with its famous Horse Fountain. The cakes, the pastries and the speciality hot chocolate all slip down a treat.

Café Streif
Getreidegasse 50 *Area: Left bank, Mozarts Geburtshaus*
Tel: 662 843181
Open: 10.30-01.00 (Sun, Bank Holidays & during the Music Festival 11.00-24.00)
A split-level 1970s café in the Festival District that's heavy on oak, though the sombre feel is alleviated somewhat by mirrors and plenty of lighting. The bar is at the back, with leather banquette sharing the seating with bentwood cane chairs. There is a small terrace outside in the pedestrianised street. Soups, steaks, sausages and sauerkraut head the menu. Some excellent Austrian wines to drink.

Café Tomaselli
Altermarkt 9 *Area: Left bank of Salzach above Residenz*
Tel: 662 844 4880
Open: 07.00-21.00 (Sun from 08.00, Jul & Aug till 24.00)
The most renowned of Salzburg's many elegant cafés, established as a coffee house in 1703. It acquired its magnificent coat of arms 50 years later and was taken over by Karl Tomaselli in the mid-19th century. His father, originally from Milan, had been a tenor in Salzburg before moving to Vienna in 1807, and it was Karl who renamed the place after his family. Tourists and the good citizens of Salzburg are equally charmed by the wonderful marquetry wall panelling, chandeliers, polished oak-block floor, cane-backed chairs, and brass hat and coat and umbrella stands. A girl circulates with cakes on a tray, constantly replenished from the display, which in turn is restocked by their own patissier; in fine weather these goodies can be enjoyed out on the terrace. One of the favourite drinks is weizen gold from a private Salzburg brewery.

Café Wernbacher
Franz Josefstrasse 5, A-5020 *Area: Right bank, east of Mirabellplatz*
Tel: 662 871460
Open: 08.30-24.00 (Sun till 18.00)
When it opened just after the Second World War, this handsome café (note the brass-panelled 'glass' ceiling) specialised in Italian cuisine. Its kitchen has now gone native, but pasta is still on the menu, and the wine list includes Italy as well as Austria and France. Snacks take in soups, sausages, egg dishes and wiener schnitzel. Outside is a terrace of tables under the trees.

Winkeler Café
Mönchsberg 32, A-5020
Tel: 662 847738/9 *Area: Left bank, west of Festspielhaus*
Open: 11.00-23.00
Closed: Monday except in tourist season
Visitors to Salzburg should leave time for the 20-minute walk up Mönchsberg, or they can let the public lift from Anton Neumayerplatz do the donkey work. The view is superb, and the reward for the climb above the Old Town is a rest for refreshment at Winkeler Café with its delightful terrace and tempting ice creams. It's licensed and also has a full restaurant menu, and one of its specialities that alone makes the effort worth while is the spectacular sweet *Salzburger Nockerl* soufflé, whose shape is inspired by the three hills of Salzburg.

BURNING PASSIONS

We all know Sigmund Freud is the father of psychology. Many of us know he enjoyed a cigar. The big question is: did Freud's passion for stogies light his journey into the human soul? Was it smoke that lit the fire?

When you next catch sight of a Viennese café-goer lighting their cigar, consider this simple fact: *some of the world's most original thinkers have stoked their genius with a smoke*.

Edison, Freud, Churchill, Hemingway, Orson Welles and Kennedy to name but a few, all understood how a good cigar can help illuminate the mind. Indeed, scratch beneath the wrapper of history and it seems the brightest moments of these careers happened in the company of rolled tobacco.

Sitting in the relaxed hubbub of a Viennese café, it's time to ask whether the seismic discovery of the human subconscious — made here in Vienna — could have happened without the stimulus of a good cigar?

Welcome to the world of Sigmund Freud. As a man who smoked an average of 20 cigars a day, it's fair to say that the father of modern psychology probably knew as much about *fillers* and *binders* as he did about the *ego* and the *id*. And stogies were there from the start of his scientific journey.

From the autumn of 1902, the unofficial birthday of psychoanalysis, Freud and a group of colleagues met each Wednesday at his home in Vienna to debate the latest research. They smoked like volcanoes.

In full view of Freud's legendary couch, the members of the Vienna Psycho-Analytical Society (as they later called themselves) filled the great man's house with cigar smoke and his ash-trays with stubs. It wasn't that you had to be a cigar smoker to join, you understand, but under the gaze of the great smokestack himself the two sort of went together.

As well as being present at the birth of psychoanalytic theory, cigars rapidly found their way into the consulting room too. Puffing through his sessions with clients, and hidden from view behind a screen, the great man's cigar smoke was the only evidence he was still in the room. As a former colleague and patient de Saussure remembers in *Freud As We Knew Him*, "Contact was established only by means of his voice and the odour of the cigars he ceaselessly smoked."

The stimulating effect of the cured *nicotiana* leaf may well have had a hand in leading Freud to discover the subconscious — arguably one of the most important discoveries of human history. But as to Freud's subconscious relationship with the cigar, the great man left us guessing. "A cigar is sometimes just a cigar," he once said, enigmatically.

The emphasis, we like to think, was on the word "sometimes".

Scratch the surface of Belgium's polished euro-veneer, and you're soon knee-deep in pleasure. You don't, after all, open up you city to the tens of thousands of ex-pat staff of the European Parliament and NATO without providing catering facilities to match. It was only ever a matter of time before Belgium became a gourmet mecca – and they had the head-start of producing over 350 different types of beer. Belgium's heart beats fastest in Brussels, a city with a truly cosmopolitan flavour. Here, café culture is king and endless hours can be whiled away at some of the finest monuments, palaces and cathedrals in Europe. Belgium's love of chocolate is well documented (they make a staggering 172,000 tons each year), but the city is also fast becoming the gastronomic destination of Europe, with a varied cuisine that runs the entire gamut from hearty rustic fare through to wallet-punishing gourmet. The cities of Bruges and Antwerp vie for the claim of housing the most medieval architecture, the largest collections of Old Masters, and the best pavement cafes for people-watching, while a rural alternative to city life can be found in the untouched gorges and timeless villages of the Ardennes.

Toerisme Vlaanderen

Brussels

There's only one way to find out what really makes Brussels tick – and that's over a glass of traditional Lambic beer at one of the many pavement cafes that crowd the Place du Grand Sablon. Besides acting as a showcase for the city's finest architecture, the square doubles as the capital's number one people-watching venue and is within easy striking distance of Brussels' other main attractions, including the Musées Royaux des Beaux-Arts and the capital's most famous statue – the cheeky Manneken-Pis. If you want to know why they call the statue cheeky, you'll have to go and see it for yourself.

Café Amadeus
13 rue Veydt *Metro: Louise*
Tel: 2 538 3427
Open: 18.30-01.00, also Sunday brunch 10.00-15.00
Closed: Mon

A wine bar and restaurant in what was once the studio of the sculptor Rodin. The candle-lit rooms are a mixture of baroque, Greek statues, Venetian chandeliers, lacquer-painted walls, cluttered period furniture (a haberdasher's counter displays the pastries) and a trompe l'oeil of an entire street. Beyond the large double doors is the glass-covered courtyard, where there are two main eating areas, one for snacking, the other for formal meals, and a bar area with high stools lined up against a long marble counter. Casked raspberry beer is a speciality, and there's a good wine list, with plenty available by the glass. Eat as much as you like Sunday brunch is served from 10.00 till 14.00. Produce fresh from the market is used in the cooking, which covers both traditional and modern; oysters in season.

L'Amour Fou
185 chaussée d'Ixelles (on pl Fernand Cocq) *Metro: Porte de Namur*
Tel: 2 514 2709
Open: 09.00-03.00 (Sat & Sun from 10.00)

A long, narrow bar in Ixelles, with a handsome parquet floor and rich wooden counter, its walls hung with works of local painters. A good place to relax in the daytime with a drink, a snack and a look through the newspapers on sticks. Sandwich bar at lunchtime. Good cocktails later on. Passiflore, a tea room in the same ownership as L'Amour Fou, is at 97 rue du Bailly, Tel: 2 538 4210.

A la Bécasse
11 rue de Tabora *Metro: Brouckère*
Tel: 2 511 0006
Open: 10.00-00.30 (Fri & Sat till 02.00, Sun 11.00-24.00)

An 'ancient drinking hall' down a narrow alley, with a spartan bar reminiscent of a German Bierkeller: long tables of scalloped oak, a low beamed ceiling and the bar loaded with glass steins and stone jugs. The draught beers (*gueuze, lambic*) are served in earthenware jugs to accompany some good salads or to enjoy on their own.

Le Corbeau
18 rue St Michel *Metro: Brouckère*
Tel: 2 219 5246
Open: 10.00-01.00 (Fri & Sat till 03.00)
Closed: Sun

A classic Belgian tavern near the Place des Martyrs, a favourite sightseeing spot. Le Corbeau has an amazing variety of glasses – the most spectacular (and potentially the most likely to result in a faceful of beer) is the 50cm high *chevalier*. Food is served until midnight except on Friday and Saturday, when the eating stops two hours earlier and the singing and dancing take over the room and often the tabletops – it gets very lively! Music festival early September.

L'Entrée des Artistes
42 pl du Grand Sablon *Metro: Louise*
Tel: 2 502 3161
Open: 08.00-02.00
One of the many bars on the Place du Grand Sablon, which also has numerous antique shops and a Saturday antiques and bric-a-brac market. And Notre Dame du Sablon is perhaps the loveliest Gothic church in the whole city. L'Entrée is a favourite spot for people-watching – particularly at one of the outside tables. Inside, there's a long oak bar and two floors of wooden tables and chairs. The walls are covered with photographs of actors and other celebrities. Le Patron is a Harley-Davidson fan and organises the occasional HD night, when the street outside is stacked with the machines. Food is served noon till midnight.

Le Falstaff
19-25 rue Henri Maus *Metro: Bourse*
Tel: 2 511 8789/511 9877
Open: 09.00-03.00 (Sat & Sun 09.30-05.00)
Café, restaurant, patisserie, ice cream parlour, banqueting hall – the renowned Falstaff is all these, and is also classified as a Historical Monument, so no alterations can be made for 500 years. Its location two minutes from the Grand'Place and close to the Bourse makes it a popular choice for both Brussels residents and tourists. The café part alone, done out in splendid art nouveau and art deco styles with dark wood and huge mirrors, covers several rooms, and there's a covered terrace at the front. The house tipple is half and half – Gancia with sparkling Luxembourg wine – and there's also a good choice of beers (5 draught, 20 bottled) and a Brittany cider to go with the Belgian cuisine – anything from a snack to a full meal.

La Fleur en Papier Doré
55 rue des Alexiens *Metro: Anneessens*
Tel: 2 511 1659
Open: 11.00-01.00 (Fri & Sat till 03.00)
A dark old locals bar in a 17th-century building, its walls covered with pictures and writings and doodles of Magritte and the Belgian surrealists and Dadaists who once frequented the place. Join the entertainingly mixed clientele and guzzle your *gueuze* with a salad, spaghetti or croque monsieur.

Le Greenwich
7 rue des Chartreux *Metro: Bourse*
Tel: 2 511 4167
Open: 10.30-01.30
A large, bright, old-fashioned bar with art nouveau decor, marble tables and wood panelling. The atmosphere (in the daytime at least) is quiet and intense, partly because many of the customers are giving their full attention to games of chess or Go. Cold snacks keep the brains sharp.

Hallowe'en
10 rue des Grands Carmes *Metro: Bourse or Anneessens*
Tel: 2 514 1256
Open: 12.00-01.00 (Fri & Sat till 02.00)
Closed: Mon
The name of this city-centre bar tells you what to expect: the decorations are mainly depictions of scary monsters and the like (two evil-looking bats

stand on guard at either end of the bar) and the ceiling is covered with Hallowe'en bunting. Tables with candles in skulls are named after Jekyll and Hyde, Dracula and so on. Waiters wear a cassock and hood, but service comes with a smile, and not a fang in sight. On Saturday evenings actors entertain, performing anything from horror stories to love stories, and there are occasional magic shows and screenings of horror films and magic. Food is served till 23.00.

t'Kelderke
15 Grand'Place *Metro: Gare Centrale*
Tel: 2 513 7344
Open: 12.00-02.00
A cellar restaurant in a splendid position on the Grand'Place, one of the most stunning squares in the world. The menu encompasses Belgian specialities including mussels and *carbonnade à la flamande*. Le Cerf, on the same premises, offers lighter snacks and live music.

Café Métropole
31 pl de Brouckère *Metro: Brouckère*
Tel: 2 219 2384
Open: 09.00-01.00
A comfortable, stylish and civilised café in the luxurious turn-of-the-century Hotel Métropole, with lofty ceilings and marble decorations on the walls and tinted mirrors. There's also a terrace on the pavement. A good place to sit in plush-upholstered comfort for a quiet drink and a light bite after meeting, as all Brussels does, in the splendid lobby. The hotel also has a cocktail piano lounge; the house cocktail is L'Italiano, made with grancia.

Pablo's
51 rue de Namur *Metro: Porte de Namur*
Tel: 2 502 4135
Open: 12.00-00.30 (later Fri & Sat)
Closed: L Sun
There's usually a party atmosphere at this glass-fronted restaurant, café and cocktail bar serving all things Mexican, including the background music (they participate in the Brussels jazz rally on the last weekend of May). The usual mix of tacos, enchiladas and quesadillas is on offer plus pitchers of Margarita, a bucket of six beers, several tequilas and a variety of cocktails. Meals are served from 12.00 to 15.00 and from 18.00 to 24.00.

Poechenellekelder
5 rue du Chêne
Tel: 2 511 9262
Open: 11.00-24.00 (Fri & Sat till 02.00)

The name means 'puppet cellar', and owner Michel de Triest's amazing collection of over 600 puppets and mannequins, along with various collector's pieces connected with the history of Brussels, mannekin pis, and old societies like the crossbowmen, still leaves space for a steady stream of customers at Poechenellekelder, a café on three levels with the bar tucked away at the back. He stocks a good range of snacks, including tartines and croques with cheese, paté and ham, spaghetti and the very popular *tête pressée* (brawn). For liquid refreshment, the impressive choice runs to some 40 beers (the strongest is the bottled Bush Beer at 12%), plus fruit juices and genevers (schnapps) with ten fruit flavours, including pear, cherry and melon, and teas, coffees, punches and hot Oxo (!). 70 seats inside, with a further 50 on the pavement in the summer. Jazz music.

Au Soleil
86 rue du Marché au Charbon *Metro: Bourse*
Tel: 2 513 3430
Open: 10.00-02.00

Once a men's clothing shop, now a café tailor-made for a pause for a drink and a snack, particularly in the summer at an outside table in the traffic-free cobbled side street. Outside are some original signs; inside, the decor features some splendid old ads and wooden fittings. Busiest in the evening.

Sounds
28 rue de la Tulipe *Metro: Porte de Namur*
Tel: 2 512 9250
Open: 11.30-04.00 (Sat from 19.00)
Closed: Sun & midsummer

A well-loved bar behind Place Fernand Cocq, with live jazz several nights a week and a cosmopolitan crowd of regulars. Note that the café is closed in mid-summer, traditionally re-opening on October 1st with a major jazz event. Sounds is owned by an Italian from Umbria, so specials include Italian dishes. If the summer is hot they stay open later, bringing the large garden into use. If the weather is bad, they go on holiday!

De Ultieme Hallucinatie
316 rue Royale *Metro: Botanique*
Tel: 2 217 0614
Open: 11.00-02.00 (Sat from 16.00, Sun from 15.00)
Closed: Sun

The area is not the most exclusive in the city, but this is certainly one of its most famous addresses, with marvellous ornate art nouveau decor in a well-preserved period house and a fiercely Flemish heritage. It scores on several levels – a tavern for classic Belgian snacks and Belgian beers, a more formal restaurant, a night club in the converted stables. It's a favourite business person's rendezvous at lunchtime, while early in the evening a different crowd stops for refreshment en route to the Opera House.

Antwerp

To really get under Belgium's skin there's no better place than Antwerp. As well as 'doing history' very well in the historic central Grote Markt, the city also manages to act as a magnet for the cream of Belgium's artists and designers. Consequently, café culture is booming and the nightlife is unparalleled. Daytime also has plenty to offer with two museums (Provincial Diamond Museum and Grobbendonk Diamond Museum) celebrating the city's 85 per cent share of world trade in uncut stones; the largest Gothic cathedral in Belgium; and the Rubenshuis, former home of the city's most famous son, Pieter Paul Rubens.

DEN BENGEL

5 Grote Markt *Area: On main square (Grote Markt)*
Tel: 3 233 3290
Open: 09.00-03.00

This large city-centre bar is one of the oldest in the Grote Markt (Grand-Place), with an unusual and amusing feature of cameo portraits of the customers when they were babies! Known as the chatterbox bar or chattering café, Bengel means 'rascal' and indeed some of the rascals' rascal children have grown to be customers and their photos are also on the walls. On the first floor is a big room for parties.

Café Beveren

2 Vlasmarkt *Area: Southwest of cathedral*
Tel: 3 231 2225
Open: 12.00-late (Fri & Sat very late!)
Closed: Tue

The place where music fans congregate for a spot of nostalgia and a glass or two of beer — the speciality is their own Bolleke Koninck. There's an amazing 60-year-old pipe organ here, with a repertoire of 37 played in strict rotation. In the front are a piano accordion, a saxophone, drums and lights — a fully working piece of inter-war music technology in this funny little bar with a terrace on the corner of the quay (Van Dijckkai). At the other end is an old juke box with songs from the 1950s and 1960s.

La Cirque Belge

13-14 Van Dijckkai *Area: Eastbank of Scheldt, SW of Grote Markt*
Tel: 3 232 9439
Open: 10.00-02.00 (Sat & Sun till 05.00 or 06.00)

A long-established bar, recently renovated but retaining its character, and also a restaurant specialising in mussels, waffles and pancakes. It also boasts 85 of Belgium's best beers behind its spacious horseshoe-shaped counter. And on Thursday, Friday, Saturday and Monday there's live music, the space vanishes and the place is packed.

De Groote Witte Arend
18 Reyndersstraat *Area: Southwest of cathedral*
Tel: 3 226 3190
Open: 11.30-24.00 (Fri & Sat till 02.00)
Closed: Tue (also Wed in winter)

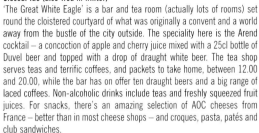

'The Great White Eagle' is a bar and tea room (actually lots of rooms) set round the cloistered courtyard of what was originally a convent and a world away from the bustle of the city outside. The speciality here is the Arend cocktail – a concoction of apple and cherry juice mixed with a 25cl bottle of Duvel beer and topped with a drop of draught white beer. The tea shop serves teas and terrific coffees, and packets to take home, between 12.00 and 20.00, while the bar has on offer ten draught beers and a big range of laced coffees. Non-alcoholic drinks include teas and freshly squeezed fruit juices. For snacks, there's an amazing selection of AOC cheeses from France – better than in most cheese shops – and croques, pasta, patés and club sandwiches.

Jan Zonder Vrees
2 Krabbenstraat/8 Palingbrug *Area: Northwest of Grote Markt*
Tel: 3 232 9080
Open: 09.00-01.00 (Fri & Sat till 03.00)

Jan Zonder Vress, 'Fearless John', is a character remembered in ancient legend. The 14th-century story goes that one day, to test his fearlessness, John's cousin dressed up as a ghost to frighten John. Fearless John ran him through with his sword and immediately saw what he had done. Not knowing what to do, he ran away. On his journey he took up many just causes, made a good name for himself and returned a hero to the people of Flanders. One of the favourite dishes at this popular place by the Grote Markt in Old Antwerp is the Jan Zonder Vrees omelette, and there's a well-priced menu of the day. Good coffees, five beers on draught, 30 bottled.

Kathedraal
17 Handschoenmarkt *Area: Next to cathedral*
Tel: 3 232 4014
Open: 11.00-24.00 (Sat & Sun till 01.00 or 02.00)
Closed: Wed in winter

A small modern bar next to its restaurant. It has a simple lunch menu – fish soup, croques, salads of speck/chicken/smoked fish, prawns, croquettes, baguette sandwiches, omelettes. The pleasant pavement terrace is typical of the cafés found in squares all over Europe, but still sadly rare in the UK.

Kulminator
32-34 Vleminckveld *Area: South of Police HQ*
Tel: 3 232 4538
Open: 11.00-24.00 (Sat from 17.00, Mon from 20.00)
Closed: Sun, New Year & early Aug

In a side street five minutes' walk from the historic centre, Kulminator is the HQ of OBP, a beer consumers' organisation, and the list of beers is of epic length: there are some 600 of them, all served in their own glasses at the proper temperatures! One of them is the German beer Kulminator, served very cold in a small glass mug. Some of the bottled beers (*gueuze*) are served in a basket as with an old Burgundy; indeed, there are vintages going back to 1979. Behind the bar is a hotchpotch of stacked beer crates of all different kinds, and shelves loaded with ranks of bottled beers lined up like soldiers. Classical music plays gently in the background, and people sit reading the newspapers at scrubbed wooden tables. Cold snacks of bread and cheese or sausage are always available. Outside seating.

De Muze

15 Melkmarkt *Area: Just east of cathedral*
Tel: 3 226 0126
Open: 12.00-04.00

A well-known jazz café – the music starts at 22.00 every day except Sunday – but even then there's music if the players feel in the mood. De Muze is on four levels; the ground floor has bare red brickwork with a broad oak bar and cane chairs, while in the open-plan upper levels the chairs are bentwood. Drinks include six draught beers and a big choice of bottled beers and genevers, and there's a variety of snacks and light meals (croque monsieur, chili con carne, moussaka, apple tart).

Paeters Vaetje

1 Blauwmoezelstraat *Area: Opposite cathedral*
Tel: 3 231 8476
Open: 11.00-02.00 (Fri & Sat till 05.00)

Beer drinking is taken very seriously in Belgium, and the 100 beers served at this small split-level bar all have their own particular serving glass, complete with imprinted logo! The glass shelves behind the old marble-topped mahogany bar are stacked with them. Two narrow spiral staircases lead up to the mezzanine and upper-floor levels, where the tables are old four-seater marble-topped mahogany types and the ceiling's exposed mahogany beams reflect the early trading days with the Far East. An old stove heats the place in winter, and the excellent home-made soups provide further warmth. The snack menu is supplemented by blackboard specials.

Pelgrom

15 Pelgrimstraat *Area: South of Handschoenmarkt*
Tel: 3 234 0809
Open: 12.00-01.00

The entrance leads from the cobbled street down some stairs to vaulted cellars which for many centuries were used by merchants to store their wares for the two annual fairs held in Antwerp. There is a private museum (open weekends) where you can see how the burghers lived in the 16th century. Service at Pelgrom is by waiters dressed in costumes that could have been painted by Brueghel. Specialities: food is Belgian-French cuisine; beers include Poorters and Pelgrom Grand Cru; excellent coffees.

De Vagant

25 Reyndersstraat
Tel: 3 233 1538
Open: 11.00-02.00 (Sun from 12.00)

In business for 460 years, this prestigious bar is very proud of its stock of 220 Belgian gins. In a side street close to the Cathedral, it is a serious place, where classical music plays and, sitting at long wooden tables on wooden chairs, you can read the daily and weekly papers and drink genevers (or beer or other spirits). The house cocktail is a mixture of white and lemon genevers, boosted by other liqueurs and fruit juices. Next to the bar, and at the entrance, are a shop and a restaurant in the same ownership.

SILENCE IS GOLDEN

With the average Belgian drinking 150 litres of beer a year – and with over 500 varieties to choose from – you'd think there'd be a lot of squabbling over who gets to wear Belgium's 'brewing crown'. But ask any local and you're guaranteed one answer... the Trappist monks

If only silence was always this fruitful. Visit one of the biggest beer drinking nations on the planet, and you'll discover that Belgium's favourite tipple is the result of centuries of silent contemplation. Dig a little deeper, and you discover that the taste and science behind these unique beers is inextricably linked with the history of the Trappist monks.

CAUGHT IN LA TRAPPE
Ever since the Last Supper, wine has been associated with Christianity – and monks have tended vineyards to make Communion wine. The Trappists were no exception. In the Middle Ages, an Abbot named Armand-Jean de Ranc was so fed up with the hypocrisy of the established church that he broke away from the Cistercians to form a stricter order. Based at La Trappe (hence 'trappist') in Normandy he followed the strict laws of St. Benedictine. Meat was banned, days were to be spent in silence – and there was no mention of beer.

FROM GRAPE TO GRAIN
While the Trappists went about their silent lives, Napoleon had his sights set on the church and soon monastic life in France was all but destroyed. The Trappists fled to Belgium where they found fields sown with barley and wheat rather than vines. Wine wasn't readily available and so they turned to the native brew – beer. The monks quickly became specialists in brewing, perhaps because they had more time than most to mull over the process, but also because they had the education to develop their craft scientifically.

AGEING GRACEFULLY
While the beer varies from monastery to monastery (there are six in Belgium) each order brews to the same recipe. Above all, every monastery uses live yeast and caramelised sugar in the brew-kettle – prompting re-fermentation in the bottle and a beer that gets better with age. From the drinker's point of view, that produces 'doubles' weighing-in between 6 and 9%, and mighty 'triples' that can pass the 11% mark. If sipping a glass of Trappist beer feels more like a four-course meal than a drink – it's no accident. Historically the beers were regarded as 'liquid bread' and used to see the monks through periods of fasting. Lent must have been wonderful.

CREAM OF THE CROP
Chimay (Abbaye Notre Dame de Scourmont)
As the first beer to be labelled, it's not surprising that Chimay is also the biggest seller. If you want to push the boat out, try a magnum bottle of Blue Grande Réserve – aged for a minimum of five years.

Orval (Abbaye Notre Dame d'Orval)
Orval is Belgium's oldest brewing monastery, and the only one open to the public. According to legend, Orval was built by an 11th century Countess, who dropped her gold ring in a local lake and swore she would build a monastery if she could get it back. Minutes later a trout jumped out of the water with the ring in its mouth – hence the logo.

Bruges

Having climbed the 366 steps that lead to the top of Bruges' central Belfort, it's difficult to over-hype the view that greets you. A mosaic of winding streets, slender canals and medieval architecture all confirm the city's claim of being the 'Venice of the North'. Back on ground level the best way to see Bruges is by canal boat. You can hop on and off the boats at will to visit some of the numerous museums and galleries – notably the Groeningemuseum, home to possibly the best collection of Flemish art in the world, and the Melmingmuseum, housed in a medieval hospital. In between cultural 'hits', why not while away a few hours with a glass of Flemish beer in a canalside café?

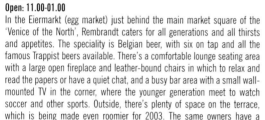

't Hof van Rembrandt

10 Eiermarkt *Area: Off the Markt (Large square)*
Tel: 50 33 7450
Open: 11.00-01.00

In the Eiermarkt (egg market) just behind the main market square of the 'Venice of the North', Rembrandt caters for all generations and all thirsts and appetites. The speciality is Belgian beer, with six on tap and all the famous Trappist beers available. There's a comfortable lounge seating area with a large open fireplace and leather-bound chairs in which to relax and read the papers or have a quiet chat, and a busy bar area with a small wall-mounted TV in the corner, where the younger generation meet to watch soccer and other sports. Outside, there's plenty of space on the terrace, which is being made even roomier for 2003. The same owners have a restaurant at 17 Eiermarkt.

Taverne Curiosa

22 Vlamingstraat *Area: 2 mins walk north of Markt*
Tel: 50 34 2334
Open: 10.00-01.00 (Sat till 02.00, Sun 12.00-24.00)

A stairway just off the main market square leads down to a medieval cellar with an oak bar and leather-bound straight-backed chairs at oak tables. It's a spacious bar-restaurant in two rooms with low, vaulted ceilings and a stone-flagged floor. They serve some 60 beers, five on tap; grills are a popular choice at lunchtime, after which tea is served; snacks are available up to 30 minutes before closing. Seasonal mussels are always worth ordering.

't Zwart Huis

23 Kuiperstraat *Area: Just north of Eiermarkt*
Tel: 50 34 1516
Open: 18.00-02.00 (later Fri & Sat)
Closed: Sun

When the soot-black brickwork was given a major clean and the whole premises refurbished some years ago, the name (The Black House) stuck. Steps lead into the principal room, which has, in the far corner, a long oak bar set with bar stools. The high beamed ceiling also looks down on another very spacious room with stout wooden tables and chairs on a solid wooden floor. Food is served in one part, and on Monday there's salsa dancing upstairs. The bar is a popular spot with the cast after the show is over at the theatre next door.

Ghent

If you believe what many of the guidebooks say, then the very best Ghent has to offer is standing in front of Jan and Hubert Van Eyck's celebrated altarpiece 'the Adoration of the Lamb'. But with the largest number of listed buildings in the country, including two medieval castles, five abbeys, 59 churches and 19 museums it's difficult to see how a single painting can make it to the top spot. In the old town, meandering waterways prove a serene means to soak up Ghent's unique atmosphere, and any sights that can't be reached on water can be visited by horse-drawn carriage. It's no wonder that for many, Ghent proves the highlight of their trip to Belgium.

Dreupelkot
13 Groentenmarkt *Tram: St Veerleplein*
Tel: 9 224 2120
Open: 11.00-02.00 (or even later)
The best place in Ghent for lovers of genevers. There are more than 180 Belgian gins with a multitude of flavourings (orange, lemon, passion fruit…) and strengths (30%-54% abv). This is where the owner serves; his restaurant is next door and there's a beer bar at the end. You can see a caricature of him on the arch over the side passage entrance to the place. The room has bare brick walls, a shelf down one side and plain wooden bar across the end, and an upturned barrel in the middle to rest your drink, unless you do the right thing and knock it back in one!

't Galgenhuis
5 Groentenmarkt *Tram: St Veerleplein*
Tel: 9 233 4251
Open: 12.00-03.00
Closed: Mon
Probably the oldest and smallest café in Ghent; its name means 'the gallows', and it was the 17th-century gallows house in the vegetable market. Today's visitors hang around for snacks served in the pretty little bar, while those in search of a full meal head downstairs into the basement where, below the level of the River Lys, the restaurant is open lunchtime and evening. On the beams are some bon mots such as 'Don't talk too much or you'll hang yourself'. Outside terrace.

Waterhuis

9 Groentenmarkt *Tram: St Veerleplein*
Tel: 9 225 0680
Open: 11.00-02.00 (Fri & Sat till 03.00 or 04.00)
A pretty bar down a cobbled terrace by the River Lys. It stocks 160 beers, with lots on tap, so the students who frequent the place have plenty of choice. Sandwiches and snacks and nourishing soups are available here, while for a bigger meal the sister restaurant is just next door.

Liège

Wandering the cobbled streets around Place St-Lambert, it's easy to think you've found provincial Belgium. Don't be fooled – life in Liège is distinctly up-tempo. Alongside the historic centre you'll find some of the best café culture and nightlife in the country – a happy by-product of Liège's university. A walk up to the citadel gives you a birds-eye view of the city, from where it's easy to pick out the magnificent Cathédrale St-Paul and the equally stunning Palais des Princes-Evêques. Shopaholics should visit on a Sunday when a mile of the river Meuse's embankment is transformed into La Batte flea market.

La Brasserie Cathédrale
pl de la Cathédrale *Area: Place de la Cathédrale*
Tel: 04 222 1386
Open: 08.00-24.00 (Fri & Sat till 02.00)
A classic French-style brasserie with tables set out under plastered beams. Outside there are lots of wicker chairs and tables where people take breakfast or a coffee or aperitif in the evening sunshine. The terrace is heated, and in December parents can watch their children ice-skating in the square from there or from the upstairs room. To eat: sandwiches, salads, grilled sausages, kebabs, crêpes, omelettes. To drink: five draught beers, 30 bottled, lots of spirits, French wines.

Bruit Qui Court
142 bd de la Sauvenière *Area: 4 mins walk from L'Église St Jean*
Tel: 04 232 1818
Open: 11.00-24.00
An air of civilised calm prevails in the lofty mid 19th-century Grande Salle with vaulted ceiling, large ferns, subtle lighting, soothing Latin-American music and charming service. There's a good choice on the menu, and a very good French wine list. A comprehensive range of beers, too, and coffee from Colombia, Kenya, Ethiopia and Jamaica. The coffee is served with a dish of whipped cream, salt, condensed or evaporated milk and a piece of chocolate.

Les Carmes
2 rue Saint-Gilles *Area: Southwest of cathedral*
Tel: 04 223 6435
Open: 24 hours
However late the party ends, Les Carmes is ready for the survivors: it's open 24 hours a day, every day of the year. Their breakfasts are legendary, with eggs fricassee providing the sort of early morning sustenance that's just what the doctor ordered after a night's merrymaking. Later perhaps a glass of Rivaner from the Mosel, a beer or a coffee – all served with a welcome smile.

Danish Tavern
1 rue Pont d'Avroy *Area: Just east of cathedral*
Tel: 04 222 3343
Open: 08.30-24.00 (Fri till 01.00, Sat till 02.00)
There are naturally some Danish specialities on the menu in this tavern, while among the drinks the influence is wider: French, with lots of Burgundian liqueurs and marcs; Scottish, with beer and 15 Scotch whiskies; Irish, with beer sold by le half and le pint. But in the morning it's time for breakfast and here they're ready to serve you coffee and offer a newspaper to read. A lot of oak is used in the tavern (floor, staircase, bar top) and decorative features include Bergerac blue glass bottles on the shelves.

L'Elysée *Area: East of cathedral, junction with Rue Pont d'Avroy*
153 bd de la Sauvenière
Tel: 04 222 2393
Open: 09.00-24.00 (Sun from 10.00, Sat 10.00-02.00)
They dub themselves 'un coin de Paris à Liège' – a corner of Paris in Liège.
The brasserie is at the junction with Rue Pont d'Avroy, a main shopping street
leading from the Cathedral. It is on two floors, ground and basement, with
floor-to-ceiling windows at street level giving a great feeling of space. A long
oak bar with the patina of age is set with leather-upholstered bar stools, and
there's a heated terrace on the boulevard. Here the best-dressed Liégeois
come for refreshment – wines, beers and their speciality, *café liégeois*, a
dessert of coffee, ice cream and whipped cream. They have coffee from
Sumatra, Columbia, Kenya and Ethiopia! Friday night is music night.

A Pilori
7 pl du Marché *Area: Opposite Town Hall*
Tel: 04 222 1857
Open: 09.00-23.00 (Sat 10.00-24.00, Sun 10.00-20.00)
In a building dating from 1632, this is one of the city's best known and best
loved cafés. It stands in the old market place right opposite the Town Hall
and has been at the centre of political life through the ages; it's also a
favourite with legal people from the nearby Palais de Justice. The bar front
is made of carved oak, and there are small oak tables and chairs sitting on
a flagstoned floor; the ceiling has seriously old exposed beams and posts to
support them. A covered terrace is used in summer. Snacks include croques
and baguettes, and at lunchtime soup, omelettes, pasta and steaks.

La Taverne St Paul
8 rue Saint Paul *Area: Next to cathedral*
Tel: 04 223 7217
Closed: Sun
Open: 10.00-02.00 (or even till 05.00!)
A well-established bar, perhaps the oldest bar in Liège, certainly the oldest
in its original state. Here's where the bourgeois start their evenings with a
beer before going on to the main entertainment – or perhaps staying here,
as this is a place with bags of character: beautiful rose aurore French
marble fireplaces, handsome wood panelling and furniture, marble-topped
tables, outside seating, delightful staff. Saturday night piano bar. As its
name suggests, the tavern is close to the Cathedral of St Paul, built at the
beginning of the 19th century to replace an earlier building destroyed by
revolutionary French guards.

Some countries trace their history through their architecture; others through works of art. The Czechs do buildings and books as well as anybody – but if you want to feel the true pulse of the nation, reach for a beer.

Sip from a chilled glass of Pilsner Urquell or Budweiser Budvar and you're drinking liquid history.

Through centuries of invasions and occupations, Czech brewers simply kept doing their stuff. The town of Pilsen (now Plzen) got so good at it that their 'pilsner' is copied the world over. The citizens of Budweis (now Ceské Budejovice) made their own contribution to global history in 1265 with a brew that still inspires countless good times… and international law suits. Both cities are well worth a visit.

Look through the golden prism of your glass of beer, and there's much else to marvel at in this wonderful country. The romantic time warp that is Prague, the turreted hamlets of Bohemia, the enchanting spa towns of Carlsbad and Marienbad (now Karlovy Vary and Mariánske Lázne). But in the company of the thirstiest beer-drinkers on the planet – sinking 160 litres a year per head – there's one Czech experience you can't refuse. Standing on Charles Bridge at sunset, or strolling the cobbles of a Bohemian town, you know that history is calling you to the bar.

Prague

Sitting in the sun-drenched slice of history which is Prague's Old Town Square, you might find yourself wondering which corner of the city to treat yourself to next. Don't think too long. One of the charms of pocket-sized Prague is that you can be there almost as fast as you can find it in the guidebook. Whether you cross the open-air museum that is Charles Bridge and head for the castle, stroll the boulevards of Wenceslas Square or meander the alleys of the Old Town, everything is just minutes away. And because it's Prague, every street will take you past more timeless buildings, more history, and more great cafés. Enjoy!

Café Archa

Na Porící 26, Prague 1 *Metro: Námestí Republiky or Florenc*
Tel: 2 23 24 149
Open: 09.00-21.00 (Sun from 13.00)

Pictures and posters with rock music and theatrical themes provide the main decorative inspiration at this modern Old Town building on two levels. Serving office workers and local residents, it's a café in the modern style doing a good trade in cakes, coffees and snacks.

Grand Hotel Europa Kavárna

Václavské nam 25, Prague 1 *Metro: Mostek or Muzeum*
Tel: 2 2422 8117
Open: 07.00-24.00

The most beautiful building on Wenceslas Square, the Hotel Europa dates from 1889, when it was called the Archduke Stephan. However, between 1903 and 1905 it was completely renovated in the art nouveau style by well-known architects Bendelmeyer Hüschmann & Letzel, a firm which exists to this day. The upper part is a hotel, while the ground floor is occupied by the spacious café with its oval gallery. The chandeliers and wall lights are now fed by electricity, but the light is subdued, keeping the warm glow that it always had. More substantial meals can be had in the main restaurant. Outside, on either side of the entrance, there are raised terraces with smart brass chairs and tables where you can watch the elegant passers-by.

Café Franz Kafka

Siroká 12, Prague 1 *Metro: Staromestská*
Tel: 2 231 8945
Open: 09.00-21.00 (Fri & Sat 10.00-22.00)

The Jewish Czech writer Franz Kafka was born in Prague in 1883, when the city was in Bohemia, and this café is located in the Jewish quarter. Its grained panelled walls and booths with their dim lighting somehow reflect the writer's dark humour. The floor is tiled, the bar stands to the right, and there are some outside tables. Around the walls are some of Kafka's bons mots, some in German, his chosen language, some translated into Czech. Traditional fare includes goulash soup, chicken stew and rice, and there are some well-priced wines.

FX Café

Belehradská 120, Prague 2
Tel: 2 25 12 10 (office)
Open: 11.00-06.00

This long-hours café attached to the Radost night club serves excellent vegetarian snacks including pitta bread sandwiches, pizzas, nachos and good pastries. Somewhat narrow and a bit cramped, it relies on a quick turnover. Sunday brunch and poetry readings. Ten minutes walk from Wenceslas Square.

The Globe Bookstore and Coffee House

Pstrossova 6, Prague 1 *Metro: Národní trída or Karlovo námestí*
Tel: 24 91 62 64
Open: 10.00-24.00

A long-established bookstore-cum-coffee shop that's a favourite with expats with its impressive selection of English-language books. The atmosphere is always welcoming and friendly, and the buzzy café serves home-made sandwiches, bagels, salads, cheesecake, apple pie and other

goodies. There are monthly readings by budding authors, and the café has a number of internet computers and laptop connections.

Café Imperial
Na Porící 15, Prague 1 *Metro: Náměstí Republiky*
Tel: 2 231 60 12
Open: 08.00-01.00
Built in 1914, the café occupies the ground floor of the hotel. It was particularly innovative at the time, the high walls and ceiling decorated in pierced ceramic, depicting hunting scenes and the flora and fauna in Eastern Europe. Immediately after the Second World War, it was commandeered by the upper communist echelons as their own refreshment venue and to entertain like-minded foreign dignitaries, and closed to the public. After the fall of the communist regime in 1989 there was a dispute as to its ownership, and until April 2000 it remained entirely closed. The café part is open again, serving traditional fare at kind prices in a very special atmosphere.

Café Louvre
Národní trída 20, Prague 1 *Metro: Staroměstská*
Tel: 2 29 72 23/29 76 65
Open: 08.00-late
Café Louvre was established in 1902, but was closed between 1948 and 1992 when the socialists regarded it as being bourgeois and therefore unsuitable, so it was used as offices. Today it has been restored to its former elegant condition and offers a broad choice of coffees and Czech, American and English breakfasts, and a wide selection of other dishes during the day, including some for vegetarians. A parlour is available for hire, with a non-smoking room, and there's also a seven table billiards club. The symbol of the Café is Ganymede (cupbearer to the Gods) offering refreshment to Zeus in the form of an eagle. The café is located on the first floor, with a view from the tall windows of the busy street below. At night it becomes a rock café.

Kavárna Meduza
Belgicka 17, Prague 2 *Metro: Náměstí Míru*
Tel: 2 225 15 107
Open: 11.00-01.00 (Sat & Sun from 12.00)
Outside the centre in a pretty, quiet, residential, treelined street, Meduza is well known among Prague café society. The unobtrusive entrance gives way to a spacious old-style café with a mixture of styles of furniture. It's a bit like the reception room of a large residence, which it once was. Charming, relaxed and comfortable, this is an ideal spot to read a book or newspaper in peace, or to play a game of chess over a cup of coffee and a snack.

Café Milena
Staromestske námestí 22, Prague 1
Tel: 2 260 843 *Metro: Staroměstská*
Open: 10.00-20.00
Standing in the Old Town Square, this is the home of the Franz Kafka Society, and is named after one of his lovers, Milena Jesenka. The building also houses an art gallery where publications on his life and works are available. Decorated in 1930s style, the civilised café is on the first floor, looking out to the famous Astronomical Clock, installed in 1410, remodelled in 1490 and ticking and cuckooing more or less non-stop since 1572. The black chairs and pillars contrast with the white ceiling, walls and marble-topped

tables, lit with art deco wall uplighters. Live music is played on the upright piano daily between 16.00 and 18.00. Besides all sorts of coffees and teas, there's a big selection of cakes, strudels, filled pancakes and ice creams.

Kavárna Obecní Dum

námestí Republiky 5, Prague 1
Tel: 2 200 27 63 *Metro: Náměstí Republiky*
Open: 07.00-23.00 (kitchen 12.00-16.00 & 18.00-23.00)

Built in the last period of the Austro-Hungarian Empire, between 1905 and 1912, Obecní Dum, the Municipal House, is Prague's most important art nouveau building, with neo-renaissance and neo-baroque bits thrown in. To the right of the imposing entrance, facing out on to Republic Square, is the grand restaurant, while to the left is the elegant café. The building, which stands on the site of the Gothic Royal Court Palace was intended to satisfy many of the social and cultural activities of the city folk and includes the Smetana Concert Hall, the city's main classical concert venue. The interior of this remarkable building is decorated with works by leading early 20th century Czech artists, including the best known of the art nouveau exponents, Alfons Mucha. It was from here that Czechoslovakia declared its independence from the Austro-Hungarian Empire in 1918. Popular with both residents and visitors to Prague, the café welcomes a constant low of customers relaxing inside or sitting out on the terrace that stretches the length of the café front. Coffees, aperitifs, beers and wines are served by smartly dressed waiters throughout the day, along with snacks and brasserie-style dishes.

Café de Paris at Hotel Paríz

U Obecního domu 1, Prague 1 *Metro: Náměstí Republiky*
Tel: 2 422 2151
Open: 10.00-24.00

Situated next door to the extravagant art nouveau Municipal House (Obecní dum – see above), Hotel Paríz is the work of the celebrated architect Jan Vejrych and suffers little in comparison with its neighbour. The Pariz was declared a historic monument in 1984 and the Café de Paris (along with its splendid restaurant) were immortalised by the nation's most illustrious author Bohumil Hrabal in his *I Served the King of England*. This classy café in the foyer of the hotel, where the day starts with a variety of breakfast options, still speaks of the golden age of almost a century ago, the time when café society reached its pinnacle, led mainly by such luminaries of the country's German-Jewish community as Franz Kafka.

Premiera Caffé

Parízská 18, Prague 1 *Metro: Staroměstská*
Tel: 2 231 03 67
Open: 08.30-01.00

An elegant café that spreads out on to the pavement under the trees in the smart street leading away from the Old Town Square towards the river. Baguettes and breakfasts are offered between 08.30 and 11.00, giving way to brasserie snacks – goulash soup, pasta, salads, pancakes and pastries. The local red and white wines are served in 20cl glasses, imported varieties in 10cl glasses.

Café Patio
Národní 22, Prague 1 *Metro: Národní třída*
Tel: 2 491 8072
Open: 08.00-23.00 (Sat & Sun from 10.00)
In the centre of town, halfway between Wenceslas Square and the River Vltava, Prague's Café Patio has been designed on several levels with interconnecting rooms. Exotic music, a stylish interior with an assortment of lanterns hanging from the ceiling, a ship of the line steaming towards the main entrance and a pagoda on the way to the basement antique shop are just a few elements to catch the eye and ear. The very reasonably priced salad bar menu changes daily and you can enjoy a grand array of freshly-made pastries washed down with fine Illy coffee served by friendly staff. A selection of local and foreign newspapers for browsing is available. Kafka did not visit Café Patio, but never mind – the café's motto is: *L'Art de Vivre!*

La Provence
Stupartská 9, Prague 1 *Metro: Náměstí Republiky*
Tel: 2 900 54 510-512
Open: 11.00-02.00

La Provence is tucked away in a quiet street between the Old Town and Republic Squares, and its aspect is of a Languedoc timber-framed shop-cum-café. Inside is more rustic, with timber furnishings and bare brick walls. Incorporating all things Mediterranean, it offers snacks and meals, drinks and entertainment, with origins in France, Italy and Spain – salad mistral or niçoise, carpaccio or linguine, gazpacho or pinchitos along with many others. A restaurant, a café and a tapas bar, on two floors; the entertainment swings from jazz on Mondays, to French songs to the piano on Tuesdays, dancing on Wednesdays, and so on. The upstairs part is called Banana Café, with go-go girls and cocktails.

Café Relax
Soukenická 7, Prague 1 *Metro: Náměstí Republiky*
Tel: 2 248 18 892
Open: 10.00-23.00 (Sat & Sun from 13.00)
In the north-east of the city centre, a short step from the River Vltava, a tributary of the Elbe, lies this comfortable, welcoming student café, offering well-spaced tables and a random selection of chairs, even a central rug to make it feel more homely. The high ceiling and full height windows enhance the feeling of spaciousness. Serving the excellent Illy coffee, this well-named café attracts the young, who come during the day to read the papers or their current study book, or to play board games; the evenings are more boisterous.

Café Savoy
Vitezna 1
Tel: 2 24 53 97 96
Open: 09.00-23.00
This 19th-century café, eyecatchingly decorated with restored murals, is one of the best known in the city. The atmosphere is calm and civilised, the service attentive, the music soothing attentive and the hors d'œuvre selection excellent.

I DRINK… THEREFORE I AM

Most nations revere their big thinkers before their big drinkers. Czechs remember the men who could do both. We visit the cafés where the legends were born

GOOD KING WENCESLAS – WENCESLAS SQUARE

Ask any native of Prague, and they'll tell you the only place to meet in this city is 'under the tail'. Accept the offer and you've fixed your rendezvous not just next to the epic statue of the Saint on Wenceslas Square – but 'under the tail' of the nag he's perched on.

Wenceslas was, of course, the 10th century Duke who brought Christianity to Bohemia, was later made a saint and went on to make it big in Christmas carols. Pick a café – there are over 20 to choose from – and hum the tune to yourself.

TOLSTOY – SLAVIA, SMETANOVO NABREZI 2

If a future generation was looking for one building to sum up the Czech passions of high thought and alcohol, it would have to be *Café Slavia*.

Maybe it's the stunning views of the castle and the river Vltava below, but *Slavia* is a uniquely soothing place. And starting with legendary 19th century novelist Tolstoy (*War and Peace, Anna Karenina*), great minds have come here for nourishment. Café Slavia also happens to be the spot where trouble-makers like the young Vaclac Havel met to stir each other up. Given the number of Prague bars which boast him as a pre-Revolution regular it's a wonder any dissident writing got done at all.

KAFKA – MILENA, STAROMESTSKE NAMESTI 22

On a sunny day it's hard to imagine a more charming place on earth than Prague's *Staromestske namesti*. Surrounded by spires and chiming clocks, it's the town square by which all others should be judged.

So it's doubly confusing, then, to find one sandwich-board directing you into *The Museum of Torture Instruments*, and another pointing to *Kafka's Café*.

While Franz was born and raised in Prague's Jewish quarter, there's no concrete proof the great man ever got squiffy here. But the fact that *Milena* doubles up as Kafka Society and Kafka Library makes this place decidedly… Kafkaesque.

MOZART – MOZART MUSEUM, BETRAMKA, MOZARTOVA 169

If Wolfgang had lived in the age of aerosol 'tagging', he might have felt the urge to daub '*Mozart woz ere*' across the city. In fact, the city's entrepreneurs have done it for him. Building on the fact that Mozart wrote *Don Giovanni* in Prague, the capital's concert halls, churches and even puppet theatres fight back with a giddying programme of his work.

To experience 'deep Mozart', head across Charles Bridge to the Betramka Villa (now Mozart Museum) where the prodigy wrote the overture to *Don Giovanni* the night before the premiere. Sip a cappuccino in the tasteful café, and muse on life's riches.

Slavia Kavárna
Smetanovo nábrezí, Prague 1 *Metro: Národní třída*
Tel: 2 24 22 09 57
Open: 08.00-24.00
In a neo-classical building on the banks of the Vltava, this Slav Café is approached up a broad but austere staircase, with a glass wall separating the stairwell from the reception, from which you are shown to your table. The café area stretches along the first floor, looking out at the National Theatre. Traditional filter coffee and national dishes are offered and served by formally dressed staff, and the customers are mostly residents of Prague who have been coming here for years.

U Prince
Staromestske námestí, Prague 1 *Metro: Staroměstská*
Tel: 2 242 138 07
Open: 10.00-01.00
In the corner of the Old Town Square is a robust building with a vaulted ground floor. The solid stone walls and paved floor are furnished with robust wooden tables and chairs. Many's the local family and tourist visitor who've refreshed themselves here, perhaps with a Staropramen lager. Outside, under an extending canopy, is a formal terrace of tables in the square with comfortable basket-weave armchairs, secluded by greenery on either side. Here you can get a range of traditional Czech dishes, and some of the more familiar Western European ones, served professionally and cordially by smartly dressed waiting staff.

Valmont Café
Parízská, Prague 1 *Metro: Staroměstská*
Tel: 2 232 72 60
Open: 10.00-23.00/24.00
On the edge of the Jewish quarter, Valmont is a smart modern café-bar with the look of a traditional Parisian brasserie. Tubular chairs with basket-weave seats and backs spread around outside on the patterned cobbled pavement. A stone's throw from the river Vltava, it is also not far from Rudolfinum, an imposing building in neo-classical style; it houses the beautiful Antonin Dvorak concert hall. The tall arched openings have french windows that open on to the street. A smart set choose to pause at the café after a stroll from their hotel or a cultural visit to the concert hall.

Kavárna Velryba
Opatovická 24, Prague 1 *Metro: Národní třída*
Tel: 2 24 91 23 91
Open: 11.00-02.00
A just-below-street-level café with club and art gallery; velryba means whale but no one seems to know how it came by the name. The popularity however, is obvious, especially among the intellectual crowd, and the reason for that is the very reasonable prices charged for the snacks. The kitchen closes at 23.00. Great whisky selection.

France

A quick look at a map will dismiss any notions of discovering quintessential France – the truth is that she's too big to be pinned down. People rarely visit 'France' – they explore one corner of the jigsaw that makes up this wonderful country. Whether it's mixing with the glitterati at Cannes, cycling past fairytale chateaux in the Loire valley, enjoying the 200km of alpine skiing trails in Chamonix or visiting the hilltop villages of Provence – there are enough different sides to France to keep you busy for a lifetime.

But no matter how you spend your days here, they all end the same way – with a good meal. French cuisine is the envy of the world, and even the humble picnic is elevated to a work of art. The country that gave the world foie gras, Roquefort cheese and the soufflé has nothing to prove to anyone. Epicurean delight doesn't stop at food, with the regions of Champagne, Burgundy and Bordeaux producing some of the best wines on the planet.

France is just as good an artist as she is a cook, and it's hard to think of another country that has produced so many major players in every field, from poetry to fine art, from photography to cinema. Spend some time in Paris' numerous galleries and it soon becomes clear that without the likes of Matisse, Monet and Duchamp – Western art wouldn't be what it is today.

Paris

To really get to know this city, pull up a chair at a terrace café, order a carafe of rosé and keep your eyes open. Paris happens at street level – and open air museums like the Champs Elysées, Rue de Rivoli, Jardin des Tuileries and Place des Vosges offer some of the best 'people watching' on the planet. You can live on sight alone in this unashamedly seductive city. Getting up from your table, you'll find the buildings just as captivating as the crowds. Whether you're looking down from the hilltop of Montmartre or gazing at Notre Dame from a riverboat on the Seine, Paris preens herself in front of your stare. Look for flaws in the surface, and you simply won't find any. Up close, the masterpieces of the Impressionist galleries in the Musée d'Orsay, the jaw-droppingly expensive jewellery in the windows of Place de la Concorde and the effortlessly hip bargains at Clignancourt market all tell the same story: Paris is the capital of style.

L'Angevin
168 rue Montmartre, 2nd *Metro: Bourse or Sentier*
Tel: 1 42 36 20 20
Open: 10.00-02.00
Closed: Sun & Mon
Wine and cheese are the two main attractions at L'Angevin, a pleasant, civlised bar in art deco style where the patron, Jean-Pierre Robineau, and his black-aproned staff have a warm welcome for friends and strangers alike. The wine selection is mostly from western France, the Loire and the South, and one of the more unusual offerings is an organic Coteaux du Loire made from the chenin grape. They also have a range of Côtes du Rhône.

L'Apparement Café
18 rue des Coutures St-Gervais, 3rd *Metro: Saint - Sébastien Froissart*
Tel: 1 48 87 12 22
Open: 12.00-02.00 (Sat 16.00-02.00, Sun 12.30-24.00)
Just minutes from the Picasso Museum, and itself once an art gallery, this is a laid-back place of real character, with various rooms named like the rooms in an apartment (the pun is on the French words for apartment and apparently). Each room has its own idiosyncratic decor, for instance the 'library' with wooden seats and bookcases, from which visitors are welcome to take their pick for a browse with their drink. 'Le petit salon' is furnished with 1930s armchairs and sofas. Board games are also available.

Bouillon Racine
3 rue Racine, 5th *Metro: Cluny-La-Sorbonne*
Tel: 1 44 32 15 60
Open: 12.00-23.30
Since this is a listed historic building, nothing can change here – which is just as it should be. Camille Chartier opened this delightful belle époque café/restaurant in 1906 and it became one of the most popular workmen's dining halls in Paris, establishing the tradition of taking bouillon (soup) at the counter. Later much favoured by students, it was completely renovated by a young Belgian entrepreneur in 1996, restoring its marvellous bevelled, mirrored panels and intricate woodwork to their pristine splendour. The tipple is beer (Belgian beers on draught, available by glass or jug), and the cooking is Belgian, with classics such as waterzooi among the favourites; and beer is an integral part of many of the dishes.

Carette
4 pl du Trocadéro, 16th *Metro: Trocadéro*
Tel: 1 47 27 88 56
Open: 07.30-24.00
A classic *salon de thé* established in 1926 right opposite the enormous Chaillot Palace and the vast terrace that provides the most impressive view of the Eiffel Tower from across the Seine. Carette is open all day, every day for coffee, tea, superb pastries and light savoury snacks, with a few *plats du jour* providing elegant lunching. There's also a busy takeaway trade and a home delivery service.

Au Chai de l'Abbaye
26 rue de Buci, 6th *Metro: Mabillon*
Tel: 1 43 26 68 26
Open: 08.00-02.00 (Sun 11.00-23.00)
Chai de l'Abbaye is a favourite watering hole and meeting place in Rue de Buci, a bustling, high-class open-air food market that runs along to Rue de Seine. Bright, friendly and inviting, it manages to preserve something of a local feel while being in the heart of touristy St Germain. The buzzy atmosphere, the long list of wines by the glass, the Poilâne tartines (Auvergne ham; Cantal; goose rillettes; smoked salmon), the salads, the charcuterie and the hot snacks, the super ice creams and sorbets are excellent reasons for a visit, and the long opening hours are a bonus.

Café Charbon
109 rue Oberkampf, 11th *Metro: Saint-Maur or Parmentier*
Tel: 1 43 57 55 13
Open: 08.00-02.00 (Sat & Sun from 09.00)
Rue Oberkampf is considered one of the hot spots in up-and-coming Ménilmontant, and one of the cafés at the heart of this revival is this beautifully restored fin-de-siècle former dance hall. The decor is its chief charm: fading murals above tall mirrors show top-hatted gentlemen being entertained by crinolined can-can girls. Barrels are racked up by a steel girder and pulley system at the bar, providing a large selection of beers. There's also a range of wines, with a dozen available by glass or half bottle. A lively spot, especially when the DJ's doing his stuff at the weekend.

La Coupole
102 bd du Montparnasse, 14th *Metro: Vavin*
Tel: 1 43 20 14 20
Open: 07.30-02.00

La Coupole is the most renowned of the art deco brasseries that sprang up after the famous 1925 exhibition of decorative arts. A great favourite with the American set, this vast place opened its doors in 1927, since when it has remained one of *the* places for people-watching and an almost compulsory stop on a tourist trail that might otherwise have little reason to lead to Montparnasse. The columns, painted by different artists, are an eyecatching feature of the decor, whose centrepiece is a revolving modern sculpture. A full brasserie menu is served from 11.30, with classics like foie gras, salmon and steaks, and some excellent zingy-fresh shellfish; before that they serve coffee at the bar and breakfast on the *terrasse*.

Les Deux Magots
6 pl St-Germain-des-Prés, 6th *Metro: Mabillon*
Tel: 1 45 48 55 25
Open: 07.30-01.30
Closed: 3-4 days late Jan

This is the most famous of all the arty cafés in Paris, founded in 1875 and long associated with leading lights of French and American literature and art, from Verlaine, Rimbaud and Mallarmé to the surrealists, Picasso, Saint-Exupéry, Sartre, Simone de Beauvoir, Ernest Hemingway and Truman Capote. The literary connection is still maintained by the owners, with a prestigious annual prize, but tourists are now a major source of business at this prime spot for watching Paris pass by on the ever-busy Boulevard St-Germain. Les Deux Magots was the name of a shop selling Chinese silk that occupied this spot until it became a café; the name was kept, and to this

day the statues of the two Chinese wise men stand guard over a room with rich red banquettes, brass-edged tables and walls of mirrors. But outside is really the place to be, sitting at one of the many tables on the Boulevard pavement or round the corner in the Place opposite St-Germain church enjoying a speciality hot chocolate with a slice of pastry and a slice of la vie parisienne. The waiters in their long aprons and black waistcoats rush around all day long, covering, it was once estimated, an average of 12 kilometres during each shift!

L'Ecluse
15 pl de la Madeleine, 8th *Metro: Madeleine*
Tel: 1 42 65 34 69
Open: 11.30-01.00
With high-class neighbours that include Caviar Caspia and the outstanding grocer and traiteur Hédiard (and Fauchon across the road), L'Ecluse at Place Madeleine is one of a chain of five superior wine bars specialising in the wines of Bordeaux and appealing equally to Parisians and visitors to the city. This branch has the look of a private wine-imbibers' club, with seats comfortably clad in velvet, marble panels set into the bar front and the little tables, and wine paraphernalia everywhere. An amusing *carte des vins* lists and describes the extensive range of wines (many of them available by the glass – *verre dégustation* and *verre amateur* – as well as by the bottle) and includes an aide-memoire for tasters. Food is taken seriously, too, and the menu offers a fair selection of straightforward hot and cold dishes, plus cheeses and desserts.

Also at:
64 rue François 1er, 8th. Tel: 1 47 20 77 09
15 quai des Grands-Augustins, 6th. Tel: 1 46 33 58 74
13 rue de la Roquette, 11th. Tel: 1 48 05 19 12
1 rue Armaillé, 17th. Tel: 1 47 63 88 29

L'Européen
21bis bd Diderot, 12th *Metro: Gare de Lyon (RER)*
Tel: 1 43 43 99 70
Open: 06.00-01.00
A busy brasserie in classic Paris style, and a boon for rail travellers using Gare de Lyon, whose main entrance is right opposite. The decor features extravagant chrome, Lalique-style floral lamps and star-cluster chandeliers, and the seats in the front section are on wheels like executive office chairs. A long bar counter with high stools accommodates travellers in a hurry for the terminus and the terminally thirsty, while the rest of the capacious room is set with tables for dining. Breakfast is served from opening time and the full brasserie menus come on stream at 11.00. L'Européen is an excellent alternative to the catering outlets in the station itself, with a wide choice of dishes (*fruits de mer* and *choucroute* are specialities), reasonable prices and affable, capable service – in short, 'une brasserie très parisienne'.

Café de Flore
172 bd St-Germain, 6th *Metro: Maubert-Mutualité*
Tel: 1 45 48 55 26
Open: 07.00-01.30
The neighbour of *Les Deux Magots* and another of the great cafés *littéraires*, this cradle of existentialism has a 1930s interior and plenty of seats outside.

In the 1930s and 1940s Simone de Beauvoir and Jean-Paul Sartre, Camus, Genet and Marcel Carné were regulars, and Picasso met his mistress Dora Maar here while taking a break from working on his masterpiece *Guernica*. It is still very much a place for intellectual chit-chat, but is also one of the must-visit tourist spots on the Left Bank; service runs professionally under white-aproned waiters.

Le Fouquet's
99 ave des Champs-Elysées, 8th *Metro: George V*
Tel: 1 47 23 70 60
Open: 09.00-02.00
A notable Parisian landmark, the prestigious Fouquet's (pronounce the 't') is a real institution, the most famous boulevard café-restaurant on the most famous boulevard in the city. Refurbished in the summer of 1999, it continues to attract the rich and famous, the stars and the wannabes, and the main entrance floor is a rollcall of famous stars, their names engraved in brass plaques.

Harry's Bar
5 rue Daunou, 2nd *Metro: Opéra*
Tel: 1 42 61 71 14
Open: 10.00-04.00

1911 saw the opening of this renowned outpost of America, and 90 years on visitors going through the famous swinging wooden doors will discover a piece of America where the walls are lined with college banners and the spirits of Gershwin and Hemingway and Fitzgerald still linger. The barmen are shaker champions and will mix a different cocktail for any day of the year, including the Harry's Bar inventions the Bloody Mary and the Sidecar. Among the time-honoured snacks are the hot dogs, smeared with Harry's special blend of Dijon mustard, the club sandwich, home-made chili, savoury tourtes, brownies and fresh grapefruit salad.

Café de l'Industrie
16 rue St-Sabin, 11th *Metro: Bréguet Sabin*
Tel: 1 47 00 13 53
Open: 10.00-02.00
Closed: Sat
Dating from the 1880s, this is one of the happiest, most relaxed cafés not just in the area but in the whole of Paris. In the three dimly lit rooms the faded cream walls are a merry jumble of bric-a-brac, including saucy pre-war prints, photographs of the old film stars, plants, masks, spears, Oriental rugs and crocodile skins. The rooms open on to a little indoor garden. The customers are mainly lively youngsters from the Bastille district. Drinks, snacks and full restaurant meals are served.

Café de la Mairie
8 pl St-Sulpice, 6th *Metro: Odéon*
Tel: 1 43 26 67 82
Open: 07.00-02.00
Closed: Sun (except in June)
Students and writers follow in the footsteps of Ernest Hemingway, F Scott Fitzgerald and Samuel Beckett to meet at this small corner bar with outside tables. Good snacks include croque monsieur made with *Poilâne* bread, omelettes and composite salads. The amazing Church of Saint-Sulpice, just

along the road, is one of the great buildings of Paris. It took 135 years to build and it was actually never finished, the south tower being crude and obviously incomplete – you couldn't trust builders even in the 17th century! The church and the spectacular fountain in the square are both the work of the architect Visconti.

Café Marly
Cour Napoléon, 93 rue de Rivoli, 1st *Metro: Louvres-Rivoli*
Tel: 1 49 26 06 60
Open: 08.00-02.00

One of the most chic and fashionable cafés in the city, Café Marly boasts an impressive setting is the grounds of the Louvre, right opposite the Pei glass pyramid. Tables and chairs are arranged outside on the terrace (a long marble-floored forecourt, lined with great stone columns, leading down to the Cour Napoléon itself). Inside, the decor is splendidly extravagant: Venetian chandeliers light black and gold furnishings with grey velvet chairs and sofas, and the magnificent loos are decked out in marble and black china. The chic turns almost to magic at night, when the courtyard is floodlit. Steak and salmon tartares and Caesar salad are fixtures on a menu that changes every two months with the seasons.

Brasserie Café de la Paix
12 bd des Capucines, 9th *Metro: Opéra*
Tel: 1 40 07 30 20
Open: 09.00-00.45

Running along two sides of the Grand Hotel Inter-Continental (a building listed as a Historic Monument), this is a spacious corner café with a sumptuous Second Empire interior by Charles Garnier, whose masterpiece, the very grand and sumptuous Opéra Garnier, can be seen from the glass-

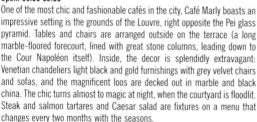

roofed pavement terrace. A classy place, popular with better-off tourists and better-off local workers, with a brasserie menu of snacks and classics such as oysters, grilled salmon and steak tartare.

La Palette
43 rue de Seine, 6th
Tel: 1 43 26 68 15
Open: 08.00-02.00
Closed: Sun, ist 2 wks Aug & 1 week Feb

A popular rendezvous for shop owners and students from the nearby Ecole des Beaux Arts. Palettes and paintings brighten the dark interior, and outside on the terrace is a bronze statue depicting the arts. Food is served lunchtime only: the favourite snacks are guillotines – open ham sandwiches made with toasted Poilâne bread.

Pause Café

41 rue de Charonnne, 11th *Metro: Ledru-Rollin*
Tel: 1 48 06 80 33
Open: 07.45-02.00 (Sun till 20.30)

A hugely popular and successful café in the burgeoning Bastille area. A changing exhibition of contemporary artwork hangs on the walls, and the red and yellow decor is vibrantly cheerful. Drinks are reasonably priced, and the food specialities include dishes cooked *à l'ardoise* and savoury *tourtes* served with salad. When the sun shines there's fierce competition for a seat on the terrace. Pause Café featured prominently in the film *Chacun Cherche Son Chat*.

Le Petit Fer à Cheval
30 rue Vieille-du-Temple, 4th *Metro: Saint-Paul*
Tel: 1 42 72 47 47
Open: 09.00-02.00

2003 sees the 100th birthday of this very popular and very pretty little café on a main street of the Marais, one of the oldest and most atmospheric parts of Paris. The name means 'horseshoe', and the horeshoe-shaped marble-topped bar is the only original one left in Paris. The mirrored walls and mosaic floor are other period features, along with old wooden Métro seats and a tall pewter water-fountain; the toilets are in stainless steel, reminding some visitors of Captain Nemo's *Nautilus*, others of Flash Gordon's spaceship. The menu runs from tartines, sandwiches and salads to andouillette, steak tartare, bavette and confit de canard, and there's a decent selection of well-priced wines by the glass.

Les Pipos

2 rue Ecole-Polytechnique, 5th *Metro: Cardinal Lemoine*
Tel: 1 43 54 11 40
Open: 07.30-23.30 (Sat till 02.00)
Closed: Sun & Aug

A friendly little corner *bar à vins* with an impressive selection of wines by glass and bottle. Beaujolais wines are the speciality, bought direct from the vineyards by the enthusiastic owner. There's also an extensive range of armagnacs going back more than 30 years. The place attracts a wide cross-section of Parisian society, and tourists also enjoy the buzz. Live accordion and guitar music makes Friday and Saturday nights particularly jolly.

Raimo

51-61 bd de Reuilly, 12th *Metro: Dugommier*
Tel: 1 43 43 70 17
Open: 09.00-24.00
Closed: Mon & Feb

The decor is unremarkable, the ices anything but! M. Raimo, from a long line of Italian ice-cream makers, runs one of the capital's very best ice cream parlours, in business for 50 years and priding itself on the quality of the fruit and other produce bought from Rungis market. Favourites among the 40+ flavours include three chocolate (white, milk and dark), Cardinal (strawberry, raspberry, lemon) and Raimoise (pear and praline). Hot and cold savoury dishes are available at lunchtime, but it's the ice creams that bring people out to Raimo, which is located just beyond the handsome lion fountain at Place Félix Eboué, Metro Daumesnil.

Le Reflet

6 rue Champollion, 5th *Metro: Luxembourg (RER)*
Tel: 1 43 29 97 27
Open: 10.00-02.00

In a tiny street running parallel to the Boulevard St-Michel, Le Reflet is popular with business people during the day. At night, students from the nearby Sorbonne take over, along with filmgoers and movie buffs (the Médicis Logos cinema is opposite). The decor is black, and the ceiling lighting is made to look like the sort of rig you might find on a film set. Black and white stills from the movies line the walls. The menu runs from tartines through salads to hot dishes such as lasagne and chili. The bar specialises in cider. Jazz plays in the background, with live music Monday evening.

Le Sancerre

35 rue des Abbesses, 18th
Tel: 1 42 58 08 20
Open: 07.00-01.30

Wines from the Loire, Rhône and Saône regions accompany some very good snacks, with a good selection of beers and whiskies in support. Daytime jazz, evening rock with a young crowd.

Le Select

99 bd du Montparnasse, 6th *Metro: Vavin*
Tel: 1 42 22 65 27
Open: 07.00-03.00 (Sat till 04.00)

Le Select is still going strong after 80 years, and the decor, the clientele and the general feel of the place are not very different from the day it opened as an American Bar. A wide variety of drinks includes great cocktails and more than 60 whiskies, and snacks, light meals and excellent home-made pastries are served throughout the day at this Montparnasse stalwart opposite another (*La Coupole*). The spacious terrace is very popular in summer.

La Tartine

24 rue de Rivoli, 4th *Metro: Saint-Paul-Le Mareil*
Tel: 1 42 72 76 85
Open: 09.30-22.00
Closed: Tues & L Wed

Little has changed down the years in the decor of this lovely old Marais bar à vins, where old-fashioned globe lights and vintage booths maintain the period feel. Trotsky was once a regular at La Tartine, which from the start has provided good wine and simple snacks at very reasonable prices. It first saw the light of day in the early 1900s, and today's customers trot along for the tartines made with the wonderful *pain Poilâne* and for something from a very impressive range of wines available by glass or bottle.

Terminus Nord

23 rue de Dunkerque, 10th *Metro: Gare du Nord*
Tel: 1 42 85 05 15
Open: 08.00-01.00

Eurostar arrivals at Gare du Nord have only to cross the road to be sure of a memorable first experience of the food and the atmosphere of Paris. Terminus Nord, with its superb 1925 decor, good food, convivial atmosphere and on-the-ball service, also has a large and loyal local following, and is one of the undoubted stars in the Café Flo firmament. It's open for breakfast early in the morning, and the full menu (fruits de mer, choucroute, foie gras, grills and steaks among the specialities) comes on stream at an early 11.00. A drink at the bar or in the glassed *terrasse* can be had at any time, but it's worth allowing an extra hour or two to sit down to a full meal and to start or end a visit to Paris relaxed and content.

FAME OR BUST

For any Frenchman surveying the celestial bodies of Brigitte Bardot, Catherine Deneuve, Iñes de la Fressange and Vanessa Paradis, two words spring to mind: 'magnificent bust'. We can tell you why...

Pause to consider the careers of four of France's most glamorous daughters, and you start to find some odd parallels between these very different women.

Two of them (Bardot and Deneuve) were discovered by, and fell in love with, the same man. Two have had global album hits (Bardot and Paradis). Three of our divas (Deneuve, Fressange and Paradis) have been the 'face' of Chanel. Three have starred in over 130 movies between them (Bardot, Deneuve and Paradis). But in the mind of any Frenchman, there's one accolade that crowns the lives and careers of all four women and that's being voted 'bust of the nation'.

Perhaps we should explain. Rewinding back a couple of centuries to 1792 – and the declaration of the First Republic – one of the first acts for the spin-savvy revolutionaries was to announce a national emblem. Showing a deft touch for PR, the committee announced: "the new emblem of the State will be the figure of Liberty..." captured as the striking image of the bare-chested woman in the floppy hat.

The nation fell in love with her at first sight. And although no one quite knows why, the emblem became known to every Frenchman as Marianne.

For the next two hundred years, throughout wars, revolutions and counter-revolutions, Marianne popped up everywhere. Decorating coins, bank notes and medals under every government, she was finally installed as a statuette in every town hall.

But what's all this got to do with Bardot, Deneuve, Fressange and Paradis? And where's the 'magnificent bust'? Patience, we're about to reveal all.

The year was 1969, and in the hamlet of Thiron-Gardais the local Mayor was about to launch a minor revolution of his own. Caught up in the liberal mood of the 60s, and apparently a bit of a movie buff, the Mayor decided to take down the statuette of Marianne and replace it with a bust of Bardot.

France went bonkers. For half the country, the idea of choosing the star of French cinema's first nude movie scene (*And God Created Woman*) as the face of the nation was an outrage. For the other half, the gravity-defying neckline of the Bardot bust was the best thing they'd ever seen. Mayors across France voted with their feet, and busts of Bardot went up everywhere. Brigitte became the new Marianne.

The tradition lives on today. The country might wait ten years, it might wait 20. But once in a while a new diva appears who 'does it' for the men of France – and a new Marianne is proclaimed. As classics like *Belle de Jour* and *Le Dernier Metro* launched her career, Deneuve became the face of the nation. In the fashion-hungry 80s, it was the turn of super-model Iñes de la Fressange to lend her sculpted cheek bones to a new Marianne. And in the multi-media 90s, it was singer/ actress/ model Vanessa Paradis who made it into marble.

Stand back from any of these incarnations of French womanhood, and you have to hand it to them... magnificent bust.

Bordeaux

You know you've arrived in Bordeaux when a vintage Claret wraps itself around your taste buds. There's no experience quite like it. And round here there are no end of opportunities to indulge – whether it's in the cellar of a specialist wine merchant, visiting a local vineyard or dining on truffles and foie gras in Place de la Victoire. Like the wines of the region, Bordeaux itself is well-balanced and refined – but not without body. As well as the grand architecture of the Musée des Beaux-Arts and the manicured gardens in the Place Gambetta, there's a less formal side to the city in its 24-hour café and bar culture.

Café Le Bal
Eurl le Bal des Grands Hommes
Tel: 5 56 48 55 24 *Area: Place des Grands Hommes nr Grand Théâtre*
Open: 08.00-19.30
Closed: Sun
Her Majesty Queen Elizabeth, accompanied by the French Minister for Foreign Affairs, opened the imposing glass building that dominates the square in 1992. It stands on three levels, and the ground floor includes a daytime café selling good pastries and light brasserie-style lunchtime snacks. Many of the ingredients come straight from the market which occupies the floor below and which the café overlooks from a balcony.

Le Café Bordelais
15 allées de Tourny *Area: East off Place des Grands Hommes*
Tel: 5 56 51 73 16
Open: 11.00-01.00/02.00 (Sat from 12.00)
This bar à vins/restaurant is on the north side of the Allées de Tourny just up from the Place de la Comédie, where the Grande Théâtre is one of the most spectacular buildings in town. Le Café Bordelais has a terrific wine list – lots available by the glass – that changes every week and is among the best for choice in a place where wine is its lifeblood. On a corner site, the terrace is cobbled in hand-thrown yellow and red quarry tiles; it is enclosed

53

in glass under a green awning and was clearly once part of the pavement. Before becoming a restaurant it was a garage, so the interior is spacious, with a mezzanine area of the bar for dining. Food specialities are cassoulet and *fondant au chocolat*. Staff are professional and attentive.

Le Castan
2 quai de la Douane *Area: West bank of Garonne nr Palais de la Bourse*
Tel: 5 56 81 85 02
Open: 09.00-02.00
Closed: Mon
In a prime location right by the River Garonne, this is one of the celebrated *grands cafés* of France, a unique establishment famous for its extraordinary sparkling stone grottoes, which form a natural alcove for a variety of ceramic sea pictures dating back to the days when Bordeaux was the main embarkation point for travellers. These pictures were produced at the Boulenger factory in Choisy-le-Roi. Outside, there is additional seating for those who prefer to bask in the sun while having a drink or a meal. Seafood and oysters are the speciality of this distinguished old place.

Chez Ducou
14 allées de Tourny *Area: East off Place des Grands Hommes*
Tel: 5 56 81 61 61
Open: 12.00-02.00
One of many eating and drinking establishments on the famous tree-lined Allées de Tourny, Chez Ducou is a popular brasserie with a long zinc bar and an assortment of caps, kepis and casquettes surrounding a caricature bust of General de Gaulle. The atmosphere is busy, chatty and amusing, and on the walls are some very amusing photographs. Every evening they have a variety of live music to entertain the varied crowd that assembles in the bar or out on the terrace.

Le Cintra
4 cours 30 Juillet *Area: Next to Grand Théâtre*
Tel: 5 56 44 27 05
Open: 07.30-02.00
Le Cintra is an attractive café decorated in the style of the 1900s: a mahogany-fronted bar with banquettes under a leaded glass backlit ceiling leads on to a small room, and stairs ascend to the restaurant area. The terrace has tables for some 30 people, shaded by the red blind and red and white parasols, an ideal spot for breakfast, a light lunch or aperitif as the sun goes down on cocktail hour. Good variety of salads and plenty of wines by the glass. Next door on one side is the Hotel des Quatre Sœurs, where Wagner stayed in 1850, while on the other is the Grand Théâtre, an 18th-century gem that inspired Charles Garnier to build the Paris Opera House in similar style.

Café de la Comédie
52 cours du Chapeau Rouge *Area: Near Grand Théâtre*
Tel: 5 56 51 27 30
Open: 07.30-02.00 (Sat & Sun from 08.00)
A popular café on the side of the Grand Théâtre, open long hours for drinks and a selection of sandwiches, salads and charcuterie. Beyond the wide, open frontage is a red granite bar counter with a mahogany-panelled front and Edwardian decor of upside-down silk lampshades on brass fittings. Red upholstered bar stools and chairs and banquette seating stand on granite floor tiles to match the countertop, and mirrored walls give the place a spacious feel.

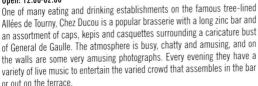

Beyond the bar is another room leading out on the Rue de la Maison Daurade behind, and with the doors open a cool breeze wafts through the place.

Café La Concorde

50 rue du Maréchal Joffre *Area: North of Place de la République*
Tel: 5 56 44 68 97
Open: 08.00-22.00
Closed: Sun

A city-centre brasserie/café with a winter garden. There are seats for 180 in its lofty rooms with their handsome plasterwork and mirrored walls, and tables and chairs outside overlooking Place de la République, the Palais de Justice and the Saint André hospital, sheltered by a green awning. This is where the legal boys come – the law school is next to the Palais. On the food front are fixed-price and à la carte menus, plus an hors d'oeuvre buffet, a dish of the day and as many oysters as you want.

Café Gourmand

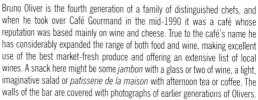

3 rue Buffon *Area: West off Place des Grands Hommes*
Tel: 5 56 79 23 85
Open: 11.00-01.00 (Mon from 15.00)
Closed: Sun

Bruno Oliver is the fourth generation of a family of distinguished chefs, and when he took over Café Gourmand in the mid-1990 it was a café whose reputation was based mainly on wine and cheese. True to the café's name he has considerably expanded the range of both food and wine, making excellent use of the best market-fresh produce and offering an extensive list of local wines. A snack here might be some *jambon* with a glass or two of wine, a light, imaginative salad or *patisserie de la maison* with afternoon tea or coffee. The walls of the bar are covered with photographs of earlier generations of Olivers.

Les Noailles

12 allées de Tourny *Area: East off Place des Grands Hommes*
Tel: 5 56 81 94 45
Open: 08.30-24.00

The street in which Les Noailles is located is the renowned Allées de Tourny, part of the Triangle of Bordeaux that has contained the fashionable restaurants and bars for some two centuries. This one is decorated in the style of 1936. A bar-brasserie serving drinks and *grillades* throughout the day from midday to midnight, it has a wide open frontage and a permanent terrace of tables under a green awning. The waiters are resplendent in their white shirts, black waistcoats and trousers, and long white aprons below the knee in classic style. A good choice of wines as you'd expect, or a simple kir with your friends.

Le Bistrot des Quinconces

4 pl des Quinconces *Area: Next to Esplanades des Quinconces*
Tel: 5 56 52 84 56
Open: 07.30-01.00/02.00

Any time of day is the right time to drop in to this art deco style bistro: a bite on the hop, a business lunch, teatime refreshment after a hard day's shopping, an aperitif with friends after work, an intimate evening or a celebration party with friends for dinner. The welcome is always warm and the staff are never too busy to help. Some evenings there's a live jazz trio. There's a spacious terrace at the front, well shaded by a huge green blind, and while a lot of the interior is laid out for eating at mealtimes, there's a bar and bar area where you can drop in at any time for a drink.

55

Café Régent
46 pl Gambetta *Area: Next to Porte Dijeaux*
Tel: 5 56 44 16 20
Open: 08.00-01.00

Very reliable and very popular with local residents and shoppers, the brasserie-style Régent occupies a commanding corner of a square dating back to the time of Louis XV; in another corner is the 18th-century arch of the ancient Porte Dijeaux. The café is very spacious inside, and all the windows open up on to the pavement. The interior is set out in squares with banquette seating, while outside, the small round tables are set with cane chairs, south-facing to get the sun. Ice creams are a speciality.

Lyons

Wandering the narrow cobbled streets of Vieux Lyons, it doesn't take long to realise that you're in the gastronomic capital of France. There are more restaurants per square metre here than anywhere else in the world, and the business of eating is taken very seriously indeed. Whether you like your cuisine 'haute' or prefer the more rustic fare served in one of Lyon's 'bouchons', the best way to work up an appetite is to climb to the top of Fourvière hill to take in the views of the meandering river Saône. Getting up from the table, it's time to visit the rococo Basilique de Notre-Dame or relax in one of the two Roman theatres set into the hillside. The theatres are a relic of a time when Lyons was the capital of Gaul – and fast forwarding to the present day it's well worth getting a ticket for the plays and concerts held here on summer evenings.

Bar Américain
24 rue de la République *Metro: Cordeliers*
Tel: 4 78 42 52 91
Open: 06.30-01.00

A unique fact about the Bar Américain is that is the only café in France to have been listed on the Paris Bourse (stock market), and the charming patronne will happily tell visitors all about its history, which goes back some 170 years. Faithful renovations include a wonderful trompe l'oeil ceiling of clouds and angels, and some engraved mirrors with bronze trappings; a number of 19th-century paintings have been added. Good fresh food is always on offer and there's usually an interesting guest beer on tap.

Café Bellecour

33 pl Bellecour *Metro: Bellecour*
Tel: 4 78 37 03 63
Open: 07.00-20.00 (Sat 09.00-15.00)
Closed: Sun & Aug

An old-fashioned brasserie with a large summer terrace that makes a perfect spot for a refreshment break for visitors to the heart of the city in this, the largest square in Lyons, a huge gravelly expanse famous for its statue of Louis XIV as a Roman emperor. Salads and a *plat du jour* at lunchtime.

Café Chantecler

151 bd de la Croix Rousse *Metro: Croix-Rousse*
Tel: 4 78 28 13 69
Open: 07.30-01.00 (Sun 08.30-21.00)

A place for beer-lovers. Draught bitter is brewed on the premises, so it's not a total surprise that the patron is an Englishman, Raymond Rushforth. The smoked-oak panelling, surrounding veranda and terrace make this a pretty much ideal spot to enjoy a drink and perhaps a plat du jour. Live music on Thursdays at this café in what was once the silk weavers' district of Lyons.

Le Cintra

42 rue de la Bourse *Metro: Cordeliers*
Tel: 4 78 42 54 08
Open: 07.00-05.00
Closed: Sun

Le Cintra is a fun café-restaurant and piano-bar all in wood, with a coffered ceiling, a classic tiled floor and motifs in brass. This has been a popular choice for cocktail drinkers and beer fans (there are nine beers on tap) and diners (last orders 02.00) ever since it opened 70 years ago.

Grand Café des Négociants

1 pl Francisque Regaud *Metro: Cordeliers*
Tel: 4 78 42 50 05
Open: 07.00-24.00 (Fri & Sat till 01.00)
Closed: 1 May

A wonderfully traditional *grand café*, from the five-light chandeliers, period hatstands, leather banquettes and tall arched mirrors to the immaculate waiters in their long white aprons (*rondeaux*). People come from near and far to this marvellous place in the Cordeliers district between the Rhône and the Saône to enjoy a wide selection of drinks and their choice from the extensive menus. Large terrace.

Le Régent

9 pl Bellecour *Metro: Bellecour*
Tel: 4 78 42 25 38
Open: 08.00-01.00 (Sun & Mon from 14.00)
Closed: Sun & Aug

An Italian Regency café with an interior mezzanine. The menu is based on the local cuisine, with omelettes, crêpes, quenelles and *saucisses briochées*. There's also a good choice of teas and draught beer at this centrally located café.

CHAMPAGNE SUPERNOVA

It is, quite simply, the most celebrated drink on earth. Used to launch ships, revolutions and kingdoms across the centuries, champagne is never far from the headlines. We explore the individuals and historic moments connected with the King of Wines.

Working from the philosophy that 'in victory you deserve it, and in defeat you need it', Napoleon always made sure he had a good supply of the stuff before setting out on a campaign. In fact, imagine a world without champagne and life suddenly looks a lot less bubbly. Wedding toasts would be flat, New Year's Eve would loose its sparkle and ship launches would no longer go with a bang.

That this sublime liquid exists at all is all thanks to the efforts of a teetotal French monk, Dom Pérignon. The cellar-master's task of looking after the communion wine at Hauteville Abbey was made all the more difficult by the fact that the casks kept exploding. Try as he might, he was unable to rid the wine of what he called 'stars'. Dom Pérignon finally threw the towel in and concentrated on developing his 'méthode champenoise'. Just as well, really.

Much of the great man's success is owed to the geography of the Champagne region whose chalky soils are ideal for the three varieties of grape used: Pinot Noir, Pinot Meunier (both red) and Chardonnay (white). Champagne's northerly location also meant late harvesting and cold winters (causing fermentation to stop early and start up again in spring, hence the bubbles).

Admittedly, the art of capturing the 'mousse' has come a long way since the seventeenth century, but some things haven't changed. The grapes are still picked by hand as a damaged grape can affect the colour of the Champagne. After pressing, the grape juices are left to settle – and blended – before the first fermentation. Then it's into the bottle for the second fermentation (typically three to seven years) with each bottle turned every day by a 'remueur'. Which only leaves one problem: how to get rid of the unwanted yeast? It was the legendary Veuve Clicquot (Widow Clicquot) who found that by drilling holes in her antique table and placing the bottles in upside-down, the sediment would fall to the neck where it could be frozen and removed. Champagne was ready to go global.

After much historical wrangling (including the 1911 Champagne Riots – not half as much fun as they might sound) the geographical boundaries of the Champagne Viticole were set out. And it's an exclusive club; only bubbly produced in these 312 villages can be called champagne. Today, Moët et Chandon produce over half of the world's champagne and their cellars in Epernay boast a staggering 65 million bottles. It's heady stuff and a far cry from Dom Pérignon's early experiments. The last word goes to Lord Keynes, whose dying lament should be a lesson to us all: "I wish I'd drunk more champagne."

Nice

Riding in a convertible along the Promenade des Anglais – with a sea breeze ruffling the palm trees overhead and the smell of baked langoustines drifting from a waterfront restaurant – it's impossible not to be swept up in the sheer indulgence that is Nice. The good news is that lots of the best things in this ritzy city are affordable too. After all, this is the birthplace of the salad niçoise – a dish that manages to be delicious, good for your health and gentle with your wallet at the same time. A world away from the buzzing social centre that's the beach, Nice has a medieval town dotted with Baroque churches and pretty market squares – blessed every morning with the riches of Provence. Take your pick from cheeses, vegetables and fruit that look almost too good to eat.

Bar des Fleurs

13 cours Saleya *Area: Off Place P Gaultier opposite Chapelle de la Miséricorde*
Tel: 4 93 62 31 33
Open: 05.00-02.00 (Oct-Mar 05.30-20.00)
Café, bar, tabac and PMU (tote) point that's used by both stallholders and visitors to the famous flower market, which is open every afternoon and is a great place for strolling. You buy your ciggies, get a drink and place your bet in that order down the lefthand side, or take a table in the very spacious room and study form over a cup of coffee. Croissants and *pains au chocolat* are made on the premises, and ice creams and crêpes are other popular choices. Lit by globe lights, it becomes a brasserie at lunchtime.

Le Gambetta

pl de la Libération (pl Général de Gaulle) *Area: Next to Gare de Provence*
Tel: 4 93 84 76 07
Open: 07.00-24.00 (Sun till 15.00)
A neighbour of once-grand but now derelict station of the *Chemins de Fer de Provence*, this café is also a brasserie (seafood a speciality) and up a couple of steps inside the tables are set for meals. Leaded lights and engraved glass panels are eye-catching decorative features.

Le Globe

56 bd Jean Jaurès *Area: Just south of Gare Routière*
Tel: 4 93 62 31 74
Open: 07.00-23.00/24.00
On the same street as the excellent Museum of Modern and Contemporary Art, Le Globe has been serving a faithful clientele for more than a century. During the morning the customers are mainly locals, many from the hotel and restaurant industry, while as the day draws on the tourists begin to make their presence felt. Around the walls are tiled tableaux of local coastal scenes – Cap d'Ail, Cannes, Nice, Antibes, Villefranche and St-Jean.

Le Grand Café de Lyon et du Centre
33 ave J Médecin *Area: Corner of Rue Clemenceau*
Tel: 4 93 88 13 17
Open: 07.00-24.00

An art deco style pavement café, one of a genre that is becoming increasingly rare. It stands on the corner with Rue Clémenceau, about halfway up Nice's main shopping street and opposite the Nice Etoile shopping arcade. Always busy, especially as a welcome pit stop when the shops are open, it offers a day-long choice of snacks, crêpes, croques and speciality ice creams. At lunchtime much of it becomes a brasserie. Lots of beers, both draught and bottled.

Le Café du Palais
1 pl du Palais *Area: Next to Palais de Justice*
Tel: 4 93 85 77 63
Open: 07.00-02.00 (Oct-Mar till 21.00)
Closed: Sun

Facing the Palais de Justice in an attractive square behind the flower market, the café is decorated in Belle Epoque style, and outside there are seats for 100 set at little round tables. Lunchtime *plat du jour*, otherwise pastries and rolls, coffees and cocktails.

Les Ponchettes
3 pl Charles Félix *Area: Near Chapelle de la Miséricorde*

Tel: 4 93 92 16 13
Open: 07.00-01.00

Place Charles Félix bustles in the morning with the life of the market but at night when the weather's good half of Nice seems to be here to party. You can always get a table inside at Les Ponchettes (named after the arcaded gallery on the seafront), but outside is where everyone wants to be on a fine night. Music plays inside, while on the street it's the hubbub of animated conversation. Snacks are served, but people mostly order drinks or ice creams.

Chez René, Bar Socca
2 rue Miralhetti *Area: Just south of Place Garibaldi*
Tel: 4 93 92 05 73
Open: 08.30-21.00 (Oct-Mar till 22.30)
Closed: Mon

Bar Socca and restaurant Chez René face each other on a street in Old Nice. The popular orders here are chips, pizza, and the local specialities *socca*, which is a bit like a poppadom, and *pan bagnat*, a round loaf scooped out and filled with a Niçois mixture of salad, egg, tuna and anchovies. The crowd is a cheerful mix of locals and tourists who've picked up a thirst and an appetite wandering through the streets of this old part of town.

Le Rossetti
32 rue Centrale (pl Rossetti) *Area: Opposite cathedral*
Tel: 4 93 92 17 10
Open: 08.00-00.30 (Sun from 10.00)

A cosy little café in the old town, facing the baroque Cathedral dedicated to the young martyr St Réparate, patron saint of Nice. Appealing equally to local Niçois and tourists, it has a long terrace of green tables and chairs under white sunshades that stretches along to the fountain. On Sunday mornings there's a secondhand book market in front of the Cathedral.

Toulouse

Café hopping is an institution in Toulouse – good news for travellers as you don't have to worry about hurrying to your place in Capitoline square because there's another table being prepared for you just around the corner. On your way there, work up an appetite wandering the 14th century cloisters of the Musée des Augustins. With dusk approaching, it's time to grab a table at the Place Saint Georges whose pink stone buildings earned the city the nickname 'la ville rose'. A student town with all of the energy you'd expect, the streets of Toulouse fizz well into the night.

Le Bar Basque

7 pl St Pierre *Area: South of Université des Sciences Sociales*
Tel: 5 61 21 55 64
Open: 07.00-02.00

A bar of very wide appeal. Rugby fans, British visitors and students from the nearby business schools like to meet here on this corner site in a leafy square down near the river. There's not a lot of Basque about it apart from the name, the colour green and a wooden bench or two, nor is it a *bar à vins* as it claims on the awning: Beer is King of the Drinks here, reflecting the taste of its clientele. Next door is L'Annexe, where they have salsa most nights. A lively duo!

Le Café Bibent

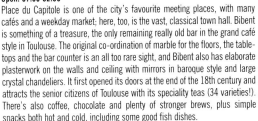

5 pl du Capitole *Area: Next to Town Hall*
Tel: 5 61 23 89 03
Open: 07.00-02.00

Place du Capitole is one of the city's favourite meeting places, with many cafés and a weekday market; here, too, is the vast, classical town hall. Bibent is something of a treasure, the only remaining really old bar in the grand café style in Toulouse. The original co-ordination of marble for the floors, the table-tops and the bar counter is an all too rare sight, and Bibent also has elaborate plasterwork on the walls and ceiling with mirrors in baroque style and large crystal chandeliers. It first opened its doors at the end of the 18th century and attracts the senior citizens of Toulouse with its speciality teas (34 varieties!). There's also coffee, chocolate and plenty of stronger brews, plus simple snacks both hot and cold, including some good fish dishes.

Chez Tonton

16 pl St Pierre *Area: South of Université des Sciences Sociales*
Tel: 5 61 21 89 54
Open: 08.00-02.00 (Sat 09.00-04.00)

Pastis is the thing to drink Chez Tonton. It's also known as 'Pastis O Metre', which represents seventeen glasses in a row. Intrepid drinkers sink all 17, one after the other. After the colour of the pastis, the decor here is all yellow, though you might not be aware of this after passing, or indeed failing, the Metre test. A favourite meeting place for the pétanque experts.

Café Le Florida
12 pl du Capitole *Area: Next to Town Hall*
Tel: 5 61 21 49 92
Open: 07.00-02.00 (Sat till dawn!)
A grand café in a magnificent arcade facing the Town Hall. The ceiling of the arcade over the pavement tables is painted with tableaux by Raymond Moretti depicting the history of Toulouse. Equally eye-catching inside this turn-of-the-century café is a wonderful mahogany bar with a zinc counter. There are two faces to Le Florida – elegant shoppers and business people pause for refreshment in the daytime, while at night the students come for a longer stay to enjoy the music and to debate the world's problems.

Le Père Léon
2 pl Esquirol *Area: Next to Musée des Augustins*
Tel: 5 61 23 90 95
Open: 06.30-00.30
Closed: Sun
A very traditional brasserie, with a stern portrait of the founding family hanging on the wall and, high above the bar, shelves of wines untouched for over a hundred years with about two inches of dust on them! There's globe lighting and cane chairs on two levels inside, and a glass-enclosed terrace and more tables on the pavement outside in this main cross street coming from the Pont Neuf, right in the heart of Toulouse.

Au Père Louis
45 rue des Tourneurs *Area: South of Musée des Augustins*
Tel: 5 61 21 33 45
Open: 09.00-22.00
Closed: Sun & 2 weeks Aug
Probably the oldest bar in Toulouse, with a few pavement tables, barrels in the bar to rest your drink on, and old paintings on the walls and ceilings depicting the bridges of the Garonne and the Canal du Midi. Open in the morning for coffee and a glance through the newspapers, at lunchtime they serve *plats du jour*. Thereafter you can get a tartine through the rest of the day. The busy time is aperitifs at 18.00, when it's packed, and as the evening wears on the students arrive, often to perform their own music. They've been producing wine and fortified wine for sale in the bar since time immemorial and among their specialities are *Quinquina* – a liqueur with bitter oranges, *Maury* (port-like) and *Muscat*.

Bar Le Quartier Latin
1 pl Rouaix *Area: South of Musée des Augustins*
Tel: 5 61 52 33 82
Open: 07.00-02.00

An agreeable little bar in a square at the bottom of the Avenue Alsace-Lorraine. A breakfast café on the way to work and a place to take a break from shopping, it becomes a sandwich bar at lunchtime and then as the day wears on it takes on a lighter tone in readiness for the cocktail hour. Between 19.00 and 21.00 on Wednesday to Saturday they offer little tapas with drinks. Then it gets very busy with a happy young crowd and stays that way into the night. One of the walls inside has a very large and striking abstract painting in oils by Nikos.

Café Wallace
15 pl St Georges *Area: Just north of Musée des Augustins*
Tel: 5 61 21 07 18
Open: 07.30-01.00 or 02.00
Closed: Sun am

A simple spacious bar where the real treat is to sit out in front or in the square in the shade of plane trees with an aperitif or one of their amazing speciality ice creams. Snacks are also available, and wines by the glass.

Looking at a car as flawless as a Mercedes, a Porsche or a BMW, it's an easy step to assume that the nation who made it must be just as polished and efficient. Surely, ask the rest of us, no country which makes cars this good can know how to party? Well, they can – and they do. The fact is that Germany has always had a café, club and street party culture to rival anything in Europe. And the news is spreading. If you've ever lifted one of the 20 million pints which get poured and drunk at Munich's Oktoberfest then you're in on the story. If you've got inside Berlin's buzzing club and café scene, you know all about the 'manic' in 'Germanic'. And if you've ever been to Cologne's seven day street carnival then you're probably getting flashbacks as you read this. Yes, maddeningly, the truth is that the country with some of the slickest cars, football and ski slopes in the world also has some of the best beer and parties. But when you've had your fill of life in the fast lane, Germany does charming back roads just as well. Somewhere in every German town – from Hamburg in the north to Munich in the south – there's a hushed café waiting for you, complete with leaded windows, starched tablecloth, and a mouth-watering slice of Käsekuchen.

Berlin

Most cities have one centre; Berlin has two. Somewhere between the two hubs, the Brandenburg Gate symbolises the country's path to re-unification. Welcome to Germany's most diverse and vibrant city! For thirty years, West Berlin soothed its strained nerves by high-living and decadence - and since the 'Ossis' of East Berlin joined in the fun in 1991 it's been party-time round the clock. When you've had your fill of the pleasure spots, head for the stunning Museum Island, with its corral of five world-class galleries. To experience Berlin as it used to be, visit the Gedächtniskirche (Memorial Church) and the Checkpoint Charlie Museum. Two sobering experiences.

Adler
Friedrichstrasse 206 *U-Bahn: U6 - Kochstr*
Tel: 30 251 89 65
Open: 09.30-24.00 (Sun from 19.00)
An old-fashioned corner café next to Checkpoint Charlie and the Museum that tells the story of the Berlin Wall. Originally a pharmacy, it became a café in the mid-1980s and was the first stop for many East Germans coming to the West. Light snacks, cakes, beers, wines and coffee are the order of the day, and when the weather's fine it's nice to sit outside.

Café Aedes
Die Hackeschen Höfe, Rosenthalerstrasse 40-41, 10178
Tel: 30 285 82 75 *S-Bahn: S3,5,7,9 - Hackeschelmarkt*
Open: 10.00-02.00 (Fri & Sat till 03.00)
Part of one the numerous imaginative modern developments in Berlin. A courtyard and the buildings around it were restored and converted into cafés with apartments above, and a cinema. Inside, Aedes is a stylish, comfortable bar, while outside there's a huge parasol covering tables and chairs to hold about 40. Good menu and wine list + 75 whiskies.

Astor
Oranienburgerstrasse 84 *S-Bahn: S1,2 - Oranienburgerstr*
Tel: 30 283 68 34
Open: 10.00-01.00 (Fri & Sat till 02.00, Sun from 10.00)
A quintessentially English bar/restaurant where fish & chips, jacket potatoes and other favourites are washed down with tea and beer by local Anglophiles and occasional packs of Brits abroad. Despite the extraordinary montage of photos and press cuttings of the Royals and other patriotic memorabilia, there are also some American specialities, particularly among the desserts.

Café Bleibtreu
Bleibtreustrasse 45, 10623 *S-Bahn: S3,5,7,9 - Savignyplatz*
Tel: 30 881 47 56
Open: 09.30-01.00 (Fri & Sat 09.00-02.00)
A highly individualistic café-bar with some quirky features that include an English telephone box and photographs of Hollywood greats from Laurel & Hardy and Charlie Chaplin to Bogart and Wayne, Bardot and Hepburn. Soft lighting and candles help to complete the intimate atmosphere in the evenings. Excellent fresh orange juice and a good selection of newspapers are two good reasons to make a stop-off here at breakfast time. Special evening menus.

Dressler
Kurfürstendamm 207-8 *U-Bahn: U15 - Uhlandstr*
Tel: 30 883 35 30
Open: 08.00-01.00
A small company with cafés in French brasserie style: art nouveau, globe lights and shaded uplighters, black and white decor, ditto staff outfits. The wall-hangings are in Expressionist style. Two thirds of the lofty interior is taken up by the restaurant, while the bar section extends outside to terrace tables. The speciality drink is the romantic 'chandelier', two glasses of pink Moët sitting prettily in a little chandelier, and there are other champagnes, German and French wines, beers, coffees and teas; great patisserie, and hot and cold snacks, salads and full meals served from 11.00. Also at Unter den Linden 39.

German National Tourist Office

Café Einstein
Kurfürstenstrasse 58, 10785 *U-Bahn: U1,2,4,12 - Nollendorfplatz*
Tel: 30 261 50 96
Open: 09.00-02.00

On the ground floor of an elegant villa-like private house built in 1898, this is an opulent Viennese-style coffee house with a lofty main room and various other majestic rooms leading through into the leafy garden. Apple strudel with a cup of superb coffee is a popular order, and full meals are served noon till midnight. A popular choice for well-to-do Berliners, especially on Sunday starting with the renowned Einstein breakfast. Service is friendly and helpful, even at the busiest times, and children are welcome as long as they are kept in check.

Filmbuhne am Steinplatz
Hardenbergstrasse 12, 10623 *U-Bahn: U2,12 - Ernst-Reuterplatz*
Tel: 30 312 65 89
Open: 09.00-03.00 (Sun till 02.00)

Opposite the HDK concert hall, this is a popular meeting place for intellectuals, a large café with a sizeable terrace beyond the tall windows. Breakfast is served from a buffet that includes lots of fresh fruit. Plenty of teas and coffees to choose from. It is incorporated into one of the many independent cinemas that are so popular in Berlin.

Hoeck
Wilmerdorfstrasse 149, 10585 *U-Bahn: U2,7,12 - Bismarckstr*
Tel: 30 341 81 74
Open: 08.00-24.00
Closed: Sun

Hoeck is named after its most famous owner, Host Hoeck, who was a gold medallist in the 1932 Los Angeles Olympics, and the walls are adorned with bottles bearing his name. The house speciality is the Berlin Kindl original Weiss Schankbier, served in a broad tumbler, an ideal accompaniment to the robust German fare on the menu, including the famous *Schweinehackse* (knuckle of pork). A listed building, and the oldest of its kind in Charlottenberg.

Kempinski
Kurfürstendamm 27, 10719 *U-Bahn: U9,15 - Kurfürstendamm*
Tel: 30 884 34734
Open: 06.30-01.00
The ground-floor café of the Hotel Bristol Kempinski is a favourite place of refreshment for the Berlin smart set, the terrace for drinks and snacks, inside for meals. Soups, salads, terrific fruity ice creams. Wine by the glass is served in a 20cl glass pot. The Bristol Bar has a an excellent cocktail list.

Leydicke
Mansteinstrasse 4 *U-Bahn: U7 - Yorckstr*
Tel: 30 216 29 73
Open: 16.00-24.00
Closed: Sun
Leydicke is a grand old family enterprise in traditional style, where the introduction of electricity is one of the few changes to have come about since the doors first opened in 1877. Fruit wines are a speciality, with gooseberry, raspberry and plum just three of the many varieties on offer, served in generous tumblers to be enjoyed in the civilised surroundings. Four candelabras provide the illumination and some yellowed newspaper obituaries framed in a glass cabinet stand as a tribute to members of the founding family.

Café Leysieffer
Kurfürstendamm 218 *U-Bahn: U15 - Uhlandstr*
Tel: 30 885 74 80
Open: 09.00-02.00 (Sat & Sun till 22.00)
Established in 1909 in what was the Chinese Embassy, Leysieffer has claims to being one of the very best confectioners/patissiers in the whole wide world. Try a cake, torte or chocolate confection on the terrace outside the shop, or in the café/bar in the gallery upstairs, with a glass of champagne or house wine or a liqueur while they wrap the gift you have chosen from the brochure. A splendid place for a little spot of self-indulgence, and an excellent source of an extra-special gift (Christmas hampers a speciality). There are other Leysieffers throughout Germany.

Pranzo e Cena
Goltzstrasse 32, 10781 *U-Bahn: U7 - Eisenacherstr*
Tel: 30 216 3514
Open: 09.00-01.00
The enterprising owners who set up shop here in 1999 are second generation Turkish waiters, but the food and wine are Italian, with some real bargains among the bottles. Open from breakfast onwards.

Rampenlicht am Sudstern
Korterstrasse 33 *U-Bahn: U7 - Südstern*
Tel: 30 692 1301
Open: 09.00-01.00 (Sun from 10.00)
Tucked away in the residential area of Kreuzberg and close to the Volkspark Hasenheide Gardens, this double-fronted café is a versatile place that serves breakfasts, light lunches and evening meals in bistro style as well as being an all-day café. It is particularly busy in the evening and the bench tables on the terrace are much in demand when the weather is kind. Plenty of choice among the wines and beers.

Rost
Knesebeckstrasse 29, 10623 *U-Bahn: U15 - Uhlandstr*
Tel: 30 881 95 01
Open: 09.00-24.00/01.00
A busy arts café with minimalist modern decor, located in a residential area just south of the overland metro line by Savignyplatz. Seating comprises stools at the slate-topped bar, benches and chairs around the walls, and outside chairs at a small line of terrace tables. There's a stage for poetry, jazz, etc, and a full programme of events.

Sale e Tabacchi
Kochstrasse 18 *U-Bahn: U6 - Kochstr*
Tel: 30 252 11 55
Open: 09.00-01.00 (Sat & Sun from 10.00)
Comfortable, bright and airy, with a full-height glass front, Sale e Tabacchi is just a block away from Checkpoint Charlie. It offers a good opportunity to combine a visit to the fascinating CPC Museum with some excellent real Italian coffee and authentic Italian food.

Wintergarten im Literaturhaus
Fasanenstrasse 23, 10719 *U-Bahn: U15 - Uhlandstr*
Tel: 30 882 54 14
Open: 09.30-01.00
A large, comfortable and impressive café/bar with a conservatory and garden terrace in Berlin's central library. There is a full programme of recitals, readings and performances to dazzle the most seasoned of café intellectuals, but customers are equally at home just reading one of the many newspapers provided. The clientele are mostly young, mostly wine-drinkers. Breakfast is available until 14.00, bistro-style cooking from 11.30.

Cologne

While the most famous thing to have come out of this city is 'eau de Cologne', the fact is that Cologne is packed with different pleasures and moods. At the top of the tourist 'to do' list there are the 'must sees' of the Dom (cathedral) and the fine art treasures of the Museum Ludwig. But if you're in the mood for museums, why not try the less trodden paths of the Popdom (a unique museum of 60s and 70s design and pop music) and the Schokoladenmuseum (Willy Wonka's Chocolate Factory brought to life). When you're ready for a good time, the Alter Markt (Old Market Square) and its myriad bars and cafés are ready to oblige.

Bootshaus Rodenkirchen
Rodenkirchener Yachthafen, Am Leinpfad 50996
Tel: 221 39 51 84
Open: 14.00-22.00 (Sat & Sun from 11.00)
Closed: Tue
This permanently moored café-bar-restaurant was established over 30 years ago and offers the pleasure, winter or summer, of sitting and watching the busy traffic on the Rhine over a beer, glass of wine or a coffee. Snacks are available, but the kitchen doesn't cater for full meals until after 17.30.

Engelbät
Engelbertstrasse 7, 50674 *U-Bahn: Zülpicher Platz*
Tel: 221 24 69 14
Open: 11.00-01.00
Engelbät offers a huge range of crepes, sweet and savoury, and the excellent Illy coffee, also wines by the glass from Germany, Italy, France, Spain and Argentina, and a range of salads. An upright piano stands in the corner of this dimly lit café that's very popular with young people including many students; enamelled adverts decorate the walls, well-used sturdy bar stools stand at the bar and the tall tables, and in the window wooden tables are set on the quarry-tiled floor. A music centre with a library of tapes and CDs stands next to the pre-war till.

Café Fleur
Lindenstrasse 10, 50674 *U-Bahn: Rudolfplatz*
Tel: 221 24 48 97
Open: 09.00-01.00 (Fri & Sat till 02.00)
A pretty corner café offering a range of coffees and teas augmented in summer by iced specials. Fleur is a popular spot for browsing through the papers or enjoying a chat over a cup or glass. The drinks list includes four white, three red and a rosé in 10cl or 20cl glasses and lots of spirits and cocktails. Snacks are served lunchtime and evening, and salads are available throughout the afternoon.

Guildenhaus
Grosse Budengasse 10, 50667 *U-Bahn: Dom/Hbf*
Tel: 221 257 5966
Open: 08.00-03.00
Housed in a building that dates back to the 13th century, Guildenhaus offers solid refreshment from breakfast time to midnight and liquid sustenance until well into the small hours. It's very popular with locals, and on May Day musicians meet here for a big party, when they play and sing and dance. Several beers are available from the hop-hung bar, and the recommended draught is the local Kölsch served in 20cl slips. The Mett, a crusty roll with a filling of steak tartare and onion, is a popular, satisfying snack. The café

is tucked away in a side street round the corner from the Cathedral, the Opera and the Old Market.

Haus Schwan
Dürenerstrasse 235, 50931 *Tram: Lindenthal*
Tel: 221 40 33 68
Open: 11.00-01.00
In a well-known street leading west out of town, this café-bar is a favourite among the gregarious townsfolk, and at Carnival time (in February) becomes the focus for organising the float for its district. Marionettes hang above the bar, along with badges representing the various districts. Good food, served at kind prices, can be enjoyed at the bleached tables set on the scrubbed oak floors to the left of the bar. Excellent local brews.

Café Orlando
Engelbertstrasse 9 *U-Bahn: Zülpicher Platz*
Tel: 221 237 523
Open: 09.00-01.00
This delightful dear little café in the student district is renowned for its home cooking. Coffee is served with a delicious little biscuit, and the prices are all very reasonable. They do eight fruit juices, eight milk shakes, chili con carne, omelettes etc, and have a very reasonable wine list.

Peters Brauhaus
Mübalengasse 1, 50667 *U-Bahn: Dom/Hbf (actually Mühlengasse)*
Tel: 221 257 39 50
Open: 11.00-24.00
In the Altstadt, and not far from the Philharmonie and the Rathaus, Peters Brauhaus serves an excellent range of beers from their own brewery. Food is mainly traditional Cologne fare – snacks like cheese, or boiled salt beef with bread, or more substantial (*very* substantial) dishes such as sausages with fried potatoes, pork with mashed potatoes, knuckle of pork, black pudding etc. Businessmen come during the day and mingle with the tourists and shoppers, while at night opera-goers mix with locals and visitors here for a good night out.

Pomp
Lindenstrasse 38, 50674 *U-Bahn: Rudolfplatz*
Tel: 221 21 11 12
Open: 09.00-02.00 (Fri & Sat till 03.00, Sun from 10.00)
A popular and very sociable meeting place with internet access, a thronging interior and pavement tables shaded by leafy trees.

Café Reichard
Unter Feltenhennen 11 *U-Bahn: Dom/Hbf*
Tel: 221 2 57 85 42
Open: 08.00-20.00
Part of a small chain of four, this seriously smart bar, tea room, restaurant and shop is one of the very best in Cologne. From the large terrace (which in summer is set with tables and chairs), or from the conservatory, you can see the front of the impressive cathedral (Dom) in the centre of the Altstadt. The shop sells pralines, sweets and cakes as colourful and as enticing as anywhere in the world. In the mornings there's a breakfast buffet as good or better than in a top-class hotel, with hot and cold food, and of course, a selection of their pastries. The restaurant has an extensive cold buffet, with

strudels among the specialities. Another real treat is the coffee, and yet another the ice cream. There's a choice of five Italian wines by the glass and two draught beers. A very impressive establishment which has remained at the top of the tree since it first opened its doors in 1855.

Vintage
Pfeilstrasse 31-35, 50672 *U-Bahn: Rudolfplatz*
Tel: 221 92 07 10
Open: 10.00-24.00 (kitchen: 12.00-15.00 & 18.00-23.00 (Fri till 24.00, Sat 12.00-24.00)
Closed: Sun
One of the very best of its kind in Cologne, this splendid café-wine bar has a wine list that is extensive, imaginative and very reasonably priced; bottles are available for retail off-sale, and if you drink it on the premises there's a modest corkage. They also stock some excellent produce from Italy, including charcuterie and olive oil, and the espresso is first-rate. The design of the place is light and modern, and the private courtyard terrace is a great spot on warm days and balmy evenings.

Waschsalon
Ehrenstrasse 77, 50672 *U-Bahn: Friesenplatz*
Tel: 221 13 33 78
Open: 09.00-01.00 (Fri & Sat till 03.00)
Waschsalon, as the name suggests, started life as a launderette where you could have a coffee while using the machines. But that didn't wash with the customers, so they used the machines in the decor – carcasses in the bar front, drums for light shades, bases of stools at the bar etc, and now the place bustles! Big and open, with bench seating under huge umbrellas in the pedestrianised street, the café offers breakfast in the mornings, from the simple to the truly filling, and at weekends a buffet brunch. Four wines are offered by the 15cl glass and the coffee is good. The food choice also includes pizzas, salads, chicken wings and fries.

Wippenbekk Café (Restaurant and Hotel)
Karlstrasse 7-9, D-50996 *U-Bahn: Deutzer Freiheit*
Tel: 221 93 53 150
Open: 11.00-01.00 (Sat & Sun from 10.00)
The views of the Rhine are a big attraction at this café in the pretty suburb of Rodenkirchen, with a conservatory open to the bar, and stepped-down terraces open to the elements. It serves Segafredo coffee and several wines by the 10cl glass, and you can prolong your stay with a snack such as soup or a ciabatta sandwich, or a meal from the à la carte menu, or the 2- or 3-course fixed price menu during the day. A haunt for tourists and city dwellers who come for the view.

Frankfurt

Goethe's famous phrase 'Rest not, life is sweeping by' springs to mind as you explore the poet's home city. And if Frankfurt was pacey in Goethe's time, then today's go-getting, high-rise city is the Manhattan of Europe. Down among the skyscrapers in Westend, you might find yourself forgetting for a moment that Frankfurt is as much about fun as it is about finance. So head for the bars of Bockenheim, and sample the stunning local white wines until you're back in the mood for relaxation. Start with a stroll around the museums on the Main's south bank. If time's pressing just see the Städel – for many, Germany's greatest gallery, where Rubens, Holbein, Rembrandt and contemporary geniuses are all ready to greet you.

Café au Lait/Bistro Maria
Am Weingarten 12, Bockenheim *U-Bahn: U-Bahn - Leipzigerstr*
Tel: 69 70 10 39
Open: 09.00-01.00 (Sun 10.00-18.00)
Café Au Lait, aka Bistro Maria, lies among residential streets out to the north-west of town. There's just enough room outside for a narrow line of pavement tables, while up some steps inside there's the bar and a good view through the windows. The place is renowned for its excellent variety of breakfasts, from the simple French to the 'extrem' for two. Apart from that, there is a daily card of hot and cold dishes, and a reasonable range of wines by the glass.

Café Bar 13
Am Wilhelmsplatz 13, Offenbach
Tel:
Open: 09.00-01.00 (Sat till 02.00)
Value for money is the order of the day at Café Bar 13, where refreshments and meals are offered from breakfast time to the cocktail hour: soups, salads, pasta, fish, vegetarian dishes and all sorts cooked in the wok. Specialities here include the breakfasts, starring the Sunday buffet served from 09.30 to 15.00, and the cocktails.

Chez Daniel
Brückenstrasse 35, Sachsenhausen *U-Bahn: U-Bahn - Schweizerplatz*
Tel: 69 61 82 47
Open: 10.00-01.00 (Sat & Sun from 17.00)
Chez Daniel is roomy, friendly and unashamedly French – the name is emblazoned across a tricolore. It is firmly established in the gastronomic centre of Frankfurt, with tables spilling out on to the pavement under aquamarine awnings. The menu is typified by snails in a calvados cream sauce, and bouillabaisse with all the trimmings, while simpler snacks take the form of filled baguettes. The wine list is strong on Alsace.

Café Extrablatt
Bockenheimer Landstrasse 141, Bockenheim
Tel: 79 40 39 99
Open: 10.00-24.00 *U-Bahn: U-Bahn - Westend or Bockenheimer Warte*
Part of a large and successful chain, this Extrablatt lies north-west of the city centre. It serves an extensive range of breakfasts, notably a buffet that extends to midday on weekdays and until 14.00 on Sundays. Other snacks include American/Italian dishes like pizzas, pasta and salads. The standard Extrablatt range of two red and two white wines by the glass, choice of beers, very good coffee and hot chocolate.

Holbein's
Holbeinstrasse 1, Sachsenhausen *U-Bahn: U-Bahn - Schweizerplatz*
Tel: 69 66 05 66 66
Open: 10.00-24.00
Closed: Mon
This very grand café-restaurant stands in a mature garden, with imposing gates and glass walls extending up through three storeys; wide steps lead up to terrace tables with basket-weave chairs under parasols. Renowned for its seafood, this is the in place to eat in Frankfurt, to meet your friends for a prosecco in the heart of the gastronomic district, Sachsenhausen.

Café Karin
Grosse Hirschgraben 28 *U-Bahn: U-Bahn - Hauptwache*
Tel: 69 29 52 17
Open: 09.00-01.00 (Fri & Sat till 02.00, Sun 10.00-19.00)
Karin is a busy city-centre café in classical style, with globe and chandelier lighting, comfortable round wooden tables, newspapers, and lots of people coming to meet friends to chat over a drink or a snack. It offers a range of breakfasts and a lunchtime menu, with dishes served by friendly, professional staff. A macaroon accompanies espresso served in the familiar gold-rimmed, green Apilco china; they even serve Ovaltine! The evenings attract thirsty locals with a decent variety of wines by the glass and good draught beer.

Café Liliput
Neue Kräme 29/Sandhof Passage *U-Bahn: U-Bahn - Römer*
Tel: 69 28 57 27
Open: 09.00-22.00
Hidden away in a city-centre shopping arcade just off the Römerberg in the city centre, this is a delightful little place, small and cosy within, and also with a garden with flowers and shrubs. Drinks range from tea, coffee and hot chocolate kir royal; for the hungry, three or four different cakes, a choice of soups and a variety of French and German breakfasts.

Living XXL
Kaiserstrasse 29 *U-Bahn: U-Bahn - Willybrandtplatz*
Tel: 69 24 29 37 10
Open: 11.30-01.00 (Fri till 03.00, Sat 16.00-03.00, Sun 19.00-02.00)
Facing the Theatre, by the Eurobank, Living XXL caters for those here for business or for culture. Look up through the glass roof and the Europe Tower looms above. This is skyscraper terrain. Fortunately, although it reaches out from the basement on two levels leading to the bar and terrace, its aspect is open space. The long bar serves good espresso, several wines by the glass and draught beers, and a good, imaginative range of dishes is served in the downstairs restaurant, which has a dance floor for evening jollity.

Opéra/Café Rosso
Opernplatz 1/Alte Oper *U-Bahn: U-Bahn - Alte Oper*
Tel: 69 13 40 215
Open: 10.30-24.00 (restaurant 12.00-01.00)
Part of the imposing Frankfurt Opera house complex, the café has a highly ornate ceiling, smart bar, elegant tables and loose-covered chairs looking out through the tall windows. It feels immediately chic with the ruched curtains and patterned tile floor, elegant globe chandeliers and gilded ornamental plasterwork. Yet it is inexpensive, and the friendly professional

service makes visitors feel instantly at ease. The menu offers a choice of wholesome, straightforward dishes, with wines by the glass to accompany. Upstairs is Opéra, a larger and even more elegant room with even more to offer.

Schiffer Café
Schifferstrasse 36, Sachsenhausen *U-Bahn: U-Bahn - Schweizerplatz*
Tel: 69 61 99 32 21
Open: 08.00-20.00 (Sat till 19.00, Sun 09.00-19.00)
Schiffer is a corner café and provisioner in a residential area south of the River Main. stands this 'L'-shaped corner café-cum-larder. Behind the bar are shelves with some of those things that get forgotten on the shopping list, the biscuits, coffee and tea and drinking chocolate, jam and preserves, demerara sugar. A tiny amaretto biscuit accompanies the espresso, the coffee being from the excellent firm of Wacker. Wine is served by the 20cl glass. A good range of breakfasts is offered, and assorted blends of tea. A tall ceiling and a floor tiled in pale beige, create a good of feeling of space, and there's a rack of papers to read.

Schirn Café
Römerberg 6a *U-Bahn: U-Bahn - Römer*
Tel: 69 29 17 32
Open: 11.00-01.00 (Sun till 24.00, Mon from 19.00)
A stylish modern café in the centrally located Veranstalungs Gallery. A horseshoe central bar serves glass-topped coffee tables at the entrance to the right, and to the left, tall tables (pedestal swagged) and a grand piano stands; all is columns and curves, and beyond the bar are restaurant tables.

Hamburg

Relaxing in a rowing boat on the Alstersee, as sunlight polishes this tranquil lake, it's easy to forget you're in the heart of Germany's foremost trading centre. Fortunately for today's traveller, Hamburg is just as good at fun as it is at business. As well as being Germany's leafiest city (with half its area turned over to parks, lakes and gardens) this buzzing port also boasts a cutting-edge café and cultural scene. To survey it all, take a lift up the 900 feet tall Herz tower from where you can see the Rathouse (town hall) and the huge port area. Ponder your next move with another sort of 'Altsterwasser'- the refreshing local lager.

Bobby Reich
Fernsicht 2 *U-Bahn: Klosterstern*
Tel: 40 487 824
Open: 10.00-24.00

Booby Reich stands at the northern end of Aussalter, one of the two main lakes in the centre of the city. It's a great place to be in summer, when tables are set out across a raft terrace. The decor consists of variations on a musical theme with marine bits and pieces thrown in.

Die Brücke
Innocentiastrasse 82 *U-Bahn: Hoheluftbrücke*
Tel: 40 422 55 25
Open: 11.00-02.00 (Sun 19.00-24.00)

A bar-restaurant whose appeal and clientele change throughout the day. Coffee and little snacks are served from opening time, joined at noon for lunch with a largely business clientele. It's back to snacks until the early evening, when the dinner menu comes into operation (last orders 23.00). From mid-evening, a mainly young set takes over till the wee hours, transforming the atmosphere into that of a loud and trendy bar.

Eisenstein
Fridensallee 5 *S-Bahn: Altona*
Tel: 40 390 46 06
Open: 11.00-01.30

Eisenstein is a trendy café-bar in a converted factory set back from the road in a side street to the west of the Altstadt. Spacious and open-plan with a sweeping bar, it is part of modern shopping mall development, and among the other shops is an excellent wine merchant. Pizza and pasta are the specialities, and Sunday brunch is served from 10.00 to 15.00. Plenty of outside seats.

Brasserie Gröninger

Ost-West-Strasse 47 *U-Bahn: Messberg*
Tel: 40 331 381
Open: 11.00-24.00 (Sat 17.00-02.00)
Closed: Sun

Beer is king at the vast and atmospheric Brasserie Gröninger, which is located in the cellars of the old town brewery – still visible through glass panels. Old brass brew-pots that were once part of the daily operations upstairs are now on display in the bar. The beer is available in anything from a small glass to a barrel holding 20 litres which is brought to your table on a stand for you and your party to help yourselves. Hearty German dishes provide the blotting paper.

Open

Eppendorferlandstrasse 31 *U-Bahn: Eppendorfer Baum*
Tel: 40 480 36 07
Open: 10.00-22.00 (Sat & Sun till 20.00)
A firm favourite with the locals, Open is a modern bar with marble bar-top and tables. Modern music (often Latin American) plays in the background and service is unrushed and unpretentious. The menu changes every fortnight.

German National Tourist Office

Munich

In a city where history, culture and sport run so deep – you'd be sticking your neck out to say that beer is Munich's number one attraction. But it is. Twenty million pints of Bavaria's best await your attention at the Oktoberfest, Munich's mammoth beer bash held every autumn since 1810. Out-of-season, beer hunters can shelter from winter snow among the stein swiggers in the cavernous Hofbrauhaus, spend Easter at the Festival of Strong Beers, and devote a strenuous summer session to supping in the historic 'biergärten' in the Englischer park. For a momentary break from the brew, take the S-bahn to the spectacular 1970's Olympiczentrum - and view the city from its soaring tower. If you're feeling dizzy, blame the revolving deck.

Arzmiller Konditorei-Café

Salvatorstrasse 2, 8000-2 *U-Bahn: Odeonsplatz*
Tal 11, Böhmler-Passage
Tel: 89 29 42 73
Open: 08.00-18.30 (Sat 09.00-18.00)
Closed: Sun
Two patisserie outlets tucked unobtrusively away, the first in the inner courtyard of the Theatinerhof (theatre house), the other through the shopping arcade Böhmler. They both use the very good Alfredo coffee, which can be enriched with one of their wide range of pastries and cakes. They also offer a good range of alcoholic drinks, which can be enjoyed away from the hubbub of traffic in these secluded pedestrian areas.

Café am Beethoven platz

Goethestrasse 51, 80336 *U-Bahn: Sendlinger Tor*
Tel: 89 54 40 43 48
Open: 09.00-01.00
A veteran dating back to 1899, this 'concert café' sells good beer, good wine (14 wines available by the glass), tasty pastries and other meals too, salads and dishes of the day, and a good, strong espresso. A bust of Beethoven stands in the middle of the café, and there's a grand piano just inside the door. Live music most nights, usually starting around 19.30.

Kaffee Dukatz
Literaturhaus, Salvatorplatz 1, 80333 *U-Bahn: Odeonplatz*
Tel: 89 29 19 60-0
Open: 10.00-01.00
There's a French theme to this very large and busy café-bar-restaurant in the Literaturhaus, with a balcony built above and behind the bar under the long, high-vaulted ceiling. Behind the bar are bottles of pastis, calvados, cognac and armagnac, and also on display is the standard document summarising the French regulations regarding the sale of liquor to minors. People come here to read, chat, meet, have lunch, read the newspapers... Meals are served lunchtime and evening.

Faun
Hans Sachs strasse 17 *U-Bahn: Fraunhoferstr*

Tel: 89 263 798
Open: 10.00-01.00 (Fri & Sat till 02.00)
This busy, busy bar, formerly a discothèque, was established in 1994 and is a great favourite with the younger crowd. The bar and tables are in light oak, the ceiling high, with art nouveau decor in aquamarine. There's plenty of seating at tables or on bar stools, and the slatted chairs and tables outside are always popular. Breakfast is served from 10.00 to 16.00, and at weekends until 21.00! The main menu offers a good selection of dishes, including some game (rabbit, duck, venison), and two lunchtime specials widen the choice. Many regulars drink the Munich Weissbier – it's bottled and comes up cloudy; alternatives include wine by the glass, good espresso and a selection of teas. Lots of newspapers and magazines on sticks if you're alone, but on Friday nights everyone talks to everyone at this very friendly and sociable place.

Café Freiheit
Leonrodstrasse 20 *U-Bahn: Rotkreuzplatz*

Tel: 89 134 686
Open: 09.00-01.00
Going northwest from the centre of town, in the Neuhausen district, this comfortable café is run by affable young girls for a clientele of both local residents and students. The all-Italian wine list is extensive, and the special monthly promotions are a very popular feature. The breakfast menu is served until 16.00 and dinner from 18.00. Bossanova music plays in the background. Outside tables in the summer.

Glockenspiel Café
Marienplatz 28 *S-Bahn: Marienplatz U-Bahn: Marienplatz*
Tel: 89 264 256
Open: 10.00-01.00
Closed: Sun in Jul & Aug
The entrance to Glockenspiel is in Rosenstrasse through an arcade, almost next door to the Metropolitan, and on the fifth floor, but at the back of the building, it is a terrace bar with a canopy for winter. Slatted bench seating and wicker chairs were designed to give it a Mediterranean feel, assisted by Spanish music playing. Good coffee, lots of beers and wines, cocktails, light snacks.

FASCHINATING FASCHING

Little-known outside Germany, Fasching is a street party to rival anything in Rio. The country simply goes bananas... and parties for seven days solid. We steer you to the heart of the action.

Mention the word 'Germany' to most people and they might think 'beer', 'sausages' and 'football'. Keep on prodding and you'll get 'fast cars' and the 'Black Forest'. But ask the same question of anyone who's been to Fasching and you'll hear 'salsa in the streets', 'party frenzy' and 'what a week!' Welcome to one of the best kept secrets on the Euro social calendar.

Formal details: Strictly speaking, Fasching is part of the Christian celebration of Lent. Harking back to medieval street processions, Fasching reaches its peak with parties on Rosenmontag (the 42nd day before Easter) with the fun timed to end just before Ash Wednesday. Formerly a pivotal moment in the Christian calendar – and a chance for stratified medieval society to dissolve into a week of partying – you'd have to look hard to find many religious elements in today's Fasching.

Kicking off: For most people, the starting gun for a week of madness is 'Weiberfastnacht' (women's carnival) which falls on the Thursday before Rosenmontag. In a ritual that Freud would have had interesting views on, Weiberfastnacht gives every woman in Germany a green light to chop the tie of any man they can get their hands on. Offices, bars and streets are literally full of women with flashing pairs of scissors – and men with savaged neckware. In a foretaste of the week to come, women are also allowed to kiss any man they choose.

Homing in: Just to add to the confusion of an already giddy week, Fasching has different names all over Germany. It's called 'Karneval' in the Rheinland cities of Aachen, Bonn and Düsseldorf; 'Fastnacht' in Mainz; and Fasching in Munich. But don't let the vocabulary fool you. Head for any of the cities we've named and you'll be exposed to a week of cutting-edge partying. Yes, there are the carnivals and floats by day – but it's at night that things really go bonkers. Quite simply, almost every bar throws open its doors until dawn, booze flows like the Amazon, and Germany parties like there's no tomorrow. In an unwritten law, Germans are discouraged to sue for divorce for anything that does (or doesn't) happen during Fasching.

Best of the best: If you only do one Fasching (and once is usually enough) head for Cologne. With a carnival dating back to 1341, a Prince of Festivities known as Seine Tollität, 'His Craziness', and 1.5 million revellers, Cologne breaks every record for fun. Yes, you should make an effort to get up in daylight at least once to see the mighty processions thrown by Cologne's 105 ancient carnival guilds. For the rest... party on!

Iwan
Josephspitalstrasse 15 *U-Bahn: Sendlinger Tor*
Tel: 89 554 933
Open: 12.00-02.00 (Sun from 17.00)
In a courtyard well back from the traffic on the ring road, Iwan is located behind the Swedish Embassy, whose premises it shares. It is essentially a wine bar, but there's almost no representation from Germany. There's wine from France, Portugal, Italy and Spain; snacks are available, there's a salad bar and pasta dishes are served at lunchtime. Jazz/swing music plays. The tables, bar and bar front feature lots of steely grey granite, and in the day the light streams through the virtually all-glass outside wall, while at night the red lighting over the bar creates an intimate atmosphere. Lots of bar stools, little snacks served free 21.50-23.50, balcony restaurant over the ground-floor bar.

Luigi Tambosi am Hofgarten

Odeonsplatz 18, 80539 *U-Bahn: Odeonplatz*
Tel: 89 29 83 22
Open: 09.00-01.00
It's German owned, but it's named after a well-known Italian who opened the first café here in Munich some 200 years ago. The food emphasis is on French and Italian cuisine. Tables are set in the Hofgarten, and there's a terrace at the front, while inside, the velvet-clad chairs sit at little marble tables and a sweeping gallery served by a spiral staircase looks down on the pleasant scene. Next door is the spectacular Hofgarten and Palace, while across the road Versace and other top designers have their shops.

Café Luitpold
Briennerstrasse 11 *U-Bahn: Odeonplatz*
Tel: 89 292 865
Open: 09.00-18.00 (Sat 08.00-19.00)
Opened in 1888, this was Munich's answer to the famous cafés in Paris, Vienna and Berlin, and bears the name of the then Prince Regent of Bavaria. A venue favoured from the beginning by aristocracy and literary figures, and later by musicians and artists, the café of those early years was destroyed by fire at the end of the Second World War. When rebuilt, it incorporated the boutiques of well-known high-street names. The spacious café has a patisserie in the middle, and tables extend into an inner courtyard where businessmen, shoppers and tourists flock for lunch.

Metropolitan Café
Marienplatz 22 *S-Bahn: Marienplatz U-Bahn: Marienplatz*
Tel: 89 230 970
Open: 09.00-01.00 (Sun from 10.00)
A fast glass lift carries customers up to the café, which occupies the top two floors of the Metropolitan building. It overlooks the Marienplatz, the scene of many a dramatic event in Munich's history. Uppermost is the café-bar and cocktails, below, the restaurant. In the square there are also bench café tables. Directly in front is the exotic clock where, when it strikes 11 o'clock (and also 5 o'clock on summer afternoons), two groups of figures perform, one above the other. The very elegant, airy, modern bar-café has royal blue suede chairs and beech-topped tables on stainless steel frames, recessed low-voltage ceiling lighting, and tall windows to the floor to make the most of the view. Among the items on offer are coffee, six types of tea, and a choice of eight breakfasts. The light lunch menu reflects the very international feel that prevails in Munich.

Münchner Kartoffelhaus
Hochbrückenstrasse 3 *U-Bahn: Marienplatz*
Tel: 89 296 331
Open: 11.30-01.00
Closed: Sun
Potato is king in this excellent bar-cum-restaurant, boiled, sauteéd, mashed and especially baked. There's even potato pasta and, of course, potato schnapps! A good selection of beers is served at the oak bar, which gets very busy as the evening wears on. Hot food is served non-stop from opening time through to 23.30. There are also dishes like veal or smoked salmon, but you can gamble all your chips that potatoes will creep in somewhere.

Café Reitschule
Königstrasse 34 *U-Bahn: Giselastr*
Tel: 89 333 402
Open: 09.00-01.00
The university riding school is situated beside the Englischer Garten (actually designed by an Anglophile American called Benjamin Thompson). It has a very roomy café, bar, restaurant and terrace overlooking the stables, and inside there's a window through which you can watch the indoor school. The long bar is towards the middle, with dining at one end (about 30 covers) and the café at the other (60 covers); the terrace is at the back. Some typical dishes on the menu: spinach soup, cold meats and salads, spaghetti, lamb provençale. Two-course set lunch, weekend brunch. Newspapers for browsing.

Café Roma

Maximilianstrasse 31, 80539 *S-Bahn: Marienplatz U-Bahn: Marienplatz*
Tel: 89 22 74 35
Open: 08.00-03.00

A stylish Italian watering hole with lots of tables outside under large awnings, with space heaters for warmth. This is the beginning of fashion street – all the top names have premises – and the Munich Kempinski is also here, so the faces are here, too. Breakfast with the papers starts the day; then comes lunch, and later on the fun starts, with wine lovers, indeed lovers, coming to sip and laugh with their friends.

Schlosscafé im Palmenhaus

Schloss Nymphenburg Eingang 43 *Area: NW of city centre. Tram: 17*
Tel: 89 175 309
Open: 09.00-18.00 (summer till 18.30)

A very elegant café occupying the long side of the lofty glass palm house in the grounds of the magnificent castle. Visitors like to stroll through the well-groomed symmetrical gardens, with their moat and lakes, before passing through the tall hedge into an enclosed garden with the Palmenhaus and its terrace. The café is a very popular venue, especially at the weekend; on Sundays between 10.00 and 14.00 they play live music.

Schumann's American Bar

Maximilianstrasse 36, 80539 *S-Bahn: Marienplatz*
Tel: 89 229 268
Open: 17.00-03.00 (Sun from 18.00)
Closed: Sat

Charles Schumann gave his name to this American-style cocktail bar when he opened it in January 1982. A prolific author on American cocktails, and of stories around them (*Tropical Bar Book; Artistry of Mixing Drinks; Whisk(e)y Lexicon*), he has decorated the bar in black, with mirrors: the bar, the stools and the tables are all black, and the cupboards and wood panelling are stained dark brown going to black at the frames. The lighting is carefully directed to light surfaces, while maintaining the intimate club-like atmosphere, underscored by gentle jazz piano music. Early evening visitors are besuited businessmen and some elegant couples. There's an impressive list of single malts, and several champagnes.

Hungary

With a riverside location matched only by Paris, coffee houses that would turn Vienna green with envy, and Turkish baths to rival anything in Istanbul, Budapest really is the city with it all. And then, of course, there's the rest of Hungary – a country to satisfy any appetite. Outside the capital Mother Nature has been rather generous to the Hungarian countryside – with peaks, forests and plains acting as a playground for outdoor fun. And despite its landlocked position on the map, Hungary also has its fair share of water. In fact with over 1,000 lakes – including the 600 square kilometres Lake Balaton – Hungary is as cool a summer destination as anywhere on the Med. On the subject of liquid pleasures, it's unlikely you'll leave Hungary without sampling a glass or two of their fabled Bull's Blood wine. But travel east of Budapest to the vineyards of Eger and Mátra and wine lovers will think they've died and gone to heaven (with its huge cellars and magnificent caverns, Eger is the heart of Bull's Blood country). Gastronomes won't be disappointed either with mouth-watering dishes such as pörkölt (goulash) and jokai babieves (spicy bean soup). Among all these treats, perhaps the most memorable part of a visit to Hungary is the soundtrack. Whether it's listening to the strains of a Gypsy violin, relaxing in the elegant grounds of Brunswick palace for the annual Beethoven festival or checking out Debrecen's Jazz Days festival, it's clear that they're a nation with a lot to make a noise about.

Budapest

Standing on one of the many bridges that stretch across the Danube as the evening sun drops behind Castle Hill, you're in the perfect place to plan your next day in Budapest. On the other hand, you could just enjoy the moment – and let the capital plan things for you. At every turn, Budapest's buildings and monuments flaunt the city's historic past – so whether you've planned it or not, 'sightseeing' happens naturally. Highlights of your tour will almost certainly include the Museum of Fine Arts and the lovingly restored Central Market Hall. After a day on your feet there's no better way to unwind than by taking a dip in one of the capital's magnificent thermal baths. If there's a city that does hot water more lavishly than Budapest, then we'd like to know about it.

Café Angelika
1 Batthyany Ter 7 *Buda Metro: M2 - Batthyány Tér*
Tel: 1 212 3784
Open: 10.00-20.00
Café Angelika is a civilised, atmospheric café housed in the former crypt of St Anne's Church in Old Budapest, right by the Danube. In summer, a terrace gives views of Parliament across the river, while in winter patrons sit inside in cosy niches lit through dark stained glass and enjoy a variety of coffees and home-made cakes. A nice old-fashioned place and a favourite rendezvous for a good gossip.

Coquan's Kávé
Ráday utca 15 *Pest Metro: M - Kálura Tér*
Tel: 1 215 2444
Open: 09.00-17.00 (Sun from 11.00)
A small, friendly, American-style gourmet bar with a great line in coffees. The high ceiling, ochre walls and wooden floor, legacies of its days as a grand shop, provide a naturally light environment, enhanced by halogen spots over the bar. Coffee cocktails provide an added kick.

TIMELESS TOKAY

It can age for 200 years or more in the bottle, costs up to £200 for a single glass, and has provoked entire nations to war. But trace the legend of Tokay Aszu back to its source – and you find a mouldy grape in the hills of Hungary.

Louis XV of France called it the "wine of kings, and the king of wines", Voltaire dedicated a poem to this "amber beverage that weaves the golden threads of the mind", and big-shots from Schubert to Goethe have swooned over it. This is, clearly, a wine we need to take seriously. In fact the deeper you get into the 'visitors' book' of Tokay, the more gripping the story becomes. Peter the Great of Russia, for example, kept a regiment of Cossacks permanently in Tokay to make sure his personal supplies got through; Prince Rakoczi of Transylvania used a consignment of Tokay to persuade Louis XIV to back him in his war with the Habsburgs. When the flow of European history is being changed by a case of wine, we should at least have a glassful.

ROTTEN LUCK
The wines of the Tokaji region – a hundred miles east of Budapest – had been a favourite with the Romans and marauding Magyars since the time of Christ. But Tokay's big break dates to 1570, when grapes that were 'aszu' (shrivelled and infected with fungus) were found to be the unlikeliest ingredient for the world's finest dessert wine. The harvest of the aszu grapes – still done as it always was – would horrify a devotee of mass wine production. The grapes are not picked by the bunch, but individually selected to catch them at just the right stage of decay. In years of exceptional quality, even sweeter Eszencia wines are made from the virgin juice that drips un-pressed under the weight of the grape itself.

LYING LOW
One of the extraordinary qualities of this extraordinary wine is that – with 60 per cent sugar – it ferments more or less indefinitely. Today, in the miles of historic caves around Tokaji, some cellars still shelter wines that have quietly sat through two centuries of seismic change (the fall of the Austro-Hungarian empire, two world wars and the rise and fall of communism). The Tokay, meanwhile, just got a little sweeter.

TIME FOR A DROP
When a 19th century Hungarian poet described Tokay Aszu as "a golden flame locked up within a bottle", he might have been referring to the price as well as the taste. Prepare to get your wallet singed. For anyone wanting to sample the spell-binding fragrance of a pre-war vintage (dominated by pear and peach with hints of chocolate and almonds) a price tag of £1,000 a bottle awaits. For the rest of us, £10 buys a non-vintage bottle of Tokay. Delicious, but 195 years short of its sell-by date.

Incognito
VI Liszt Ferenc tér 3 *Pest Metro: M - Oktogon*
Tel: 1 267 9428
Open: 10.00-24.00 (Sat & Sun from 12.00)
The long-time favourite of the young of Budapest, with battered old furniture and the sleeves of rare jazz LPs that cover the walls just visible in the dim light. The trendy set flock here to sip their coffees and beers and spirits and cocktails, and listen to jazzy beats, having probably started the evening at one of the other bars on not-as-quiet-as-it-was Liszt Ferenc square.

Café Mozart
VII Erzsébet körút 36 *Buda Metro: M2 - Moszkva Tér*
Tel: 1 267 8586
Open: 09.00-23.00 (Sat till 24.00)
A wide selection of coffees and pastries can be enjoyed at this Mozart-themed place. The jazzed-up garden furniture is topped only by the waitresses in tight-laced baroque costume and the mirthmaking murals depicting scenes from the life of the great composer.

Café New York (New York Kavehaz)
Erzebet Korut 9-11 *Buda Metro: M2 - Moszkva Tér*
Tel: 1 322 3849
Open: 09.00-24.00
A once glorious meeting place for the literati of Pest at the turn of the century. Now primitive scaffolding supports a frontage which was rammed in 1956 by a Russian tank. Inside, however, is in sumptuous contrast: a riot of art nouveau decor — twisted columns, wrought iron and gilding — seduces visitors into abandoning thoughts of tea and sandwiches and ordering cocktails, caviar, a mountainous concoction of cream and chocolate, and fabulous coffee.

Ruszwurm
1 Szentharomsag Utca 3
Tel: 1 375 5284
Open: 10.00-20.00
Closed: Wed
Popular with tourists visiting Castle Hill, this tiny salon nestles among the old cobbled streets high above the city. Its linzertorte was already renowned in Hapsburg Vienna by the turn of the century. Today its two small rooms still evoke the era, with pastel-coloured walls, a chandelier, antique-filled glass cabinets and a ceramic stove. This is an elegant spot for sipping iced coffees and ice creams in summer and a range of coffees, teas and hot chocolate in winter.

As with previous editions of the *Café Crème Guide to the Cafés of Europe*, one of the privileges of reviewing Europe's cafés is acknowledging the very best of the best.

In the fifth year of our European Café Awards, it's our pleasure to name the establishments below as the winners of the following categories:

☆☆☆ Grand European Café of the Year

☆☆☆ Best French, Italian, Portuguese, Spanish and UK Café of the Year

☆☆☆ Best Café of the Year for the rest of Europe

If you're lucky enough to visit one of these establishments in their Award-winning year, we hope you agree they represent the cream of European café culture.

Grand European Café of the Year
☆☆☆☆☆☆☆☆☆
Majestic Café, Oporto, Portugal

Majestic by name, majestic by nature. Immortalised by the national poet Antonio Ferro in 1922, this remarkable café has long been the favourite haunt of Portuguese intellectuals. Today, the sumptuous establishment and its legendary wine list, menu and ambience have been declared a National Monument by the Ministry for Archaeology and Architecture.

FRANCE
☆☆☆☆☆☆☆☆☆
La Coupole, Paris

One of the most renowned brasseries that sprang up after the 1925 'Exhibition of Decorative Arts', this art-deco masterpiece has been a 'must' for everyone living in or visiting Paris. Whether you're here to take in the decor (including columns painted by different artists and a revolving sculpture) or indulge in the art of people-watching, the opportunities here are world-class.

ITALY
☆☆☆☆☆☆☆☆☆
Antico Caffè Greco, Rome

Situated on Rome's high altar of fashion, the Via Condotti, the Antico Caffè Greco has always liked to choose its clientele carefully. The list of regulars – including Goethe, Casanova and Wagner – is about as exclusive as you can get. Settle into a velvet upholstered chair beneath the gilded mirrors, and you'll soon be feeling a million dollars.

PORTUGAL

☆☆☆☆☆☆☆☆

**Majestic Café,
Oporto**

see Grand European Café of the Year

SPAIN

☆☆☆☆☆☆☆☆☆

**Nuevo Café
Barbieri, Madrid**

Ask a Madrileño to name their single favourite feature of this legendary café, and they'll probably want to list five or six. Supported by lovely 19th century columns, the Nuevo Café Barbieri also boasts a beautiful curved bar, elegantly fading mirrored walls, seductive lighting and acres of voluptuous red velvet. Pondering which is your favourite feature, choose from the giddying menu of 20 varieties of coffee.

UK

☆☆☆☆☆☆☆☆☆

**Konditor & Cook,
London**

Sitting cheek-by-jowl with the trendy Young Vic theatre, Konditor & Cook rises to the occasion with a superb range of cakes and pastries (supporting dazzling performances from the café's savoury headliners). Bright and lively – and home to a buzzing theatre crowd – Konditor & Cook shows off the best of coffee, cooking and charisma that London has to offer.

**BEST OF THE
REST OF EUROPE**

☆☆☆☆☆☆☆☆

**Café Reichard,
Cologne, Germany**

Whether you're looking outside towards the view of the Dom, or inside towards the mouth-watering menu, Café Reichard is a show-stopper. The pralines, sweets and cakes are heavenly, the breakfast buffet rivals anything from a top hotel, and the panoramic views from both terrace and conservatory are jaw-dropping. A worthy winner.

Europe	1998	**Caffè Florian, Venice, Italy**
	1999	**El Pabellon del Espejo, Madrid, Spain**
	2000	**Les Deux Magots, Paris, France**
	2001	**Café Landtmann, Vienna, Austria**
	2003	**Majestic Café, Oporto, Portugal**

Austria	1998	**Café of the Year**: Café Sperl, Vienna
		Special Award: Hawelka, Vienna
	1999	**Café of the Year**: Hotel Sacher, Vienna
		Special Award: Valena, Vienna
	2000	**Café of the Year**: Tomaselli, Salzburg
		Special Award: Café Diglas, Vienna
	2001	**Café of the Year**: Café Landtmann, Vienna
		Special Award: Niemetz, Salzburg

Benelux	1998	**Café of the Year**: Café Luxembourg, Amsterdam
		Special Award: Café in den Vogelstruys, Maastricht
	1999	**Café of the Year**: De Groote Witte Arend, Antwerp
		Special Award: De Ultimatie Hallucinatie, Brussels
	2000	**Café of the Year**: Amadeus, Brussels
		Special Award: Tomas, Eindhoven
	2001	**Café of the Year**: Le Falstaff, Brussels
		Special Award: Café Americain, Amsterdam

Denmark	2000	**Café of the Year**: Victor, Copenhagen
		Special Award: Franck A, Odense
	2001	**Café of the Year**: Opera Cafeen, Copenhagen
		Special Award: Café Gertrud, Odense

France	1998	**Café of the Year**: Café Marly, Paris
		Special Award: Les Pipos, Paris
	1999	**Café of the Year**: La Cigale, Nantes
		Special Award: Pause Café, Paris
	2000	**Café of the Year**: Les Deux Magots, Paris
		Special Award: Les Flots Bleus, Marseilles
	2001	**Café of the Year**: Bouillon Racine, Paris
		Special Award: Excelsior, Nancy
	2003	**Café of the Year**: La Coupole, Paris

Germany	1998	**Café of the Year**: Café Einstein, Berlin
		Special Award: Luigi Tambosi am Hofgarten, Munich
	1999	**Café of the Year**: Wintergarten im Literaturhaus, Berlin
		Special Award: Café Reitschule, Hamburg
	2000	**Café of the Year**: Café Adler, Berlin
		Special Award: Bobby Reich, Hamburg
	2000	**Café of the Year**: Hollandische, Hanover
		Special Award: Et Kaduffke, Dusseldorf
	2003	**Best of the Rest**: Café Reichard, Cologne

Ireland	1999	**Café of the Year**:	Bodega, Cork
		Special Award:	Bridge Café Bar (Bewley), Dublin
	2000	**Café of the Year**:	Thomas Read, Dublin
		Special Award:	The Palace, Dublin
	2001	**Café of the Year**:	Clancy's, Cork
		Special Award:	Kaffe Moka, Dublin
Italy	1998	**Café of the Year**:	Caffè Florian, Venice
		Special Award:	Antico Caffè Greco, Rome
	1999	**Café of the Year**:	Osteria Caffè Italiano, Florence
		Special Award:	LaTega, Verona
	2000	**Café of the Year**:	Babington's, Rome
		Special Award:	Giubbe Rosse, Florence
	2001	**Café of the Year**:	Quadri, Venice
		Special Award:	Antica Caffè della Pace, Rome
	2003	**Café of the Year**:	Antico Caffè Greco, Rome
Portugal	1999	**Café of the Year**:	Martinho da Arcada, Lisbon
		Special Award:	Majestic Café, Oporto
	2000	**Café of the Year**:	Café Nicola, Lisbon
		Special Award:	Pavilhao Chines, Lisbon
	2001	**Café of the Year**:	A Brasileira, Lisbon
		Special Award:	Gambrinus, Lisbon
	2003	**Café of the Year**:	Majestic Café, Oporto
Scandinavia	2000	**Café of the Year**:	Fazer, Helsinki
		Special Award:	Theatercaféen, Oslo
	2001	**Café of the Year**:	Operabaren, Stockholm
		Special Award:	Grand Café, Hotel Driftselskap, Oslo
Spain	1998	**Café of the Year**:	Café Gijón, Madrid
		Special Award:	Café de l'Opera, Barcelona
	1999	**Café of the Year**:	El Pabellon del Espejo, Madrid
		Special Award:	Pilar del Toro, Granada
	2000	**Café of the Year**:	Café Comercial, Madrid
		Special Award:	Café Iruña, Bilbao
	2001	**Café of the Year**:	Café de Oriente, Madrid
		Special Award:	Els Quatre Gats, Barcelona
	2003	**Café of the Year**:	Nuevo Café Barbieri, Madrid
United Kingdom	1998	**Café of the Year**:	Mud Dock Café, Bristol
		Special Award:	Picasso, London
	1999	**Café of the Year**:	The Troubadour, London
		Special Award:	Madisons, Belfast
	2000	**Café of the Year**:	Le Metro, London
		Special Award:	Café Concerto, York
	2001	**Café of the Year**:	Browns, Bristol
		Special Award:	Arches, London
	2003	**Café of the Year**:	Konditor & Cook, London

If pleasure was an Olympic sport, then Italy would hold every record – and regularly claim all three places on the podium. Travel this magical country and the facts speak for themselves. When it comes to cities, nowhere does urban better than Rome, the 'capital of capitals'. Looking for the perfect beach? No one does sea and sand better than Amalfi and Capri. In fact, whether your passion is food, coffee, cars, fashion, lakes or mountains, Italy always likes to have the last word. The rest of us can only look and wonder. And wherever you go in this country, you're never far from that great institution, the Italian caffè. Whether it's a sumptuous 'star bar' on the Via Veneto in Rome, a pair of tables tucked under the awning of a sleepy Tuscan grocery store, a chic meeting-spot in Milan, or a buzzing terrace-bar on Venice's Piazza San Marco, every Italian caffè wants you to do the same thing: relax, enjoy the company of your friends, and pick something mouth-watering from the menu. In a country that invented the cappuccino and the espresso, you know you're going to be in safe hands.

Rome

It takes a lot of confidence for a city to call itself 'caput mundi' (head of the world). But when that city is Rome, there's all the evidence you need to make the title stick. Reaching back into Rome's past, you could trawl the planet and find nothing to match the scale of the 2,000 year old Colosseum and Forum. And as churches go, St Peter's has been a world-beater since it was completed in 1626. From the glitzy shopping of the Via Condotti to the marbled glory of the Piazza Navona, Rome tells you at every turn that this is as good as it gets. If you're feeling slightly humbled, head for a quiet caffè on the intimate Campo dei Fiori and discover that Rome does 'intimate' better than anyone else too.

Babington's

Piazza di Spagna 23 *Metro: Spagna*
Tel: 06 6786027
Open: 09.00-20.15
Closed: Tue

The Piazza di Spagna, so called because it was the location of the Spanish Embassy for centuries, is a compulsory stop on the sightseeing round, and the Spanish Steps, which run down from the Trinità dei Monti church, are a magnet for tourists and Romans alike. In the piazza itself is a real surprise, a reminder not of old Italy but of 19th century England. Two Victorian spinsters Anna Maria Babington from Derbyshire and Isabel Cargill from New Zealand set up shop in this prime location, bringing a touch of English class Fortnum & Mason-style to the citizens of Rome. It remains as one of Rome's poshest places for enjoying a pukka cup of tea (a dozen varieties), but there's no shortage of stronger tipples. Food runs from an excellent breakfast selection to burgers, curries, savoury pancakes, omelettes and some splendid salads, with cakes, pastries and ice creams for sweeter teeth.

La Bevitoria

Piazza Navona 72 *Bus: Corso Rinascimento or Vittorio Emanuele*
Tel: 06 68801022
Open: 11.00-01.00 (Fri & Sat till 02.00)

A friendly little wine bar in a square dominated by Bernini's extravagant masterpiece Fontana dei Quattro Fiumi – the Fountain of the Four Rivers. The price at the tables inside is the same as at the bar, but to sit outside costs extra. On balance, this is the most pleasant bar in the square, with a touch of history in the cellars where the remains of a stadium built by the Emperor Domitian can still be seen. Drink mulled wine in winter.

Canova

Piazza del Popolo 16 *Metro: Flaminio*
Tel: 06 3612231
Open: 08.00-24.00

Pavement café, cake shop, tobacconist, bar and restaurant/tea room in a piazza just inside the city's historic northern gate, the Porta dei Populi. It's a busy place, and one of the smartest in town, done out in modern style, with friendly, efficient staff who wear brass badges on their Canova-labelled waistcoats. Once known for its extreme right-wing clientele, it now attracts aspiring film stars, who come here to be seen (as they do across the square at equally fashionable arch rival *Rosati*, once the haunt of the intellectual left). Here, you get the late afternoon sun – or you go to *Rosati* to avoid it!

La Casa del Tramezzino

Viale Trastevere 81 *Metro: Viale Trastevere*
Tel: 06 5812118
Open: 07.00-03.00
Closed: Mon pm

The eponymous *tramezzino* is the speciality of this café south of the river on the main thoroughfare in the Trastevere ('across the Tiber'). Tramezzino is a smart Italian word for sandwich, apparently coined by Mussolini during a campaign to ban foreign words. And sandwiches is what they are, all freshly made, as they have been for more than 30 years, and scrumptious in any language; and the choice is the best in all Rome. Also ice creams, and hot meals at lunchtime. You can eat outside under parasols with privet hedges in troughs separating you from the pavement.

Il Delfino
Corso Vittorio Emanuele 67 *Bus: Corso Vittorio Emanuele*
Tel: 06 6864053
Open: 07.00-21.00
Il Delfino is a very smart and very popular café-bar in an atmospheric and historic setting inside the 16th-century Datti Palace. Established in 1938, it offers coffee, beer and a good selection of wines at the self-service bar, while on the eating front sandwiches, speciality grills, pizzas and an extensive cold buffet are the most popular options, with ice cream to round things off.

La Diligenza Rossa
Via Merulana 271 *Bus: Basilica Santa Maria Maggiori*
Tel: 06 4881216
Open: 09.00-22.30
Closed: Mon
Chicken roasted on a spit over an open fire (*pollo cotto a legna*) is the speciality of the popular Red Coach, which stands a little way down the road from Piazza Santa Maria Maggiore, quite close to the Brancaccio Theatre. The menu also includes cold dishes. The building has a pretty baroque-style decor that stands out among its rather plainer neighbours.

Goffredo Chirra
Via Torino 133 *Metro: Repubblica*
Tel: 06 485659
Open: 06.30-02.00
Closed: Sun
This renowned amazing wine merchant is also licensed as a bar, so customers can sip a glass of wine with a sandwich while deciding whether to have their Balthazar (16 bottles) of Moët gift-wrapped. They also sell preserves, teas and coffees. The walls are stacked eleven shelves high with wines, aperitifs and spirits.

Antico Caffè Greco

Via Condotti 86 *Metro: Spagna*
Tel: 06 6791700
Open: 08.30-20.45
Goethe was just one of the many notables who visited this historic and very grand café on Rome's premier shopping street, and others passing through the portals include Hans Christian Andersen, Casanova, Wagner and mad King Ludwig of Bavaria. In the early days (it opened in 1760) the majority of the customers were artists or foreign visitors, and at the beginning of the 20th century it was adopted by American visitors. In the 1950s it was finally and formally recognised as a historic institution. Beyond the bar, there is a series of rooms with gilded mirrors, portraits on oil and velvet-upholstered chairs around marble tables; at the far end is a larger room with glass-fronted library shelves.

Bar del Mattatoio
Piazza Orazio Giustiniani 3 *Bus: Piazza di Bustina*
Tel: 06 5746017
Open: 06.00-21.00
Closed: Sun
Mattatoio was Rome's main slaughterhouse from 1891 until 1975, when the vast buildings began to be put to many other uses, including car pound, stables and multi-cultural social centre. In the middle of the square by the main entrance, this down-to-earth bar and tobacconist's kiosk is run with a smile and ready wit by a husband-and-wife team who have been here for years. The early opening time, which once catered for butchers and slaughterers, is now convenient for revellers who've got slaughtered in nearby Testaccio clubland.

Café Notegen
Via del Babuino 159 *Metro: Spagna*
Tel: 06 3200855
Open: 07.00-01.00 (Sun from 10.30)
The bohemian spirit that was a feature of this area after the Second World War lives on in the basement of this convivial café, where there is a stage and seating for political debate, side shows, fringe theatre, even cabaret. On the ground floor, the bar sells good coffee, drinks and snacks, and at the back there's a restaurant area. Beers and pizzas at night.

Antico Caffè della Pace
Via della Pace 3-4, 5-7 *Bus: Corso Rinascimento*
Tel: 06 6861216
Open: 09.00-02.00 (Mon from 15.00)
Once just an ordinary little corner bar, this is now probably the most fashionable bar in the old part of Rome, with cascading greenery and a prime location in the Trastevere. Film stars and other celebrities come here for drinks or coffees, and often move on to the restaurant in the same premises.

Caffè Palombini

Piazzale K Adenauer 12 *Metro: Magliana*
Tel: 06 5911700
Open: 07.00-24.00 (Sat till 13.00)
Palombini is one of the leading café-bars in a vast site that was originally developed for a massive fascist-inspired exhibition (E42) due to be held in 1942 but abandoned after a series of arguments and the outbreak of war. After the war, work resumed (no longer with a fascist connection, of course) and the site was renamed EUR (*Esposizione Universale Romana*). Palombini is a favourite meeting place, especially for the young, with its huge patio and garden setting. It gets very busy at lunchtime, when they open the buffet, and on summer evenings queues form for the outside tables. Service is excellent, and they roast their own coffee, blend it and sell it under the Palombini badge.

Café de Paris
Via Vittorio Veneto 9 *Metro: Barberini*
Tel: 06 4885284
Open: 08.00-01.00
Closed: Tue in winter
The Café de Paris has been a great success ever since it opened in 1956, benefiting initially from the post-war revival of Rome as a holiday city, and then from the boost the city got from staging the 1960 Olympic Games. Its greatest times came when it was featured in the film *La Dolce Vita*. Brando used to pop in while filming in Rome. Great cakes and a terrific tiramisu. Outside seats.

Caffè Piccarozzi
Piazza della Repubblica 62-63 *Metro: Repubblica*
Tel: 06 4745845
Open: 07.00-24.00
Closed: Sun
This handsome café stands on the north-east side of the vast semi-circular Piazza della Repubblica. Order a drink and a snack inside or out in the colonnade, where you can enjoy the magnificence of the architecture and watch the world go by in grand, semi-circular piazza with its monumental Fountain of the Naiads, whose naked nymphs so shocked the Roman clergy in 1911 that it was quickly boarded up and remained in that state of modesty for some years.

Rosati
Piazza del Popolo 4/5a *Metro: Flaminio*
Tel: 06 3225859
Open: 07.30-23.30
In a piazza that was once a favourite venue for public executions, Rosati is one of the most fashionable bars in Rome. Once a favoured meeting place of the intellectual left (Moravia and Pasolini were regulars), it is a very smart, efficiently run bar with outside tables on the opposite side of the piazza from *Canova* (see entry), opened in 1922 and decorated in the later art nouveau style, with a green marble-topped oak-panelled bar. A two-flight oak staircase leads up to the restaurant. Piano bar Friday and Saturday evenings in winter. Excellent home baking in the original oven, and some wicked cocktails.

Sant'Eustachio Il Caffè
Piazza Sant'Eustachio 82 *Bus: Corso Rinascimento*
Tel: 06 6861309
Open: 08.30-01.00
One of the city's most renowned coffee bars, with messages from the world's great and good extolling the quality of its coffee. When at this café, do as the Romans do and join a long queue to be served the tiniest volume of the most intensely flavoured espresso (*schiuma* is espresso with a frothy top) or the most delicious cappuccino, maybe even the *ciocolatto* (coffee, chocolate and cream), or a granita (crushed ice coffee) on a hot day.

Bar Alla Scrofa

Via della Scrofa 104 *Metro: Spagna*
Tel: 06 6869552
Open: 06.30-20.30
Closed: Sun

Dating back to the very end of the 19th century, this is a pleasant neighbourhood bar in a street that leads from thc Pantheon up to the Piazza del Popolo just inside the city's old northern gate. It has a couple of tables inside and four outside, and sells good home-made ice cream and snacks. Via della Scrofa (scrofa means sow) has some very grand private residences (*palazzi*) with elaborate courtyards and beautiful fountains glimpsed through enormous gates. The bar celebrated its centenary in 1999.

Gran Caffè Strega

Piazza del Viminale 27-31 *Bus: Via Nazionale*
Tel: 06 485670
Open: 06.00-24.00

Strega is the Italian word for witch, but in this case it is the name of the familiar yellow-coloured Italian liqueur sold here. Tucked away down an alley by the handsome Ministry of the Interior building, this is a very good *pizzeria-birreria* with a real *forno al legno* – wood-fired oven. Salads, a cold buffet ad grilled meats are other choices, and the pastries and ice creams are good, too. There's plenty of room to eat inside and lots of tables under large parasols in the forecourt.

La Tazza d'Oro

Via degli Orfani 84 *Bus: Via del Corso*
Tel: 06 6789792
Open: 07.00-20.30
Closed: Sun

Next to the Pantheon and across the square from the Parliament building, La Tazza d'Oro (the Golden Cup) is a major importer of coffee, bringing the beans from Jamaica, Costa Rica and many other parts of the world. The place is full of sacks and beans of coffee, and glass displays show some of the coffee beans for sale (personal customers, mail order, fax, e-mail). They make Rome's best *monichella* – iced coffee with whipped cream. This outstanding place has been in the same family since 1947.

Trasté

Via della Lungaretta 76
Tel: 06 5894430
Open: 17.00-02.00
Closed: Aug

Trasté is a popular and fashionable evening spot, heralded from the outside by 'Caffè Sala da Tè' and one of the few places in Rome to specialise in tea. Inside, it is smartly modern, with low, comfortable sofas and tables in the front part which leads to a spacious room with square tables and chairs and the bar itself. A range of infusions is on sale along with the cocktails, draught and bottled beers, cocktails, milkshakes and crêpes both sweet and savoury. Magazines are provided for browsing. Not far from the cobbled, traffic-free Piazza Santa Maria, whose fountain, built in 1692, is a popular gathering place, a sort of Roman Eros.

Bar Tre Scalini
Piazza Navona 28-32 *Bus: Corso Rinascimento or Vittorio Emanuele*
Tel: 06 68801996
Open: 09.00-01.30
Closed: Wed
Tre Scalini (Three Steps) refers to the steps that led up to this long-established bar in Piazza Navona (opposite *Dolce Vita* and *La Bevitoria* – see entries) in the days when Navona was flooded with water in order to hold boat races. Both the races and the steps are now long gone, but the bar still retains its original name and style. Ice creams are a speciality – try the tartufo nero, a rich, rich chocolate variety. Piazza Navona, built on the remains of Domitian's stadium, is the hub of the historic centre of medieval Rome and probably the liveliest square in the whole city, attracting thousands of visitors every day. It's also one of the most spectacular, with three magnificent fountains, including the spectacular Fontana dei Quattro Fiumi, designed and partly sculpted by Bernini. The fiumi – rivers – are the Danube, Ganges, Plate and Nile, representing the four corners of the world.

Il Trimani Wine Bar
Via Cernaia 37b *Bus: Via Cernaia*
Tel: 06 4469630
Open: 11.30-15.00 & 18.00-03.00
Closed: Sun except in Dec
The wine bar is an offshoot of the oldest wine shop in the city, founded in 1821 by Francesco Trimani just round the corner in Via Goito. The bar offers excellent regional Italian wines and good snacks (crostini, quiche), and the shop is vast, and made for browsing, especially as there's no list of the stock.

Da Vezio
Via dei Delfini 23 *Tram: Largo Argentina*
Tel: 06 6786036
Open: 07.00-20.00
Closed: Sun, also Tue, Wed & Sat between 14.30 & 18.00
A minuscule bar in a little back street not far from the Piazza Venezia, which with six roads converging is one of the best places in Rome for watching traffic chaos. Da Vezio has just two little tables at the back and a computer with Internet access 'for the comrades' (the communist party headquarters used to be in the next street, and the walls of this little place are covered with photographs and newspaper cuttings of history's best-known left-wing revolutionaries). The place is now listed among the Bottegi Storici (Historic Shops) of Rome.

Enoteca Antica di Via della Croce
Via della Croce 76b *Metro: Spagna*
Tel: 06 6790896
Open: 10.00-01.00
Closed: 1 week Aug
One of Rome's oldest eating and drinking places, dating back to 1842 and still boasting some of the original fittings, including marble wine vats. The choice of wines by the glass (all Italian) is impressive, and you can enjoy your tipple sitting on a comfortable stool at the bar or at one of the outside tables. One of the chief attractions in the restaurant is an excellent cold buffet featuring rare cheeses from all over Italy. Capannelle Cricket Club is next door; they stage matches at the famous Capannelle racecourse along the road.

Vineria Reggio
Campo de' Fiori 15 *Bus: Corso Vittorio Emanuele*
Tel: 06 68803268
Open: 09.00-01.00 (Fri & Sat till 01.30, Sun from 17.00)
Closed: Sun
Located in the square where the area's best food market is a daily attraction, this is one of the best and trendiest of the local bars, offering wines by the glass, at least three draught beers (served with very tasty little canapés) and a wide range of food. Serving mainly locals during the day, it widens its customer base in the evening, when the pavement tables are always full. Note the original (16th-century) ceiling. Evening concerts are held from time to time in the square.

Florence

Given that almost the whole of Western art can be traced back to this one city – and the Renaissance of 1400 – you'd expect it to be rich in culture. It is. With enough important galleries, museums and churches to keep you busy for three weeks or more, the tiny city of Florence contains more art than any other city on earth. If you had to pick, then the highlights would be the canvasses of the Uffizi and the sculptures in the Bargello. Either would keep you mesmerised for an entire weekend. And when your appetite for fine art is finally sated, draw up a chair at a caffè on Piazza del Duomo, and drink in the genius that's Brunelleschi's cathedral.

PRIMA DONNAS

When Gina and Sophia hit Hollywood in the 50s, men everywhere stood to attention. Both Italians, both in their 20s, and both with legendary sex appeal, the two actresses were set for a lifetime of rivalry. Who gets your vote?

Background: Born in 1927 and 1934 respectively, Luigina Lollobrigida and Sofia Scicolone both started life in humble families in Italy. Gina went on to win a string of beauty contests and got into movies aged 19. Sophia came second in a beauty contest, and started her movie career as an extra on Quo Vadis aged 17.

Movies: Said to be 'unfilmable' at her screen test (those big lips and curves) Sophia went on to prove them all wrong. Moving to Hollywood in 1956, she climbed the movie ladder to star alongside Cary Grant, William Holden and Alan Ladd (*The Pride and the Passion, Houseboat*). For Gina, the Latin looks and fiery on-screen presence shaped a career playing prostitutes and gypsies in movies with suitably provocative titles (*Go Naked in the World, Strange Bedfellows*).

IQ: Two very sharp cookies. In later life Gina became a respected photo-journalist, interviewing the likes of Fidel Castro. Sophia was famous in Hollywood for her sharp wit and once said she was lucky to have been born wise and in poverty. Both women made big money through sharp deals with cosmetics companies.

Romantic liaisons: Gina, oddly enough, had a thing about doctors. Marrying Yugoslav doctor Milko Skofic in 1949, she also entrusted her heart to Christiaan Barnard for a while. While Sophia married Carlo Ponti in 1957 (the producer 22 years her senior who discovered her) her name has also been linked to movers-and-shakers including Cary Grant, Peter Sellers, Omar Sharif, Gary Cooper and JFK.

Career high and low: After winning an Oscar for Best Actress in *Two Women* (1960), Sophia dynamited her own PR with a one-month prison sentence for tax evasion. Gina never won a big award – but her biggest public gaffe was a mere tantrum on the jury of the Berlin Film Festival, 1986.

Quotes: Sophia on Gina: "Who? I never criticise my elders." Gina on Sophia: "Sophia plays peasants. I play ladies."

Recent news: Still acting in her 60s, Sophia fitted snugly into a role in Robert Altman's *Prêt-à-Porter* (1994). For Gina, the big hair and heavy mascara in *Falcon Crest* (1984) proved a movie-too-far. She's laid low ever since.

Overall verdict: Call us biased, but Sophia clinches our vote. The Oscar, the curves, the list of leading men – Sophia is the movie-goers movie-star. Others try to follow. None get close.

Amadeus
Via dei Pescioni 5/r *Area: North of Palazzo Strozzi*
Tel: 055 2398229
Open: 07.00-03.30 (Sat & Sun 19.00-02.00)
Amadeus is a Bavarian-style bar in the city centre, two streets from Piazza della Repubblica. Set on three levels, with the feel of a German *beerstube*, it's a great place to meet for a drink, especially on a warm summer's evening.

Enoteca Baldovino
Via San Giuseppe 18/r *Area: Southeast of Piazza di Santa Croce*
Tel: 055 2347220
Open: 12.00-24.30
Closed: Mon, also 16.00-18.00 in winter
A young Scots couple, David and Catherine Gardner, run this busy, cosmopolitan wine bar just behind the wonderful Santa Croce church. Wines are sold by the glass and snacks include pizza cooked in a wood-fired oven and salads. Daily specials include the very popular *crostone* – toasted Tuscan bread with a choice of about 50 melted toppings: brie and truffle cream, gorgonzola and honey are just two.

Osteria del Boia
Via Ghibellina 70/r *Area: East of Teatro Verdi*
Tel: 055 2638940
Open: 12.00-01.00 (Nov-Mar from 19.00)
In an old building with high-vaulted brick ceilings, robust walls and arches leading from one room to another, the welcome is warm and the coffee excellent. At lunchtime there's a bargain set menu of a two-course meal and salad with a ½ carafe of wine. In the evening snacks such as crostini and carpaccio fill the gaps.

Caffè Donnini
Piazza della Repubblica 15/r *Area: Piazza della Repubblica*
Tel: 055 213694
Open: 06.00-24.00 (winter till 20.30)
Caffè Donnini is one of several society cafés which sprang up at the turn of the last century after the square was built in honour of Vittorio Emanuele. Though smaller than when first opened, it remains a Gran Caffè in the old Florentine tradition where you can have an excellent coffee, pastry or ice cream standing at the bar, or sitting at a table inside or out.

Café Gilli
Piazza della Repubblica 39/r *Area: Piazza della Repubblica*
Tel: 055 213896
Open: 07.30-01.00 (winter till 21.00)
Gilli is a renowned old-world grand café with lofty frescoed and moulded ceilings and arched glass doorways leading to several rooms. Inside, the tables have mustard-coloured cloths with cream lace overlays; outside, the cloths are peach-coloured, all very pretty! Sepia photographs of scenes from bygone years abound, and one end of the panelled marble-topped counter has an imposing statue. Best known for its cocktails, Gilli is also a master of all things chocolate, not least some of the super cakes based on old and treasured recipes.

Enoteca de Giraldi
Via di Giraldi 4/r *Area: East of Palazzo dei Pazzi*
Tel: 055 216518
Open: 11.00-15.00 & 18.00-00.30
Closed: Sun

The charming, helpful staff are a real bonus at this cool, roomy wine bar, where the regulars include an eight-strong local choir who often come here after a practice or a performance to dine and then sing for fun. A sheer pleasure, and with the high ceiling the acoustics are great! Giraldi is also a wine merchant and seller of typical Tuscan preserves in jars, and the main counter has a tempting display of meat, cheeses and desserts for sale. The go-ahead owners offer wine-tasting courses, cookery lessons in the splendid Tuscan cuisine and excursions to local wineries.

Giubbe Rosse
Piazza della Repubblica 13-14 *Area: Piazza della Repubblica*
Tel: 055 212280
Open: 08.30-01.30

Giubbe Rosse is named after the Viennese-style red jackets that the waiters wore in its early years. Long known as a meeting place for artists, intellectuals and journalists, it comprises three rooms: the first is the bar where gentlemen come to read the papers and discuss matters political; the second much brighter room becomes a restaurant in the evenings; the third room is more cosy and intimate. There are also tables out on the pavement.

Harry's Bar
Lungarno Amerigo Vespucci 22r *Area: Northbank of river, nr Ponte alla Carraia*
Tel: 055 2396700
Open: 12.00-24.00 (winter 12.00-15.00 & 18.00-24.00)
Closed: Sun

A famous name, and a great place for passing an enjoyable hour or two. On a fine day you can join the affluent locals on the patio and admire the views of the city across the river – you can just see the Ponte Vecchio. Harry's Club Sandwich, particularly rich with mayonnaise and generous with the chicken and chips, is a meal in itself, served by unfailingly polite, impeccably trained staff. Fresh fish every day. Splendid coffee.

Caffè Italiano
Via della Condotta 56 *Area: North of Piazza della Signora*
Tel: 055 291082
Open: 08.00-24.00
Closed: Sun & Aug

A civilised, elegant and very comfortable Gran Caffè-style establishment in a quiet street behind the Piazza Signoria. Regulars relax with the newspapers in wood-panelled surroundings, or buy wines, liqueurs and coffee (beans or ground) to take home. The cakes are all made in-house, and the chocolate varieties are the tops.

Osteria Caffè Italiano
Via Isola delle Stinche 11-13/r *Area: Southwest of Teatro Verdi*
Tel: 055 289368
Open: 12.00-15.00 & 19.00-01.00
Closed: Mon

A very handsome café and restaurant behind the Verdi theatre, in the same ownership as *Caffè Italiano*. Snackers can sit at an uncovered rough-hewn

oak table and drink a glass of wine or two, perhaps with a plate of meats and cheeses. It has very high vaulted ceilings, and enormous French windows open to the street on summer nights to keep the place cool. The bar, along with half the room, has tall oak cupboards, glass-fronted, with back-lit shelves filled with wine bottles. The bar counter is a thick marble preparation area on an antique wooden base housing the refrigerated bottles of white wine, and there's a big brass cauldron filled with iced water and the white wines for sale by the glass. Large wrought bronze chandeliers hang from the ceiling, and the floor is a herringbone pattern of terracotta tiles.

Caffè Concerto Paszkowski
Piazza della Repubblica 6r *Area: Piazza della Repubblica*
Tel: 055 210236
Open: 07.00-01.30
Concerts take place every night at this long-established café, which was originally a beer house, later became the meeting place for leading politicians, and in 1991 was declared a National Monument. Inside, there is a series of high-ceilinged arched rooms, while the canopied outside seating area is surrounded by privet hedges planted in terracotta holders. Ice creams and cocktails are specialities of the house, and the snacks and pastries are all very tempting. Chocolate is made by owners Gilli. Piano bar in winter.

Caffè La Torre
Lungarno Benvenuto Cellini 65/r *Area: Southbank of river, nr Porta San Niccolò*
Tel: 055 680643
Open: 10.00-04.00
Fresh fruit juices, focaccia and savoury pancakes are the specialities of this pleasant American-style café-cocktail bar across the river in the shadow of the tower in Piazza Giuseppe Poggi. It stays open until very late, offering little dips and nibbles with your drinks. Breakfasts are a big thing here, particularly Sunday brunch, but you can also take lunch, pop in for an aperitif, sit down to a light evening meal after a stroll along the river bank, which is only yards away, or enjoy a late-night drink with some tasty nibbles.

Milan

Leonardo da Vinci used his time in Milan to study fluids and anatomy – and you could do worse than to follow his lead. Pick a table with a view of the historic Piazza del Duomo, sample the sparkling wines of Franciacorta, and eye the chic crowds as they make 'the passeggiata', the daily ritual of parading the streets in this catwalk of a city. If you've missed the Spring fashion shows, compensate by shopping in the Quadrilatero d'Oro, then parade your buys around the bars of the old town.

Baretto
Via S Andrea 3 *Metro: San Babila*
Tel: 02 781255
Open: 11.00-01.00
Closed: Sun except during spring and autumn fashion weeks
Close to the junction of Via Sant' Andrea and Via Monte Napoleone, Baretto is a smart, club-like bar with wood-panelled walls, buttoned leather-upholstered chairs and bar stools. It's a great favourite with shoppers in the Monte Napoleone, the Bond Street of Milan and home of many of the annual fashion shows.

Bar Basso
Via Plinio 39 *Metro: Lima*
Tel: 02 29400580
Open: 08.00-01.15
Closed: Tue
Behind the gargoyled facade Bar Basso is a place of two halves. One part features elegant part-upholstered chairs and polished tables (relax with the daily newspapers), the other is the eating area done over all in pine. One of the main selling points of Basso is an amazing list of 500 cocktails, many using fresh fruit.

La Belle Aurore
Via Castelmorrone *Metro: Porta Venezia*
Tel: 02 29406212
Open: 08.00-02.00
Closed: Sun
On the corner of Via Castelmorrone and the tree-lined Via Abamonti, this high-ceilinged café-bar has exposed aluminium duct air-conditioning and walls decorated with posters. Newspapers and magazines for lone browsing, or you can play chess on the boards provided. The specialities are cocktails, aperitifs and home-made desserts.

Biffi
Galleria Vittorio Emanuele II *Metro: Duomo*
Tel: 02 8057961
Open: 07.00-01.00
Biffi is very grand and very expensive, as befits its location in the vast Galleria, one of Milan's social and political hubs. Many of the shops stay open late, and so does Biffi, a great place for a drink at any time of day. On the food front, osso buco is a popular dish.

Caffè Litta
Corso Magenta 25 *Metro: Cadorna Triennale*
Tel: 02 8057596
Open: 07.00-21.00
Litta dates only from the mid-1990s but has the look of a much older café that previously stood on the site. Inside, it has a conservatory, wooden tables and chairs and a curved green marble bar with a bottle shelf above. There are also some tables set out on the pavement. Nice friendly staff in brown aprons serve a clientele largely comprising office workers and students with a good choice of sandwiches, rolls and hot and cold snacks.

Orient Express
Via Fiori Chiari 8 *Metro: Lanza, Monte Napoleone*
Tel: 02 8056227
Open: 09.00-02.00 (piano bar Thur-Sun)
Railway buffs feeling nostalgic should steam along to this café-bar in an interesting street of many café-bars to enjoy a drink, perhaps a glass of one of their own-label wines and spirits. At the back, beyond the bar, is a faithful reconstruction of a carriage of the old *Orient Express* in a station at the beginning of the century. The garden is open all year round. At night the street becomes an exciting, atmospheric bazaar with Africans selling leather handbags and carved wood laid out on blankets on the pavement, and South American Indians selling jewellery and knitwear. Popular, too, are the many fortune-tellers reading their tarot cards.

Osteria del Pallone
Alzaia Naviglio Grande/Viale Gorizia 30 *Metro: Porta Genova FS*
Tel: 02 58105641
Open: 11.00-02.00
If Orient Express is for railway buffs, Osteria del Pallone is a place for football fans (but read on!). All the cups displayed, at least 40, have been won by the local amateur team, sponsored by owner Mario Farac, himself a former professional player in Serie A (Italian Premier Division). He is football mad and has another café/bar Osteria del Calcetto at Corso Garibaldi 46 (Tel: 02 80 518 65), which displays football jerseys, as well as a bar on the

opposite side of the canal called Bar della Stazione, featuring model trains and other railway memorabilia. So whether you get your kicks from football or trains, Mario has a place for you. Three draught and seven bottled beers, evening cocktails, generous salads and cold cuts.

Radetzky Café
Largo La Foppa 5 *Metro: Moscova*
Tel: 02 6572645
Open: 08.00-02.00
Closed: 2 weeks Aug
The city's thinkers march along to this corner café to enjoy a morning chat, to read the newspapers and to tuck into the excellent *cornetti* and pastries. The full menu changes daily to include seasonal produce such as oysters, and there are some excellent home-made desserts. One side of the room has large round polished tables, the other, small square tables with cloths, and there's a stainless-steel zinc bar counter with a range of at least 30 single malts behind. Classical music plays in the background. In the evenings it's very busy with the well-dressed younger set.

Il Resentin Caffè
Via Mercato 24 *Metro: Lanza, Monte Napoleone*
Tel: 02 875923
Open: 12.00-01.30
Closed: Sun
The calling card promises something for everyone here: *'Caffeteria, enoteca, bottega delle grappe, birraria, gastronomia, tabaccheria'*. And the pastry and bread shop next door produces even more goodies. The café has two rooms, one with velvet cushions on low bench seating, the other with large polished mahogany tables and chairs. Blues and mood music provides a soothing background for a browse through the papers, and there's a lovely flower display at the bar. Specialities from the Trentino area include wines and grappa, and Resentin also has a good range of Scotch whiskies.

Sans Egal
Vicolo Fiori 2 *Metro: Lanza, Monte Napoleone*
Tel: 02 8693096
Open: 09.00-03.00 (Mon 19.00-02.00)
One of many cafés in this part of the city, Sans Egal has a smart outside seating area, with trestled railings sheltering it from the street. Inside, behind the bar, are art nouveau-style leaded coloured glass panels and mirrors. At the far end of the bar is a film screen with a silent montage of movie scenes, with background blues music. Cocktails, much more popular in Italy than in the UK, are a speciality. The menu changes daily.

Taverna Moriggi
Via Moriggi 8 *Metro: Cordusio*
Tel: 02 86450880
Open: 08.00-01.00
Closed: Sat pm, all Sun
Moriggi is a very old and very special tavern with a lofty beamed ceiling, an atmospheric bar and a large luncheon room which becomes an overspill for the bar in the evening. The food choice includes a good range of pasta and a fine selection of cheeses displayed on a large oak sideboard. The house wine is made from *fragolo* grapes, which, as the name suggests, are redolent of strawberries. Moriggi's owners grow the grapes in their own

vineyards, and there are no labels on the bottles, because under Italian law your own wine is not subject to duty if sold on the premises. Sometimes travelling minstrels play jazz and pass the hat round.

Le Trottoir
Corso Garibaldi 1 *Metro: Moscova, Lanza*
Tel: 02 801002
Open: 11.00-03.00
On the corner of Garibaldi and Via Tivoli, the well-established Trottoir is very popular with the younger set. It has a deep mahogany bar counter with lots of stools and wooden tables with bench seats downstairs, while upstairs are tables and chairs and provision for nightly live music (very varied: jazz, rock, Celtic folk, guitar). Snacks and full meals are served, and drinks include an excellent selection of malt whiskies.

Zucca in Galleria
Piazza Duomo 21 *Metro: Duomo*
Tel: 02 86464435
Open: 07.30-20.30
Closed: Mon
On the left immediately after the grand arched entrance to the stunning Galleria Vittorio Emanuele II is the renowned café Zucca, which opened with the Galleria in 1867. Verdi and Toscanini used to drop in on their way back from La Scala at the other end of the Gallery, King Umberto I came because it served the best coffee in the city, and to this day artists, painters, authors, politicians and musicians are numbered among the regulars. There is a room upstairs where you can enjoy a quick meal at midday or Sunday morning brunch. The barmen can make the cappuccino froth into little patterns. One of the specialities is *Rabrabaro Zucca*, a Milanese liqueur with a taste like Campari.

THE GOSPEL OF VESPA

Meet Italy's biggest export since the Roman chariot

When the dust settled on the Allied liberation of Italy in 1945, the sight it revealed wasn't a happy one. Anything which hadn't been destroyed by the retreating Germans had been shelled by the advancing Allies, vaporising the country's infrastructure. Italy was back to ground zero.

Cometh the hour, cometh the man. For an entrepreneur called Enrico Piaggio, the challenge was irresistible. Starting from this blank sheet, Piaggio was determined to launch a revolutionary vehicle "which puts Italy on two wheels." His own words.

In the event, he put the whole world on his scooter.

Trained in a family engineering firm which specialised in trains and planes, Piaggio instinctively trusted the prototype design — linking two tiny wheels via a flat frame in the style of an aircraft's undercarriage.

This revolutionary shape wasn't just lovely to look at, it was also hugely user-friendly. Morphing the frame into a body made engine and tank vanish from view, created a flat, stable seat for the rider, and hushed the noise to a whisper. So much so, that when Piaggio started the engine for the first time, he said: "Sembra una vespa" ("it seems like a wasp").

By 1946 the Vespa was in full production. Five years later the company had sold its 100,000th machine.

From the comfort of the 21st century, it's difficult to appreciate the impact the Vespa made on a broke, rural Italy. Priced for the pocket of every working family in the country, the Vespa was Italy's first true object of mass pleasure. This light, safe, simple form of transport was an invitation to every Italian to escape village life and explore their own identity.

Italy accepted the invitation big time.

Not only did they buy Vespas in huge numbers, they formed Vespa clubs, put Vespas in their movies, and preached the Vespa Gospel to the planet. By 1953 there were more than 50,000 members of Vespa clubs worldwide, and by 1962 the scooter had appeared in more than 60 films.

And it didn't stop there. When a Vespa made a plucky attempt at the 1km land speed record (peaking at 171kph) and an amphibious Vespa crossed the Channel, the scooter passed from phenomenon to legend.

Moving on from a vehicle of 60s teen rebellion to green champion in the 70s, the Vespa became a symbol of... well... pretty much everything.

By the time Piaggio died in 1963, his brainchild had sold 3.5 million models and become the icon of all things Italian — pasta with an engine, even!

Today, the myth has long since overtaken the scooter.

Naples

Most of us would need a very good reason to live next to a smoking volcano. For the Neapolitans, the combined charms of one of the most beautiful coastlines in the world, plus sumptuous local cuisine and 3,000 years of culture all make any future eruptions a risk they're happy to take. To sample the three Cs of Coast, Cuisine and Culture in a single day – take a morning stroll along the glorious Caracciola Promenade, follow with a lunch of fresh sea bass delicately poached 'all' acqua pazza', and then move happily on to the National Museum of Archaeology.

Café Amadeus
Piazza Amadeo 5 *Chiaia Metro: Piazza Amedeo*
Tel: 081 7613023
Open: 07.00-03.00
A popular bar in the square at the bottom of one of the funicular railways from the Vomero (the other stations are at Piazza Augusto and Piazza Montesanto). As you walk down the Via Colonna Vittoria towards the historic city centre, note the magnificent church high above you on the left; to the right are steps down to the Via San Pasquale, leading to the waterfront and promenade.

Bilancione
Via Posillipo 238/b *Posillipo Bus: Palazzo Donn'Anna*
Tel: 081 7691923
Open: 07.00-01.00 (winter till 23.00)
Closed: Wed
Bilancione has few rivals in the best ice cream stakes. Their *nocciola* (hazelnut) ice cream has scooped the *Cono d'Oro* (Golden Cone) prize ever since most people can remember. And there's a bonus: the view from the bar, which is on the road that climbs out of the Mergellina into the Posillipo and Merliani district, is a splendid one of the Bay of Naples to the port.

Gran Caffè La Caffetiera
Piazza Vanvitelli 10 *Vomero Bus: Piazza Vanuitelli*
Tel: 081 5782592
Open: 07.00-01.00
A very smart bar and tea room on the main square in the Vomero. Tables are set out under parasols in front of the café, where a huge brass cafetière (their name and logo) is displayed. Across the pavement under some trees are several more tables in a fenced-off area. The pastries and desserts are really special: rum baba, torta caprese with chocolate and almond liqueur, torta Limoncello from Sorrento. There's another chic branch (Tel: 081 7644243) at Piazza dei Martiri 30, and two in Rome (Via Margutta 61a Tel: 06 321 3344 & Piazza di Pietra 00186 Tel: 06 679 8147).

Lo Chalet Ciro de Rosario
Via Mergellina *Mergellina Bus: Mergellina*
Tel: 081 669928
Open: 06.45-01.30
Closed: Wed
Rosaria Fummo claims to sell the best ice cream in Naples (but there are several others making the same claim, including *Bilancione*). Under a canopy at the front of the bar are ice cream counters and a refrigerated display of ice creams and cream cakes, and, on the other side of the pavement, tables and chairs under a long canopy.

Caffè Gambrinus
Piazza Trieste e Trento *Royal Bus: Piazza Trieste e Trento*
Tel: 081 417582
Open: 08.00-01.30 (Fri & Sat till 02.30)
Opposite the largest opera house in Italy, this beautifully decorated café has been host down the years to monarchs, intellectuals, poets, painters, sculptors and other notables. It claims to have inspired some of the composers of classical Neapolitan songs. To the left of the café is the Piazza del Plebiscito with the 17th-century Royal Palace on one side and the Church of St Francis of Paola, modelled on the Roman Pantheon, on the other.

Caffè Lirico
Via San Carlo 7/a *Royal Bus: Piazza Municipio or Trieste e Trento*
Tel: 081 413813
Open: 06.00-23.00
Closed: Sun
In a colonnade opposite the entrance to the imposing Teatro San Carlo, Caffè Lirico is a popular meeting place for musicians, musical directors and young hopeful opera-singers. On theatre nights, of course, it throngs with the public. The alternative is to go into the magnificent Galleria to the Bar Brasiliano (Tel: 418 383, open daily 07.00-21.00) where young artists and musicians also gather.

Mario Daniele
Via Scarlatti 104-106 *Vomero Bus: Piazza Vanuitelli*
Tel: 081 5780555
Open: 07.30-22.00 (Sat till 24.00)
An elegant bar up in the wealthy Vomero district, serving good ice cream, excellent pastries and a buffet of hot and cold dishes to be enjoyed either in a cool room inside or under a canopy on the pavement. They also make their own chocolates and a speciality cake called torrone.

Venice

Take a glass of chilled champagne, add a hint of peach nectar, and you have the Bellini, the quintessential Venetian drink – best served for two in long-stemmed glasses in a gondola. A charming glide through the waterways is the classic way to explore this treasure of a city, where drowning in splendour is the only hazard for the traveller. And with its historical bridges, miles of canals and 118 islands, Venice does water better than any other city on earth. Once you've drunk in the waterscapes, jump ashore to explore some of the world's finest galleries and museums, especially the Accademia, where Titians, Tintorettos and other masterpieces adorn every wall.

Trattoria Antica Mola

Cannaregio 2800 *Area: Canneregio*
Tel: 041 717492
Open: 08.30-23.00
A canalside trattoria with strong attachments to gondolas and gondoliers. Related photographs and memorabilia decorate the place, where gondoliers gather at lunchtime. Renato Bona, a famous gondolier, in whose memory a regatta is held every year in July/August, is remembered here with his oar and its rowlock, mounted as a trophy and presented annually to the victor ludorum of the regatta.

Osteria ai Assassini

Rio Terà dei Assassini, San Marco 3695 *Area: San Marco*
Tel: 041 5287986
Open: 11.30-15.00 & 18.45-23.00
Closed: L Sat & all Sun
The markets provide the fine fresh produce which Giuseppe Galardi uses for the daily changing menus at his splendid osteria, with fresh fish the Friday speciality. He keeps an excellent range of DOC wines at the bar, and a very good selection of cheeses, pastries and tarts.

Enoteca Boldrin
Salizzada San Canciano, Cannaregio 5550 *Area: Canneregio*
Tel: 041 5237859
Open: 09.30-21.00
Closed: Sun
This large modern wine merchant and wine bar in Cannareggio has an impressive list of DOC wines, which are available by bottle or glass. Also on offer is a selection of *polpette* (deep-fried croquettes), sandwiches, and hot and cold main dishes; specialities are prawns, lasagne with rocket and fegato (liver) veneziana. You can eat or drink at the bar or at marble-topped tables.

Osteria alla Botte
Calle della Bissa, San Marco 5482 *Area: San Marco*
Tel: 041 5209775
Open: 10.00-23.00 (Wed till 15.00)
Closed: Thur
In a narrow street on the northernmost edge of the San Marco district, a hostelry with a lot of wood in its decoration and wine barrels and demijohns all around. To accompany the excellent wine are some first-rate snacks, including the well-known Venetian speciality *kale di granchio* (rice and crabmeat croquettes).

Il Caffè

Dorsoduro 2963, Campo Santa Margherita *Area: Dorsoduro*
Tel: 041 5287998
Open: 07.00-02.00
Closed: Sun
A café of great appeal at any time of the day. It opens early for coffee and croissants, and is a perfect spot to read the morning paper and enjoy the sun before it gets too hot. Day-long snacks include panini, crostini and tramezzini. In the square, people are bustling about, getting the children off to school, or grabbing a coffee on their way to college or work, or buying groceries and fresh fish. On Thursdays in summer the café hosts jazz and blues concerts from 21.00 to 23.00.

Cantina Do Mori

San Polo 429 *Area: San Polo*
Tel: 041 5225401
Open: 08.30-20.30
Closed: Sun
The Cantina is a popular wine bar that's brim full of character and charm, located in a 500-year-old building. Apart from a couple of chairs, it's standing room only in the bar, whose walls are adorned with a large collection of copper pans. They serve wonderful tapas-style snacks and an excellent selection of wines to suit all pockets.

Cantina Do Spade
San Polo 860 *Area: San Polo*
Tel: 041 5210574
Open: 09.00-14.30 & 17.30-23.00
Closed: D Thur & all Sun
Cross the Rialto bridge from San Marco into San Polo, and a few little back streets away, through a low arch, is this small cantina (cellar), with wooden walls, wooden chairs and wooden tables. It sells a huge range of wines to

accompany simple snack dishes. The cantina has existed since the 14th century and has a room where Casanova used to entertain his ladies. A secret door leads from the room to his house – useful if an irate husband turned up out of the blue!

Caffè Florian

Piazza San Marco 55-59 *Area: San Marco*
Tel: 041 5285338
Open: 09.30-24.00
Closed: Wed (in winter), 1 week before Christmas & 1st week Jan

This renowned café first opened its doors in 1720 as Venice Triumphant, and throughout its life it has been the meeting place for artists, poets, writers and politicians (Casanova, Goethe, Byron, Dickens, Dali, Proust et al), as well as a venue for art exhibitions and musical events. There are six luxurious little rooms, each with its own entrance, in different styles with plush velvet seating, marble tables, gilt-framed pictures, splendid frescoes and Murano glassware, and outside seating for around 50 in rows under the porch. A band plays in the summer.

Harry's Bar

Calle Vallaresso, San Marco 1323 *Area: San Marco*
Tel: 041 5285777
Open: 10.00-23.00

Home of the Bellini, a beguiling blend of champagne and peach nectar, Harry's Bar attracts visitors from all over the world, with windows looking on to the Fondamenta dei Fontegheto, and a view across St Mark's basin to the Giudecca and the imposing church of St George on its island. Prosecco is a popular alternative to the Bellini, and for solid nourishment there are sandwiches and snacks. The restaurant above is the place where carpaccio was invented; the views are terrific. The other Harry's in Venice is Harry's Dolci, Fondamenta San Bagio 773, Giudecca Tel: 041 5224844, a café and restaurant with outside tables under canopies by the Giudecca Canal. A very popular spot for light refreshment.

Gran Caffè Lavena

Piazza San Marco 133 *Area: San Marco*
Tel: 041 5224070
Open: 09.30-00.30
Closed: Tue in winter

A 250-year-old pavement café where Wagner was a regular between 1879 and 1883; he reputedly wrote some of his *Tristan and Isolde* and *Parsifal* here. Nowadays a small orchestra plays old Neapolitan songs and more modern Italian numbers.

Osteria al Mascaron
Calle Longa S Maria Formosa, Castello 5225 *Area: Castello*
Tel: 041 5225995
Open: 12.00-15.00 & 19.30-23.30
Closed: Sun
This lovely old bar and trattoria with beamed ceilings is a cheerful, friendly place where it's a real pleasure to relax with a glass or two of very drinkable local wine. Seafood dishes are a speciality.

Osteria Al Milion
Corte 1a Al Milion, Cannaregio 5841 *Area: Castello*
Tel: 041 5229302
Open: 12.00-15.00 & 18.00-23.00
Closed: Wed
Tucked away in a tiny square reached through a narrow passage near the Rialto Bridge, Al Milion is a very agreeable hostelry with a charming bar and a capacious dining room. On the walls are lots of framed napkin drawings by the artists who have adopted this place as their own. There are chairs and tables outside.

Quadri
Piazza San Marco 120 *Area: San Marco*
Tel: 041 5289299
Open: 09.00-24.00 (summer till 00.30)
Closed: Mon Nov-Mar
A renowned, very elegant and very happening café-restaurant that has graced the Piazza San Marco since the 17th century. Its rollcall of distinguished visitors includes Stendhal, Dumas, Byron, Wagner, Proust and Chaplin, and they're still coming. The gilded mirrors and painted panels make a very glamorous setting for enjoying a cup of coffee or chocolate, an aperitif or a cocktail, or you can sit outside in the square to listen to the café's own orchestra playing. A small extra charge is levied for this musical treat. Light snacks are served in the café and a full menu in the second-floor restaurant, where beef, seafood and liver veneziana are among the specialities to be enjoyed with splendid views. For the indulgent there are scrumptious home-made desserts, including double chocolate mousse and *gelato al forno*, baked ice cream with chopped almonds, cream, amaretto liqueur and meringue.

Enoteca Al Volto
Calle Cavalli, San Marco 4081 *Area: San Marco*
Tel: 041 5228945
Open: 10.00-14.30 & 17.00-22.00
Closed: Sun
A really terrific wine bar with a prodigious stock of wines (some 1,300!) and a splendid cold table. The scene is set by heavy oak tables, benches and stools, and the ceiling is covered in wine labels. The walls are decorated with bits of old furniture, and there is a long piece of prose, politely requesting you not to smoke, which everyone ignores! Not to be missed by wine-lovers.

Netherlands

The reason many people choose Holland for their cycling holiday is because it's so wonderfully flat. The reason millions of clubbers, art lovers and assorted hedonists choose Holland for their holiday is because it's so giddyingly varied. All life is here.

Mixing with the bustling crowd on the Nieuwmarkt Square in Amsterdam, you can find anything you're looking for in just a short stroll. World-class museums; cutting-edge galleries; tranquil canal-side cafés; bustling bars, flower markets and restaurants from every corner of the globe – they're all here. And so of course is the Red Light District.

And that's just the central square kilometre of the capital. Stray outside Amsterdam and the spectrum of local colour gets wider still. From the cobbled, old-world charm of Utrecht you can head for the modernistic buzz of Rotterdam - Holland keeps on surprising you. Quite how they pack so many moods into one small country remains a mystery. But they do.

The one feature of the local landscape you'll find everywhere you go is the famous Dutch tolerance. Holland simply wants you to do what makes you happy. Shouldn't you accept the invitation?

Amsterdam

The cobbles on Amsterdam's side streets may make for a bumpy ride, but from every other angle the bicycle is the perfect vehicle to explore this magical city. Skimming over any one of the 1,400 bridges, or past the 160 canals, a bicycle will match you to the pace of the world's mellowest capital. Whether you're heading for the glories of the Rijksmuseum, pedalling towards a meeting with genius at the Van Gogh museum, or gazing at the shimmering reflection of Ann Frank's House, Amsterdam teaches you not to hurry. En route to your destination, just do as the locals do: pick a tranquil café, order a drink, and soak up the atmosphere of this infinitely varied city.

Aas van Bokalen
Keizergracht 335 *Tram: 1,2,5. Metro: Duomo*
Tel: 20 623 0917
Open: 17.00-01.00 (Fri & Sat till 02.00)
There are much-loved Brown Cafés all over Amsterdam, and this is one of the best loved and most durable. As unpretentious as could be, it enjoys a pleasant canalside setting, with music from the 70s to the 90s and games of chess or draughts – a place for everyone. Good-value food is served until 22.30.

Café Ebeling
Overtoom 52 *Tram: 1,3,6,12. Metro: Duomo*
Tel: 20 689 1218
Open: 11.00-01.00 (Fri & Sat till 03.00)

The premises were once a bank, some of whose features have been adapted for its current role – for example, the toilets are downstairs in the old vault. The café itself is on two levels: the ground floor is a circular reading station with newspapers and comfortable sofas, and upstairs is the bar area with the kitchen behind it. A wide variety of coffees, teas, wine, beers and Guinness is on offer, as well as some light meals and snacks served until 17.30. At the far end of the long bar is a games area with pool table, pinball machine, chess and backgammon boards.

Inter-Continental Hotel, American Bar
Leidsekade 97 *Tram: 7,6,10. Metro: Duomo*
Tel: 20 556 3000
Open: 12.00-23.00
The café-bar, an outpost of 1930s America, has retained many of its best features, including the vaulted ceiling, original light fittings, some extraordinary tile murals and superb stained glass. Long reading tables make it the place for a civilised chat, a quiet study or a leisurely sweep through the international newspapers over a cup of coffee. The café is the centrepiece of the hotel, a listed art deco building designed by Willem Kromhout in 1902.

de Kleine Karseboom
Nieuwendijk 51 *Tram: 4,9,16,20,24,25. Metro: Duomo*
Tel: 20 624 9251
Open: 10.30-01.00 (Fri & Sat till 03.00)
A lovely old corner café in the road that runs up from the Royal Palace to Centraal Station. It has an inviting white wooden facade, lace curtains and pot-plants in windows. There is often a guest beer on tap and a limited range of bar snacks is available throughout the day.

Koepel Café
Kattengat 1/Hekelveld
Tel: 20 621 2223
Open: 11.00-01.00 (Fri & Sat till 02.00)
Popular with tourists, this café in the 400-room Renaissance Hotel has a covered terrace that opens up when the weather is warmer. It's a very convenient stop-off for a quick drink before leaving for the Centraal Station just around the corner; snacks and full meals are also served. Koepel means 'dome' and refers to the dome on the church building next door.

De Kroon
Rembrandtplein 17/1 *Tram: 4,9,20. Metro: Duomo*
Tel: 20 625 2011
Open: 10.00-01.00 (Fri & Sat till 02.00)
The square was once called Reguliersmarkt and was the location of Amsterdam's butter market. It was renamed in honour of Rembrandt, whose statue stands in the gardens. De Kroon takes a natural history museum as its rather bizarre decorative theme. Skeletons, animal skins, stuffed birds and butterflies are mostly displayed in glass cabinets built into the large horseshoe-shaped bar, but other ghoulish artefacts, including some fantastic snakes preserved in jars, are just mounted on the walls. Great fun for a drink and a bite to eat or just a cup of tea or coffee. It occupies the same building as several TV and radio stations, so it's very popular with media people.

Du Lac
Haarlemmerstraat 118 *Bus: 18,22. Metro: Duomo*
Tel: 20 624 4265
Open: 11.00-02.00 (Fri & Sat till 03.00, Sun till 02.00)
Occupying premises that were once a bank, this is now a beautiful grand café done out in art deco style with greenery and objects of all kinds, from bottles and model cars to crocodile skins. Good range of drinks and snacks to enjoy in the conservatory, on the raised gallery or tucked away in one of the snugs. There's a DJ for R&B on Thursday, Friday and Saturday.

Café Luxembourg
Spuistraat 22-24 *Tram: 16,24,25. Metro: Duomo*
Tel: 20 620 6264
Open: 09.00-01.00 (Fri & Sat till 02.00)
One of the best and most popular cafés in Amsterdam, through attention to detail, excellent food and super service by young, attractive staff. Food is served from opening time to 23.00 (midnight Friday and Saturday), and the vast choice runs from breakfast with scrambled eggs with smoked salmon to dim sum, Luxem-burgers, club sandwiches and veal croquettes. With abundant comfortable seating inside and more out on the pavement, it's a favourite meeting place for large groups of friends embarking on a big night out, but during the quieter daytime hours, racks of newspapers are available for those who have just popped in for a cup of coffee or a quick snack.

Het Molenpad
Prinsengracht 653 *Tram: 7,10,20. Metro: Duomo*
Tel: 20 625 9680
Open: 12.00-01.00 (Fri & Sat till 02.00)
During the daytime the locals come to read the papers and enjoy a glass of wine with classical music and the monthly-changing exhibitions of work by local artists. Later on, however, local arts students fill the dark, narrow place and the atmosphere and music become a lot more upbeat. This is also the venue for tastings and meetings organised by the local wine society. Light lunches; full evening menu.

Nieuwe Lelie
Nieuwe Leliestraat 83 *Tram: 10,17. Metro: Duomo*
Tel: 20 622 5493
Open: 14.00-01.00 (Fri & Sat till 02.00)
A relaxed, civilised place on a corner site, with tall windows, heavy brocade curtains, artwork on the walls and just enough light to make out the quirky assortment of objects dotted around the place. All the usual beers and spirits are on offer, plus orange juice and special Jordaan liqueurs produced in the local brewery. Light snacks and cold meats. Billiards and chess. Live music at the weekend – Flamenco or Klazmer (Yiddish).

Ovidius
Spuistraat 139 *Tram: 4,9,14,16,20,24,25. Metro: Duomo*
Tel: 20 620 8977
Open: 09.30-21.00 (Sun from 10.30, Thu till 23.00)
A beautiful café serving great coffee, super sandwiches and light lunches and suppers. This bright and airy modern place spread over three floors boasts some fabulous window seats, both in the ground-floor bar area and upstairs in the gallery. Next to a shopping mall, it stays open later on Thursdays to cater for the late-evening shoppers.

Papeneiland
Prinsengracht 2 *Tram: 10,17. Metro: Duomo*
Tel: 20 624 1989
Open: 10.00-01.00
In business for 300 years, this is a cosy, relaxed Brown Café tucked away in a corner of the Jordaan at the top of the Prinsengracht Canal, with the hubbub of the nearby Noorderkerk market every Saturday and Tuesday. Inside, the beautiful tiled fireplace, worn wooden benches and stools, and heavy velvet curtains on brass rails, are lit by many little lamps and candles. Sandwiches and drinks. A secret tunnel linked the café to a Catholic church during the time of the Protestant uprising.

De Prinsessebar
Haarlemmerstraat 105 *Bus: 18-22. Metro: Duomo*
Tel: 20 624 01 06
Open: 11.00-01.00 (Fri & Sat till 02.00)
Closed: Wed
Established around 1880, a family-run Brown Café with a loyal contingent of locals. The atmosphere is friendly, and the miniature models of traditional Dutch homes, which are set into alcoves around the room, are a unique feature. Some snacks are available – perhaps pancakes or bacon and eggs – but this is first and foremost a drinking place. Billiard table.

De Tuin
Tweede Tuindwarsstraat 13
Tel: 20 624 4559 *Tram: 3,10,13,14,17,20. Metro: Duomo*
Open: 10.00-01.00 (Fri & Sat till 02.00, Sun from 11.00)
One of the best of the Jordaan bars, dark and lively, set among dozens of little boutiques in a street filled with trendy shops. The walls are practically covered with posters and flyers for musical and theatrical events around town, while the ladies and gents toilets are identified by life-size nude paintings of a man and a woman on the door. A great place to enjoy a coffee with an apple tart or a beer with olives and nachos, maybe with a game of chess or backgammon.

Twee Prinsen

Prinsenstraat 27 *Tram: 3,10. Metro: Duomo*
Tel: 20 624 9722
Open: 10.00-01.00 (Fri & Sat till 03.00)
The locals are very fond of this friendly bar decorated in traditional style, with plenty of dark wood and light brown wallpaper. It's a very pleasant place to enjoy one of the many local beers on tap with a light snack or a baguette. Heated outdoor terrace.

Vergulde Gaper

Prinsenstraat 30 *Tram: 10,17. Metro: Duomo*
Tel: 20 624 8975
Open: 10.00-01.00 (Fri & Sat till 03.00)
An intimate, welcoming café with a low, marble-topped bar lit by 1930s-style lamps and tables made of oak. Pistolettes, hot from the oven and with a choice of 20 fillings, are the lunchtime fare, while in the evening they serve sausages, toasties and various other snacks.

Wildschut

Roelof Hartplein 1-3 *Tram: 3,5,12,24,25*
Tel: 20 676 8220
Open: 09.00-01.00 (Fri till 03.00, Sat 10.30-03.00, Sun 09.30-01.00)
This is a popular art deco-style café of wide appeal. Much used by businessmen for lunch or informal meetings during the day, it becomes livelier at night, when a well-dressed office set flocks here to do some intensive unwinding. This is also a favourite choice with families for a snack meal at the weekend. Meals are served from noon till 22.00. Terrace.

Eindhoven

Depending on who you are – and what turns you on – Eindhoven might just be the centre of your universe. For fans of PSV, the attraction is magnetic. For pilgrims on the trail of the electric light bulb, Eindhoven is the home of trailblazer AF Philips; his statue dominates the central square. For devotees of Van Gogh, there's the genuine thrill of a trip to the nearby vicarage in Neunen where the artist grew up. Wander the displays of local memorabilia on a sunny day, and you might just find the influences that shaped the Sunflowers.

Grand Café Berlange
Kleine Berg, 16 5611 JV *Area: East of St Catharinakerk*
Tel: 040 245 7481
Open: 12.00-02.00
In a narrow street just off the main shopping area, Berlange is a terracotta-fronted grand café with three sets of double doors. It's a popular place with young folk, who leave their bikes outside and meet for an excellent Cook & Boon coffee or a glass of freshly squeezed orange juice. Comfortably spaced tables lead through to a stage where live music is regularly played on Monday evenings and all day Sunday. Beyond, through French windows, is a pretty garden terrace.

Carousel Café-Restaurant
Markt 35 A 5611 *Area: On main market square*
Tel: 040 245 3890
Open: 09.00-23.00/24.00 (weekends till 01.00/02.00, Sun from 11.00)
The theme of this café on the main market square is the circus, with fairground horses on poles and gypsy caravan carvings and paintings being the eyecatching decorative features of the globe-lit interior. The front part has round tables and wicker chairs and extends on to a terrace under an awning and on into the square under huge blue umbrellas. Right next to these is a fully working carousel for children. At the back is a restaurant.

Grand Café Queen
Markt 7 5611 *Area: On main market square*
Tel: 040 245 2480/2873
Open: 11.00-24.00 (weekends till 02.00/03.00)
The Queen's interior is quite baroque – a cupola supported by a wall of stained glass below which is ornately carved woodwork. One of many cafés standing side by side in the mainly pedestrianised square, this is a place that attracts a predominantly younger crowd.

Tomas Café
Stratumseind 23 5611EN *Area: South of St Catharinakerk*
Tel: 040 246 5231
Open: 11.00-01.00 (Thur till 02.00, Fri till 03.00, Sat till 04.00)
The sometime home of the Eindhoven Men's Choir, Tomas has a solid mahogany bar, high ceiling and plaster-panelled walls. As you enter, you pass under the balcony (now the restaurant) into the main auditorium, which is lit by crystal chandeliers. Up ahead you can make out what was the stage, now set with comfortable armchair furniture. The staff wear jeans and grey shirts bearing their logo. Sitting at one of the large, highly polished tables you can enjoy a coffee, beer or glass of wine with the newspapers provided, and take a snack – perhaps a toasted sandwich, a salad or a pastry.

Trocadero

Stationsplein 15 5611AB *Area: Next to train station*
Tel: 040 244 9016
Open: 10.00-23.00 (Sun from 12.00)
Opposite the station, and therefore a popular spot with travellers, Trocadero has the look of a Parisian brasserie but a far from French kitchen: snacks like nasi goreng reflect the country's connection with Southeast Asia. This dish is a sort of oriental bubble & squeak, using any left-overs with fried rice as an alternative to the proper recipe. The interior is on two levels, with the bar on high, a set of tables in the window and a terrace of tables outside.

De Vooruitgang
Markt 11 5611ES *Area: On the main market square*
Tel: 040 243 3995
Open: 10.00-03.00 (Sun & Mon 12.00-01.00, Tues 10.00-02.00, Wed 10.00-01.00, Thur 10.00-02.00)
In a period building in the old market square, this grand café has two startling spiral staircases, the main one, of steel, just inside the door. The other is of wood and is completely enclosed by little windows. The decor visits the 1950s, 1960s and 1980s, getting modern the further in you go; an old Daf car (remember them?) is parked inside. A wide variety of snacks is available in the café, and a more formal menu in the upstairs restaurant. Regular DJs or live entertainment.

BENEATH THE VERMEER

If variety is the spice of life, then Amsterdam is the spice capital of the world. Sweet and sour, Jeckyll and Hyde, this is a city of extremes. Touring the city from dawn to dusk, we pick a crop of contrasting pleasures – all very different, but all uniquely Dutch.

RIJKSMUSEUM, STADHOUDERSKADE 42

Just a short walk from almost anywhere in the city, this gallery is run by people who understand that visiting a big collection needn't feel like a marathon. For just 3.50 Euros you can hire an audio tour which steers you towards the 15 most important paintings in the collection. Let your heart melt before Vermeer's exquisite Kitchen Maid, then head for coffee.

POMPADOUR, HUIDENSTRAAT 12

Stroll five minutes back into town, and you find yourself outside the Ministry of Chocolate – otherwise known as Pompadour. Step inside, sip the cinnamon-scented froth from your cappuccino and take your first taste of passionfruit-flavoured chocolate. You've died, and gone to chocolate heaven.

FLOWER MARKET, SINGEL

A trip to Amsterdam without tulips? It would be like a joke without a punchline. Dragging yourself away from Pompadour, it's a 200 yard hike along the canal to Amsterdam's floating flower market. Riotously colourful, and wonderfully cheap, you'll want to wrap the place up and take it home with you.

T-BOAT, OUDESCHANS, BY NO 143

It was meant to happen. Bobbing on a canal right opposite Rembrandt's former house is the ultimate Amsterdam experience – a floating coffee shop. The city's coffee shops aren't quite as numerous as they used to be, nor as free to sell anything other than coffee and marijuana. But for location and sheer ambience, the T-Boat remains a classic. Turn up, drop in, check out.

DE WILDEMAN, NIEUWEZIJDS KOLK 3

Another short stroll across town brings us to a swinging sign of a heavily-built man in a loin cloth. No, we're not in the Red Light District (not quite) but outside De Wildeman, one of Amsterdam's greatest boozers. With a choice of 200 bottled beers, 20 draughts, and buzzing environment – you may never want to leave. On the other hand...

THE RED LIGHT DISTRICT, OUDEZIJDS ACHTERBURGWAL

After all the excitement of the day, one last visit to a museum would bring things full circle. The Erotic Museum and its five stories of sex toys fits the bill perfectly. Outside, Amsterdam's multi-million pound sex industry cheerfully gears up for business. And whatever you're looking for, you'll probably find it. Except, maybe, tulips.

Maastricht

Saddled with the baggage of the European treaty which was signed here, Maastricht doesn't exactly broadcast 'fun' to the average tourist. A shame really - because if you find yourself wandering the bustling labyrinth of alleys around the Markt, or standing on the sun-drenched town ramparts with their breath-taking panorama of the river – then fun is the first word that comes to mind. Add in a handful of charming medieval churches, great shopping and a lively café scene and you have the ingredients for a rather wonderful little town. No wonder they came here to sign the treaty.

Grand Café 'in de Moriaan'
Stokstraat 12 *Area: North of Onze Lieve Vrouwe Basiliek*
Tel: 43 321 1177
Open: 12.00-24.00 (Sun 14.00-22.00)
Claiming to be the smallest café in the country, this is the oldest in the street by the oldest square in the country. This charming place, which has a large terrace, is full of local people with the occasional visitor from Germany and Belgium. A full range of drinks, beers, teas and coffee and a range of sandwiches is on offer along with their speciality onion soup, with salads in summer.

Café in den Ouden Vogelstruys
Vrijthof 15 *Area: On the Vrijthof, cnr of Platielstraat*
Tel: 43 321 4888
Open: 09.30-02.00
The Old Ostrich is a wonderfully cosy café with a tiled floor, and wooden walls adorned with signed photographs of past and present famous customers and regulars. Efficient, friendly service is dispensed by smartly attired waiters wearing their emblemed ancient ostrich ties. The main lunchtime fare is excellent ham or cheese sandwiches served on black bread, and one of the speciality drinks is Emperor, a Maastricht beer.

Rotterdam

Bundled into the coastal zone known in the Netherlands as the 'Randstad' (Edge City), Rotterdam is not the place to go if you're looking for 'old Holland'. Bombed in WWII, Rotterdam seized the chance to move forward - and the enthusiasm for cutting-edge buildings still shapes the city today. Gazing from the top of the vertiginous Euromast you can drink in the futuristic skyline - and take in a coffee at the same time. At ground level, landmarks like the slanted cuboid houses on stilts are still pilgrimage points for modernists. History does raise its head in Rotterdam, as in the stunning Ruysdael-Van Beuningen Museum (Rembrandt, Rubens and the Impressionists) and the old port. Overall, however, the tense of the city is future perfect.

Café 't Bolwerk
Witte Huis 1c, Geldersekade 3011
Tel: 10 414 21 42

Open: 11.30-04.00 (Fri & Sat till 06.00) *Area: Near Willemsbrug (bridge)*
A large, handsome café overlooking the Old Harbour, across which you can see groups of modern buildings of various architectural styles, including the extraordinary cube houses designed by Piet Blom (one of these is open to the public). This is a serious meeting place for café-goers, either for a drink and a snack prior to going up town to discos, cinema or theatre, or for a meal from the simple but varied menu.

Oude Sluis
7 Havenstraat 3024 *Area: Next to lock between Coolhaven and Achterhaven*
Tel: 10 477 30 68
Open: 12.00-01.00 (Fri & Sat till 02.00, Sun from 14.00)
There are some 40 beers to choose from at this corner site with two rooms and a covered balcony that overlooks the lock between Coolhaven and Achterhaven. The most eyecatching part of the decor is a series of Rubens-style scenes in plaster relief depicting customers playing cards, throwing dice or just leaning on a barrel smoking pipes. Simple wooden chairs are set at granite-topped tables, and the notably friendly atmosphere makes this a great place to relax with a beer, a snack and a newspaper.

Sijf
115 Oude Binnenweg 3012 *Area: Near Endrachtsplein*
Tel: 10 433 26 10
Open: 10.00-01.00 (Sun from 11.00, Fri & Sat till 02.00)
On the north side of a pedestrian street, Sijf is a modern café with a traditional look. A long pine bar leads to a split-level dining area at the back. It's popular with young people who come for the beer and wine and to enjoy a very generously served pork rib snack at the bar.

Le Vagabond
99 Nieuwe Binnenweg 3014 *Area: North of Academisch Ziekenhuis*
Tel: 10 436 52 93
Open: 12.00-02.00 (Fri & Sat till 03.00)
For many years before the Second World War this was a butcher's shop. It has been a bar ever since and is well known in the music world, with a DJ on the odd Saturday and live music on Sunday. A wood-panelled bar counter and jumbled assortment of pictures and ads on the wall give the place charm, and outside, ivy grows up the wall and a large tree shelters the pavement tables. Only light snacks are served – toasted sandwiches of chorizo sausage and cheese. Once a month, on a Thursday, there's a cocktail night. Each year on the birthday of Queen Beatrix 5,000 or more people congregate here on roller blades – the bar is the start and finish of the day's run.

Utrecht

After climbing 465 steps to the top of Utrecht's Domtoren (Dome Tower) you expect a pretty good view. Recovering from a racing pulse, you get just that. On a bright day the view from Holland's tallest church tower lets you see as far as Amsterdam; closer up, the charms of this pocket-sized city are laid out for you to admire. Planning an itinerary from the tower, you'll want to add Oudegracht to your list - the canal that wanders through the city. Having converted itself from working canal into shopping precinct and foodie zone, the Oudegracht is a magnet for the city's pleasure-seekers. And given that Utrecht is Holland's biggest University City, there's no shortage of them.

Brasserie Domplein

20 Domplein 3512 *Area: Next to Domkerk*
Tel: 30 232 28 95
Open: 08.00-01.00 (Fri & Sat till 04.00)

The sandwiches are the favourite snacks at Domplein, which is nearly always busy, and seriously busy at lunchtime, which can last four or five hours. Besides the sandwiches there's a selection of tapas and fish dishes, which slip down well with Brand beer on tap. All sorts come here, as it's close to the Cathedral and the centre, and because it offers good value for money. Very friendly staff, with smart uniforms of blue T-shirts and blue aprons. A striking decorative feature is a ceiling painting of the Cathedral surrounded by angels.

De Luifel

35 Neude 3512 *Area: Just north of Stadhuis*
Tel: 30 231 16 32
Open: 12.00-02.00 (Fri & Sat till 03.00)

Approaching its 400th birthday, this venerable Brown Café is a popular meeting place for students. Over the years bric-à-brac has been added to the walls – enamelled signs and adverts from France, a saxophone, a French horn, an old gramophone, even a child's rocking horse hangs from the ceiling. It's a *taperij*, meaning a place with beer on tap, and here they offer Vos, Wieckse and Heineken. Plenty of choice on the menu, with fries and salads to accompany the dishes.

De Morgenster

323 Oude Gracht 3511 *Area: Near the bottom of old canal*
Tel: 30 234 32 06
Open: 15.00-02.30 (Sat & Sun from 11.00)

A quiet 'thinkers' café on a corner near the bottom of the Old Canal that divides Utrecht from top to bottom. Lots of newspapers and magazines to read and snacks to nibble, perhaps combining a visit with a trip along the canal.

Oudaen
99 Oude Gracht 3511 *Area: In area of the Music Centre*
Tel: 30 231 18 64
Open: 10.00-02.00
Tall windows, enormous exposed beams on the lofty ceiling, a very grand fireplace and an elaborate tableau reaching up to the rafters. That's the scene at Oudaen, which is usually very busy with couples and groups sitting in leather-upholstered chairs at candle-lit oak tables. There's a long, broad, blue-red granite bar top on the right and a quarry-tiled floor with a raised timber dais at either end of the room. Drinks and nibbles.

Eetcafé de Poort
2 Tolsteegbarrière 3511 *Area: At the bottom of Oude Gracht*
Tel: 30 231 45 72
Open: 11.00-02.00 (Sun & Mon till 01.00)
A large café of wide appeal at the bottom of the Oude Gracht where it meets the canal that goes round the city. There's a stack of board games – everything from Monopoly to backgammon and chess – and lots of newspapers and magazines. On the walls are collections of musical instruments and photos of jazz musicians. In the summer when it's fine people mostly want to sit on the spacious terrace overlooking the canal.

Portugal

Looking at the list of all the goodies you can find in Portugal – Atlantic surf, Mediterranean coastline, mountains and wilderness – you begin to wonder how they pack it all into one small country. To many people, of course, Portugal means just one thing – sun. And the beaches of the Algarve 'do sun' to perfection. But travel north and you'll discover sierras dotted with Moorish castles, sleepy vineyards, forests and snow-capped peaks – all within reach.

At the centre of the country, Lisbon acts as Portugal's cultural and economic powerhouse – corralling together a world-class collection of museums and galleries, as well as a vibrant café culture to rival anything on the Iberian peninsular. But it's the diversity of people that really makes the country.

With the end of the Colonies, Portugal welcomed back 'retornados' with open arms, blending Latin and African flavours with Portuguese. So today you're as likely to spend the evening learning to salsa as listening to traditional fado music. Epicureans won't be disappointed either, with menus that look both out to sea and inland, offering delicious combinations like pork with clams. And when in Portugal there's only one way to wash it all down – with a glass of ruby port.

Portugal may still occasionally glance over its shoulder with a nostalgic air – reflecting on the past glories of her colonies and great explorers (they've even got a word for this national trait, 'saudade'). But spend just a few days in this vibrant country and you'll find it impossible not to celebrate the present.

Lisbon

Peering over the limestone ramparts of Castelo do São Jorge, Lisbon begins to play tricks on you. Look south towards the Rio Tejo – and the patchwork of terracotta roofs and whitewashed walls of the Alfama district remind you of a North African souk. Turn your head the other way and you're greeted with startlingly modern architecture. It's Lisbon's confident juggling of this jumble of old and new which makes it such an exciting city to visit. A network of historic trams makes short work of the capital's seven hills, but if you've got the leg power you'll find plenty of surprises wandering the capital's atmospheric back streets. Café culture is almost embarrassingly rich, covering the spectrum from laid-back pavement cafés in Rua Augusta to grand Art Nouveau favourites. Culture runs just as deep, with 'must sees' including the Sintra Museu de Arte Moderna and the Museu Calouste Gulbenkian (show-casing art from 2000BC to the present day, and truly one of the world's great museums).

Antiga Confeitaria de Belem
84-92 Rua de Belem *Train: From Cais do Sodré to Belem*
Tel: 21 363 8077/8
Open: 08.00-23.00
A feast for eyes and palate in a unique pastry shop-cum-café with a 150-year history. It's famous for its little tartlets with cinnamon-flavoured custard, sold by the hundred packed in tubes. The rooms are decorated in tiles up to at least a metre high, with here and there an elaborate mural in tiles depicting scenes of Belem, the stunning 16th century Jeronimos monastery.

A Brasileira
120-122 Rua Garrett *Metro: Baixa-Chiado*
Tel: 21 346 9541
Open: 08.00-02.00

Poets and other literary figures have made this place their down the years, and the most famous of them all was Fernand Pessoa, whose bust sits at a table with an empty chair for visitors to join him. This is the most renowned of Rua Garrett's many beautiful old coffee houses, elaborately decorated in art nouveau style, with cut-glass mirrors and a marble bar. Outside, the pavement tables are almost constantly occupied, but it's worth waiting for one to watch life passing by on this affluent street.

British Bar
52-54 Rua Bernadino Costa *Metro: Cais do Sodré*
Cais do Sodre
Tel: 21 342 2367
Open: 07.00-24.00
Closed: Sun
On the left as you enter this civilised but not really very British place is a bar with a brass top and rail and wood panelling, and behind the bar there are mahogany cabinet style shelves with bottles of various ports, sherries, whiskies and other spirits. Expats and others like to drop in for a small libation when coming up to town or while waiting for a train from the station almost opposite.

Cerca Moura
4 Largo Portas do Sol *Tram: 28*
Tel: 21 888 0298
Open: 11.30-02.00 (Sun till 21.00)
A visit here can be a treat of many parts, starting with a ride one of Lisbon's grand old pre-WW1 trams, an essential experience for visitors to Lisbon. From the centre take the 28 to Largo Portas do Sol, where you get a magnificent view of S Vincente Church, and down to the sea over the rooftops and the church of S Ingracia de Fora. Opposite is this attractive little bar built into the rock foundations of the massive 12th-century walls of St George's Castle. Take a coffee or cool refreshing beer or some vinho verde and maybe a light snack at one of the pavement tables, or in the little salon dug under the exposed rock.

Chiadomel
105 Rua de Santa Justa *Metro: Baixa-Chiado*
Tel: 21 347 4400
Open: 10.00-00.30
This little café provides a magnificent view of Lisbon from its perch at the top of the Santa Justa Elevador, the extraordinary lift built by a pupil of Gustav Eiffel at the turn of the century. The Elevador climbs up from the town centre into the smart Chiado and Bairro Alto, fashionable places for bars and nightlife. If you climb another two flights you arrive at this platform with chairs and tables, waiter service, and the prospect of coffee or a cool beer, a snack or an ice cream.

Doca de Santo Esplanada
Doca de Santo Amaro – Alcantara *Train: From Cais do Sodré to Alcântara Mar*
Tel: 21 396 3522
Open: 12.30-03.00 (weekends till 04.00)
A capacious and very comfortable modern café in the renascent riverside area in the shadow of the 25th of April Bridge, the third longest suspension bridge in the world. At the entrance are four huge umbrellas set among palm trees and on the left a terrace bar. Up some solid wooden steps is the main bar, well ventilated and air-conditioned, leading to a mezzanine set with basket chairs and tables. The food is either tapas-type snacks displayed at the bar, or an à la carte menu. During the summer months it gets very busy, and at the weekends it is packed and stays open almost till dawn.

Gambrinus
25 Rua das Portas de Santo Antao *Metro: Restaurdores*
Tel: 21 342 1466
Open: 12.00-01.30

An exclusive, wood-panelled, clubby bar-restaurant in a pedestrianised street just north of the Rossio. The long bar is immediately inside this entrance and beyond are three lofty dining rooms and another entrance into a little square (Largo de Santo Domingos). Service here is the best in town, and while the bar is really for drinking they'll lay up a place for you if you feel like a snack. There's a dress code – no shorts, especially in the evening. Seafood is the main speciality of the arch-ceilinged restaurant.

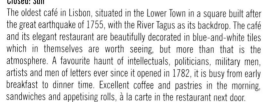

Martinho da Arcada
3 Praça do Comercio *Metro: Baixa-Chiado*
Tel: 21 887 9259
Open: 07.00-21.30
Closed: Sun

The oldest café in Lisbon, situated in the Lower Town in a square built after the great earthquake of 1755, with the River Tagus as its backdrop. The café and its elegant restaurant are beautifully decorated in blue-and-white tiles which in themselves are worth seeing, but more than that is the atmosphere. A favourite haunt of intellectuals, politicians, military men, artists and men of letters ever since it opened in 1782, it is busy from early breakfast to dinner time. Excellent coffee and pastries in the morning, sandwiches and appetising rolls, à la carte in the restaurant next door.

Café Nicola
24-25 Praça D. Pedro IV *Metro: Rossio*
Tel: 21 346 0579
Open: 08.00-20.00 (restaurant 12.00-16.00, 19.00-23.00)
Closed: Sun

Nicola is a spacious café in art deco style on the main square in the Baixa district, the city's best shopping area. The distinctive frontage is used effectively as their logo – an imposing marble arch carved in scrolls, bearing bold capital letters NICOLA supported by two stylised tapering square pillars at each end and two Ionic pillars in the middle. Out in the arcade are basket-seated chairs under sunshades where you can take your coffee or aperitif and perhaps glance through the newspaper. Good Portuguese wine list; steaks with their 'secret' sauce a speciality.

Passeio d'Avenida
Avenida de Liberdade, Praça Central next to Cinema Condes
Tel: 21 342 3755 *Metro: Avenida*
Open: 08.00-02.00 (Sat 03.00)

On the east side of one of the city's main avenues is this very good restaurant in a single-storey glass-sided permanent structure like a pavilion. In the front there are some eight or ten pavement tables, while at the other end are the kitchen and an open-air bar. Beyond are set three ranks of cloth-covered tables and elaborate white wrought-iron chairs leading to a bandstand and dance area for the nightly live music. Ice creams are a speciality.

Pastelaria 1800

7 Largo do Rato *Metro: Avenida or Intendente*
Tel: 21 388 2631
Open: 06.00-22.00 (Sat 20.00)
Closed: Sun

Built in 1857 and restored in 1924, Pastelaria 1800 is a first-class patisserie, with all the pastries made on the premises. Very popular in the morning, it also serves light lunches and suppers but closes 'early'. Original features include its decorative arch, tiled interior and facade.

Pavilhao Chines

89-91 Rua D. Pedro V *Metro: Restauradores*
Tel: 21 342 4729
Open: 18.00-02.00 (Sun from 21.00)

This unique establishment is filled with owner Luiz Pinto Coelho's amazing private collection of pottery, bronzes, militaria, pictures and paintings crowded into seven large interconnecting rooms that include two bars. The chairs are comfortably upholstered and the tables ornate with decorative marquetry. The bar counters are teak with rosewood panels supporting the tops elaborated with more marquetry and the walls are decorated in damask. The bar-café offers 40 types of tea, 100 cocktails, Portuguese wines and special sandwiches. The glasses are elegant blue-based flutes, the china blue and white. Almost everything is elegant and antique – even the washbasins in the lavatories. Classical and Portuguese music, professional service by staff in blue waistcoats and bow ties.

Real Fabrica

275/283 Rua da Escola Politecnica (ao Rato) *Metro: Rato*
Tel: 21 387 2918
Open: 08.00-02.00
Closed: Sun

A large, well-used cafeteria where the students from the polytechnic school get through beer at a very impressive rate; the beer is stored in enormous cylinders over the bar; each holds some 2,000 litres and lasts about a fortnight. A large glass cabinet displays a selection of pastries, sandwiches and snacks, and a full menu is available upstairs. Half a dozen pavement tables.

Café Rosso

53-61 Rua Ivens *Metro: Baixa-Chiado*
Tel: 21 343 2671
Open: 09.00-02.00

Approached from either Rua Ivens or 19 Rua Gambetta, this is a peaceful café tucked away in a courtyard. It's spacious and modern inside, and there are comfortable seats in the courtyard sheltered by umbrellas away from the traffic. Enormous sandwiches head the list of snacks.

ANY PORT IN A STORM

It's hard to think of a more civilised way to round off a dinner than a glass of vintage port. But the next time you take a sip, spare a thought for the Portuguese vintner who squeezed one of the world's finest wines from one of its harshest terrains.

The Douro Valley in northern Portugal is an unlikely place for a vineyard. Summer temperatures can rise as high as 50ºC, steep valley walls make for back-breaking work, and the soil is at best poor and at worst non-existent. It's the stuff farmers' nightmares are made of. But remains of Roman 'treading tanks' dating back to the third century show this is a geographical conspiracy worth its weight in gold. In fact, Rio Douro means 'River of Gold'.

SHAKY START
The first fortified wines to leave Portugal were as unpalatable as they were uncomplicated – and involved throwing a couple of pails of brandy into a barrel of wine. As well as helping preserve the wine during transport, the brandy was used to hide a multitude of viticultural sins. Not surprisingly, the drink failed to catch on.

THE BRITISH ARE COMING
At the close of the 17th century, the English weren't getting on too well with their French neighbours and various naval blockades had left England thirsty. Turning to Portugal, they decided to look for new supplies – hence the unusual sight of two Liverpudlian wine merchants sailing up the Douro in 1678. Resting in a monastery, they were offered an exceptionally smooth and sweet red wine by the abbot. By adding brandy during (rather than after) fermentation he'd been able to stop the process – producing a wine full of natural sugar. The popularity of these new 'Oporto wines' spread like wildfire and it wasn't long before English wine estates, or quintas, were dotted the length of the Douro.

SCIENCE OF PLEASURE
Today, the art of port making has become more of a science (the Instituto do Vinho do Porto ensures it's the most strictly regulated wine in the world) but at its heart the fundamentals still apply. Much of the 'treading' is now mechanized, but perfectionists still prefer to do it underfoot as this prevents the grape pips being squashed and releasing bitter tannins. Everything that's needed for fermentation is in the grape: sugars in the fruit and yeast in the skin. After just two days the process is halted by adding grape brandy and the wine is shipped downriver to Oporto. Exceptional years may be declared 'vintage' by the shipper, but it isn't something that's taken lightly as they always have to answer to the Instituto do Vinho do Porto. The last year to get the seal of approval was 1997.

PASS THE PORT
It's one thing knowing how to make port and another thing entirely knowing how to drink it. The English have had plenty of practice (draining 1.1 million cases in 2001) and most people know it should be passed to the left (possibly a naval tradition). But what do you do when you want a refill? In England, etiquette demands you ask the person nearest the decanter if they know the Bishop of Norwich (a famous port-hog). If the person doesn't seem to know what you're talking about, say loudly: "The Bishop's a marvellous man, but seldom passes the port."

Oporto

Standing on Ponte Dom Luís I, the most handsome of five bridges stretching across the Rio Douro, you'd imagine the view couldn't get any better. On the north bank the old town scrambles up the side of the valley and is crowned by the impressive Sé cathedral. Below, the waterside cafés of the Ribeira prove an ideal break from the colourful buzz of the weekday market, while to the south Vila Nova de Gaia advertises its role as the centre of Oporto's wine trade by spelling out the names of the port lodges in giant letters across the rooftops. But it's only in March when the picture is really complete as traditional square-sailed barcos rabelos deliver barrels of port from the wine estates on the Douro. A visit to a port lodge is a must, and most of them also offer free tastings. When you've had your fill, it's well worth making the effort to visit the Igreja São Francisco – a church whose sober exterior hides a lavish interior, and the Museu Nacional Soares dos Reis – the country's first museum devoted to Portuguese culture.

Majestic Café

112 Rua Santa Catarina
Tel: 22 200 3887
Open: 09.30-24.00
Closed: Sun

A remarkable art nouveau café, declared a National Monument by the Ministry for Archaeology and Architecture. It was immortalised by the national poet Antonio Ferro in 1922, when it was very much the preferred hang-out of intellectuals and men of letters. In the winter there's a resident piano player, while in the summer the pavement tables in front and the terrace at the back are more popular than inside. There's a good list of Portuguese wines, and among the specialities on the menu are cod Oporto-style, bass, hake, squid, and duck in port wine.

O Muro

87-88 Muro dos Bacalhoeiros
Tel: 22 208 3426
Open: 12.30-02.00

Two terraced houses in the old customs area of the port have become this very relaxed, informal café. A few tables on the path outside afford a splendid elevated view across the Douro river to the bodegas of the big name port wine producers. Inside, the pretty, narrow bar and its tables are looked down on by a large iron chandelier, and assorted artefacts hang haphazardly on the walls. A good place for a drink and a chat, and for straightforward traditional Portuguese cooking.

Postigo da Ribeira (do Carvao)
24-34 Rua Fonte Taurina
Tel: 22 200 4539
Open: 18.00-02.00
Closed: Mon

A spacious, split level bar-snack bar-restaurant in a narrow street in the old part of the centre of town. Original huge stone blocks form the walls and floor, and the arches and pillars over the open-plan kitchen, and three large iron posts with life-size street lamps give the impression of being outside while still enclosed. The wines on offer, all Portuguese, are sold by the carafe. Snacks are served on wooden platters – mostly seafood (their speciality) but also tripe, cheese and chorizos. It's often party time here, with live music at the weekend and at holiday times.

Confeitaria Xodo
662 Rua do Bon Jardim
Tel: 22 332 5160
Open: 07.00-20.00
Closed: Sun

Staff set about their work with a smile at this very busy local café behind the Trindade station. Offerings include excellent espresso, *galao* (coffee with milk served in a glass), pure pulped juices and substantial snacks such as the Portuguese speciality *bacalhau* (salt cod) with rice, savoury pies and cooked-to-order omelettes. Best of all are the wonderful pastries to eat in or take away. Sit at the bar or at the street window on a tall stool, or around a small table.

If there's one corner of Europe guaranteed to deliver extremes of temperature – and pleasure – then it's Scandinavia. Hurtling from 24 hours of darkness in late December to 24 hours of light in June, Scandinavia is a roller-coaster of a region where the fun never stops. Depending on the Scandinavia you want to see, you have to time your trip right. As daylight starts to dwindle in October, the citizens of Oslo, Stockholm, Copenhagen and Helsinki fight back with big cultural programmes – Scandinavian movie and theatre seasons are always timed to peak in the winter months. Then, as the calendar swings back towards the midnight sun, it's party time. Even for the most seasoned traveller, there's something giddy about sitting in a Stockholm waterfront bar at 11:00pm – with the sun still in the sky and the streets buzzing with life. Whatever the time of year, within this gigantic region, there's a smorgasbord of moods and pleasures awaiting you. Whether it's exploring the leftfield charms of Europe's mellowest capital, Copenhagen, or slamming a glass of local vodka in a Stockholm bar before you take a midsummer night's swim in the harbour, Scandinavia is right here waiting for you. Dive in.

Copenhagen

On your first morning in Copenhagen, you might find yourself asking what all the fuss is about. By midnight you'll never want to leave. Most people start their tour of this mellow capital by ticking off the 'must sees' of the Tivoli Gardens funfair, the private collection of the Carlsberg Glyptotek gallery and the Little Mermaid herself. They're all worth the trip. But it's only once you're ready to wander a little towards the alternative, that Copenhagen shows her true face. To share the relaxed Danish style of hedonism, simply take a walk from Christiania (a hippy 'free state' in the centre of town where anything goes) to the hip waterside dance bars of Holmen. Sipping a Carlsberg on your own imported sandy 'beach', with the sun setting over the water, you ask yourself just how much better things could get.

Alex
Radhusplasden 77 (Farvergade) *Area: Tivoli nr Rådhuset (town hall)*
Tel: 33 12 09 99
Open: 11.00-24.00 (Fri till 03.00, Sat 12.00-05.00)
Cosed: Sun
A convivial café on a corner site, with clever use of sunny decor and mirrors achieving a very light, cheerful effect. A good espresso coffee is produced by a spectacular domed brass Italian machine holding pride of place on the corner of the L-shaped bar. Snacks and salads are served during the day, hot food in the evening. Thursday, Friday and Saturday are karaoke nights, starting at 23.00.

Café Restaurant Amadeus
Store Kongensgade 62, 1264 Kbh K *Area: Frederiksstaden nr Frederikskirken*
Tel: 33 32 35 11/ 33 32 46 03
Open: 07.30-23.00
Close to the Royal Palace, Amadeus is a cheerful café with its own bakery open till 17.30, last dinner orders 22.00, and excellent Illy coffee to follow. All the baking is done on the premises by Denmark's acclaimed chef Allan Otto, and a mouthwatering display is on view as you enter. There's a quiet terrace at the back with tables under canvas 'gazebos'.

Hotel d'Angleterre Restaurant/Bar
Kongens Nytorv 34, 1021 K *Area: Nyhavn - nr Guinness World Records Museum*
Tel: 33 12 00 95
Open: 11.30-01.00
This luxurious and imposing 17th-century hotel across the square from the Opera and Nyhavn shows how the top and bottom of society used to rub along side by side. The bar leads to the restaurant, a classy venue for afternoon tea or a light supper before the opera, which is impressive not least for the ceramics designed in faux-Oriental style by the owner, Danish artist Bjorn Wiinblad. Special menus for special occasions such as Christmas and Easter.

Bang & Jensen Café
Istedgade 130 *Area: Vesterbo*
Tel: 33 25 53 18/40 32 02 42
Open: 08.00-02.00 (Sat from 10.00, Sun 10.00-24.00)
An early bird breakfast starts the day with a bang at this café in the so-called red light district (gets redder further back towards the station). Cheerful girls serve in the bar, which is light and airy, with tables spilling out on to the pavement and more space up some steps behind the bar. Cocktail bar Saturday evenings.

Cap Horn
Nyhavn 21, 1051 Kbh K *Area: Nyhavn*
Tel: 33 12 85 04
Open: 10.00-01.00
Once a hotel for ladies of the night, Cap Horn is now largely a restaurant, but it also welcomes visitors for a coffee at the bar or a beer on the terrace outside, served with a smile. It's a great place for watching sailing ships coming and going, or for watching the people walking up and down the quayside. Good range of bottled beers.

Chit Chat Café
Sankt Peders Straede 24a, 1453 Kbh K *Area: Strøget*
Tel: 33 33 93 39
Open: 11.00-23.00 (Fri & Sat till 01.00, Sun 10.00-17.00)
The former SMASH Café, located in the swanky/yuppie area east of the Royal Library and north of the City Hall Square. It looks very smart, with eyecatching use of steel, lovely flowers and clever lighting. Home-made luxury sandwiches, hamburgers and brasserie food – the menu changes weekly.

Café Dan Turell
Stor Regnegade 3-5, 1110 Kbh K
Tel: 33 14 10 47 *Area: Strøget - nr Guinness World Records Museum*
Open: 10.00-24.00 (Fri & Sat till 02.00)
Closed: Sun
Leatherette bench seating and a plain zinc bar top with formica back-bar suggest that the decor hasn't changed much since Dan Turell opened in 1977. It's named after a famous Danish literary figure who had fingers in many pies and was a prolific author. He died in the early 1990s and bar staff remember him as a regular visitor in the 1980s, smoking a little pipe of 'pot'. Brasserie-style snacks are available throughout the day, including salads, omelettes, pasta and bruschette – a mix of Italian and French, and daily specials add to the choice.

Drop Inn
Kompagnistraede 34, 1208 Kbh K
Tel: 33 11 24 04 *Area: Strøget - nr Dansk Skolemuseum*
Open: 11.00-04.00/05.00

An air-conditioned music café established in the 30s when jazz was king; nowadays it's more rock and blues, with live music every night. During the day it's a peaceful café with the cheapest beer in town and a rack of newspapers to read outside under the awning or inside at the roomy teak-topped bar or sitting at a wooden table on a bentwood chair.

Europa
Amagertorv 1 *Area: Strøget - nr Tobacco Museum*
Tel: 33 14 28 89
Open: 09.00-24.00 (Fri & Sat till 01.00, Sun 10.00-19.00)
Modern and glass-fronted, spreading down into the square with its bronze fountain with three storks, under upside-down umbrellas (all the spines are on top) and opposite *Café Norden*. Come here for a tea or a coffee or a beer, a snack or a light lunch, to rest your weary feet after shopping, to enjoy the sun in the morning, or to avoid it in the afternoon.

Los Flamencos
Admiralgade 25, 1066 Kbh K
Tel: 33 16 34 35 *Area: Strøget - south of St Nicholas Church*
Open: 17.00-24.00 (Fri & Sat from 13.00)
Closed: Sun
Owner Antonio imports everything he can from Spain and the dishes – tapas and main meals – are produced as they would be there, so it's all authentically Spanish, with nothing tailored to Danish tastes – and the Danes love it! Step down into the cantina – perhaps eight steps – to be greeted by soft Spanish music, and take a drink at the bar or sit in one of the capacious basket-weave armchairs set at square marble tables. If you order a bottle of house wine you only pay for what you drink.

135

DEFINITELY THE BEST LAGER IN THE WORLD

Drunk in over 120 countries, it's one of the biggest selling lagers on the planet. But under it all, Carlsberg is as Danish as... well... Carlsberg. Meet the beer that defines a nation.

Ask any Dane what the letters BC stand for, and he or she will cheerfully tell you... "Before Carlsberg". That's how big a deal the brand is over here. And downing a thirsty 108 litres per head every year – the fourth highest consumption in the world – the Danes don't need anyone to tell them about the quality of their national brew. As guests of the Carlsberg brewery, we set out to drink our way to the bottom of the legend.

BREWED TO PERFECTION

Looking at the world map of Carlsberg-drinking nations, you see a sea of green. With global sales of 5.4 billion litres a year, Carlsberg is a lager giant. They've come a long way since founder J.C Jacobsen first brewed up in his mother's bathtub 150 years ago.

You don't brew great lager for half the planet without investing in something bigger than a tub. But for all the banks of computers and mechanised processes, this is still very much a hands-on brewery. The copper tanks are still hand polished every Friday... and shine like cathedral domes. Today, as ever, Carlsberg is made on the hill in Copenhagen which Jacobsen named after his son Carl. Literally *the hill of Carl... or Carlsberg*. Sound familiar?

WIDE AND DEEP

Given that an astonishing 70 per cent of all beer drunk in Denmark comes from this one site, you'd expect to find Carlsberg everywhere in this city. You do. Crossing the capital, you can cycle right through the famous Carlsberg elephant gate. Symbolically – as well as physically – the brewery is at the heart of the city. But it gets weirder than that.

As well as fuelling countless billions of good times, the company goes one better, and its private power-station inside the factory actually supplies electricity to large sections of the city. Quite literally, they keep Copenhagen going.

There's more. The scientific history of the company is almost a history of the country. Breakthroughs like the pH system came from research at Carlsberg, and they were the ones who told Louis Pasteur that his research into yeast was, well, wrong. Today, the strain of pure yeast developed by Carlsberg is used by every lager brewer on the planet.

Walk anywhere in the city, and the brand stays with you. Copenhagen's world-class Glyptotek museum was a gift from Carlsberg that almost bankrupted the company. The Little Mermaid, that beacon for Copenhagen's tourist trade, was another present. Oh, and the company recently donated £8.5 million to build a replica of a Viking longship which makes its maiden voyage in 2005. It's enough to make you reach for a bottle.

Grand Teatret Foyer Caféen

Mikkel Bryggers Gade 8, 1460 Kbh K *Area: Tivoli nr Rådhuset (town hall)*
Tel: 33 15 16 11
Open: 11.30-21.30

A cool café in the foyer of a once-grand theatre that is now a complex of three cinemast. Classical music plays and you can have a drink, an ice cream, a sandwich or a cake before or after the film (first showing noon and then every two hours). But many people come here to relax with a newspaper in the very peaceful surroundings. Pavement tables.

Kong Kursen (Amalie Dorothea & Co's Restauration)

Kompagnistraede 4, 1208 Kbh K *Area: Strøget - nr Dansk Skolemuseum*
Tel: 33 14 46 01
Open: 11.00-22.00 (winter till 18.00)
Closed: Sun

A great selection of Danish open sandwiches and imaginative salads, meat snacks and lots of herring dishes await the hungry at Kong Kursen. Chess and backgammon are played on marquetry boards inlaid in the tops of tables set on a cool herringbone brick-paved floor. The ceiling is decorated with old enamelled Danish advertisements, and outside there are aluminium tables and chairs for balmy days. Espresso coffee, Tuborg beers and house wines for liquid refreshment.

Kafé Kys

Laederstraede 7 *Area: Strøget - south of Tobacco Museum*
Tel: 33 93 85 94
Open: 10.00-01.00 (Fri & Sat till 02.00, Sun 12.00-24.00)

Young, beautiful staff serve excellent Illy coffee, draught beer and house wines, sandwiches and salads to young, beautiful customers sitting at pavement tables in a more-or-less pedestrianised street one away from the main shopping street. The music depends on the mood, and the mood is generally cool. Each month different artists display their paintings, which are for sale.

Langelinie Pavillonen

Langelinie, 2100 Kbh 0 *Area: Kastellet*
Tel: 33 12 12 14
Open: 12.00-24.00

On the quayside near the famous bronze of the little mermaid by Edvard Eriksen, this spacious terrace restaurant-café serves a large selection of coffees, beers and snacks. It's set on three levels, two outside and the indoor restaurant atop, and provides a great vantage point for watching the comings and goings of all the wonderful craft, from small sailing dinghies to three-masters, speedboats to ocean-going ferries and liners and the Seacats.

Lapostolle Café Bar
Gothersgade 11, 1123 Kbh K *Area: Rosenborg*
Tel: 33 14 54 72
Open: 10.00-24.00 (Thur 10.00-02.00, Fri & Sat till 05.00)
An informal café-bar with a frieze of a collage of posters and a background of bossa nova and other Latin music; old bentwood chairs stand at small cast-iron base tables by a simple zinc bar; newspapers lie in the rack for you to browse over a coffee or draught beer. The dark parquet floor gives way to two narrow raised pavement terraces outside under bright yellow awnings. Snacks, salads, fish dishes and Mexican food.

Mei Chiang
Tordenskjoldsgade 1,1055 Kbh K
Tel: 33 93 03 65 *Area: Nyhavn - south of De Kongelige Teater*
Open: 12.00-01.00 (Sun till 23.00)
Once a bakery, then a lunch shop, the two back rooms are now an elegant Chinese restaurant. The bar in front has a view of the street and a glance across the front of the Opera. Behind the bar are an elaborately carved piece of pine depicting the fruits of the field and vine and mirror-backed shelving, now holding liquor bottles but once doing duty in a Spanish apothecary. Always popular in the Opera season. Really good coffee.

Café Norden
Ostergade 61 *Area: Strøget - nr Café Museum*
Tel: 33 11 77 91
Open: 09.00-24.00 (Sun from 10.00)
A very popular modern café in a pedestrian area with a fountain. Service on two floors and outside under large green awnings covers a selection of brownies, cookies, ices, soups, toasted and club sandwiches, tuna baps, salads, crêpes, nachos, peanuts and loads of coffees, juices, beers, wine and spirits. This is catering for the masses who flock here for refreshment, respite from shopping, to read the newspaper or to scour a thesis.

Café Nyhavn 17
Nyhavn 17 *Area: Nyhavn - Waterside*
Tel: 33 12 54 19
Open: 10.00-02.00 (Fri & Sat till 03.00)
Closed: 10 days at Christmas
Traditional Danish snacks of open sandwiches and a lunch menu are served until 16.30, including the special 'platte' of seven types of food served with bread. Later it becomes a bar, sometimes with live music. It retains its Scandinavian wood feel with a mahogany bar counter, a chunky brass rail held up by brass mermaid brackets, and matching tables and bentwood chairs. Lots of single malts, both Scotch and Irish.

Opera Caféen

Gothersgade 2, 1123 Kbh K
Tel: 33 12 65 83
Open: 12.00-24.00 (Fri & Sat till 02.00, Mon till 22.00)
An eyecatching feature here is a series of oil-on-canvas wall hangings depicting Italian scenes, dating perhaps from 1900 (when the café first opened in a location nearer the Opera), perhaps from its opening here in 1934. At first it was just a bar used by many of the performers and stage staff as well as the opera-goers. It still remains busy in that role, but is now a restaurant in addition. Those wishing to dine and see the Opera are strongly advised to book.

Palace Bar, Palace Hotel
Radhuspladsen 57, 1550 Kbh V *Area: Tivoli*
Tel: 33 14 40 50
Open: 12.00-02.00 (winter 15.00-01.00)
The Palace Hotel, once a coaching inn, was started in 1907 (two years after the completion of the town hall) and finished in 1910. Opening on to the City Hall Square, with cane chairs at the pavement tables and comfortable tartan-upholstered chairs within, the bar offers a good sideways view of the facade of the Seat of the City Council. In the top row are the symbols of the officials, the town crier, the lamplighters and the guard, and below is the golden figure of the 13th-century Archbishop Absalon. Good cocktails, plenty of eating choice in the Brasserie on the Square. Mainstream jazz is a regular feature.

Café Sommersko
Kronprinsengade 6, 1114 Kbh K *Area: Strøget - nr Post & Tele Museum*
Tel: 33 14 81 89
Open: 08.00-24.00 (Sun from 10.00, Thur till 01.00, Fri till 02.00, Sat 09.00-02.00)
Located just west of Nyhavn (the old port near the ferry terminals), this is a very friendly place, with newspapers to read and young people whiling away a Saturday afternoon playing backgammon. It offers a good selection of traditional Danish beers on draught, Italian coffees and wine by the glass.

Victor Café/Brasserie
Hovedvagtsgade/Ny Ostergade 8, 1103 Kbh K
Tel: 33 13 36 13 *Area: Strøget - nr Guinness World Records Museum*
Open: 08.00-01.00 (Thur, Fri & Sat till 02.00, Sun 11.00-23.00)
A busy, successful place on a corner site, with smartly clad staff and a clientele of all ages. Striking features include the ceiling, composed of opaque glass panels held in a diamond lattice in brass, and paintings by 15 different artists. From the two elaborate zinc-topped bar counters are served plentiful cocktails, draught and bottled beers, coffees Italian style and wines leading with their own-label house brand. A snack menu is printed on a long laminated card, Danish on one side, English on the other. The cooking on the main menu is French.

Helsinki

Water is everywhere, and since prohibition was lifted (in 1931), many a drop to drink. Offering a cosmopolitan mix of east and west, and a Venetian mix of land and sea, Helsinki welcomes hedonists of all denominations. Since Finland's diplomatic divorce from the collapsing Soviet Union in 1991, the city has been determined to make up for lost time – with a near carnival feel for much of the summer. Trams and ferries take you to most of the attractions, including Sibelius Park, the National Museum, and the famous Temppeliaukio Church, which has been carved into solid rock. If the domed copper roof of this amazing building brings to mind a huge still, then take the hint and sample Koskenkorva Brannvin, the local spirit – a proven antidote to those long winter nights.

Cafe Carelia
Mannerheimintie 56, SF-00260 *Area: Opposite Opera House*
Tel: 9 270 90 976
Open: 12.00-01.00 (Sat from 13.00, Sun 13.00-23.00)
This splendid café-restaurant on a corner site opposite the Opera House was in its previous incarnation a pharmacy, and much of the old interior has been retained: the bench seating, the burgundy and white diamond-patterned tile floor, the shelving, the chemist's drawers, and the mahogany-wood panelling. Illy coffee is served with Illy chocolate in smart Illy cups. The long room that runs along Runeberginkatu has the bar and smart black table-clothed tables and chairs; the other, looking on to Mannerheimintie, is for non-smokers. The speciality of the restaurant is fresh mussels.

Café Carusel
Merisatamanranta 10, 00150 *Area: On quayside in Eira*
Tel: 9 622 4522
Open: 10.00-22.00 (winter till 19.00)
Closed: Jan
There's always something to see from this café on the quay next to the marina: pleasure craft, sightseeing boats, private yachts, huge sea-going ferries – there's constantly something on the move. You can sit in the spacious, high-ceilinged circular interior, with picture windows down to the wooden floor giving a panoramic view, or out on the expansive terrace (300+ seats). A draught beer, espresso or delicious white chocolate cappucino may be taken with or without a pastry or perhaps a club sandwich.. The café hosts occasional jazz or gospel concerts.

Café Ekberg
Bulevardi 9 *Area: Hietalahti*
Tel: 9 681 18660
Open: 07.30-20.00 (Sat 08.30-17.00, Sun 10.00-17.00)
An elegant café and pastry shop located half way down a tree-lined street with the odd private gallery, towards the flea market in Hietalandenkatori (and its market hall). Away from the busy shopping centre, this is a peaceful place with an outside raised planked platform as a fair weather alternative to the simply but classically decorated room with floral drapes at the windows. More mature residents of Helsinki come and enjoy the splendid buffet breakfast, a sweet or savoury pastry with a coffee or a beer, or a late afternoon salad and glass of white wine. Along from the café is their shop with all sorts of confections, including wonderful chocolates.

Café Engel

Aleksanterink 26, 00170 *Area: Opposite Engel University & Cathederal*
Tel: 9 652 776
Open: 07.45-24.00 (Sun from 11.00, Fri till 01.00, Sat 09.30-01.00)
Named after the architect who designed the University building, Engel starts the day with a very good value breakfast menu with lots of options: The House Breakfast, French, English, and Energy. Classical music plays as customers sip and munch and chat, in the front room with the wares on display, in the piano room behind (non-smoking), or in the internal courtyard. Also available are light salad dishes, beers by the bottle and wines by the glass. In the evenings it is a busy socialising spot and wine becomes the more common refreshment. The café's walls are hung with a frequently changing exhibition of paintings. The café is associated with the Arts Cinema next door and you can get tickets here; films in Finland are not dubbed.

Fazer

Kluuvikatu 3, SF-00100 *Area: North of Esplanade (Eteläesplanadi)*
Tel: 9 6159 2930
Open: 07.30-22.00 (Sat from 09.00, Sun 12.00-21.00)
Baking is done on the premises at this very stylish café-restaurant/bakery just off the Esplanade. The rolling, cutting and shaping of the delicacics take place before your very eyes, and the range of finished goodies is mouthwatering indeed. To the left is the bar, and beyond it the restaurant, black and chrome with modern lighting.

Café Kafka

Pohjoisesplanadi 2/Svenska Teatern, SF-00130
Tel: 9 17 13 80 *Area: Parallel with Eteläesplanadi In Swedish Theatre*
Open: 09.30-19.00 (Sat from 10.00)
Closed: Sun
A stylish café with cool black-and-white decor, Kafka sits in the semi-circular foyer of the Swedish Theatre. In the café you can enjoy a peaceful refreshment and read the paper or a book away from the bustle of the shopping centre, or take your drink to the black folding metal tables and chairs outside in summer. The theatre stages musicals and comedies and has a small bookshop whose stock includes humorous books in English.

Kappeli

Eteläesplanadi 1 *Area: On Esplanade (Eteläesplanadi)*
Tel: 9 179 242
Open: 09.00-02.00 (Fri & Sat till 03.00)
A very stylish set of glass-covered pavilions in the middle of the Walk. From a central bar pavilion where they brew their own unfiltered beer, tables and chairs spill out on to the terrace, and restaurant areas at either end offer a buffet at one, table service at the other. In the basement is a bar where the favourite drinks include dark ales and a wide range of whiskies (this bar opens at 16.00).

Kiasma

Mannerheiminaukio 2 SF-00100 *Area: Inside museum of modern art*
Tel: 9 1733 6504
Open: 10.00-22.00 (Tue 09.00-17.00)
Closed: Mon
Staccato modern minimalist decor in a modern art museum facing Parliament, with a big Mannerheim statue and an oblong pond outside and

an art library across the foyer. The café serves very good espresso, and wine and beer to go with salads.

Ravintola Seahorse
Kapteeninkatu 11, SF- 00140 *Area: Eira*
Tel: 9 628 169
Open: 10.30-24.00 (Sat till 01.00)
Established in 1934, this restaurant/café is a bastion of true Finnish food and culture. The food is top-notch: salmon or wild mushroom soup, herrings in various ways, baked perch, steaks with morel and cranberry garnishes and sauces, anchovy butter, meatballs, pancakes and strawberries, cheese and cloudberry jam, blackcurrant sorbet – all at very reasonable prices, with teas and coffees, draught beer and wines by the glass to accompany. The mural at the end is an artistic impression of two sea horses swimming, and the chairs and a row of bench seating are repro in style. This café stands in a quiet suburb south of the city centre towards Eira, while an offshoot is in the northern suburb of Niemenmaki.

Robert's Coffee House
Kanavakatu 5, SF-00160 *Area: Near Katajanokan Terminaaali*
Tel: 9 1733 4458
Open: 09.00-17.00 (Sat from 10.00)
Closed: Sun, also Sat unless there's an exhibition in the building
An altar to coffee and tea in the docks along from the market by the quays where all the long-haul ferries come in. It occupies the middle of a long building, with a bar at either end and a granite-tiled terrace with folding metal chairs and tables outside. Inside are sacks of coffee piled up among the quiet comfortable wicker chairs set at tables. Among other offerings are three types of espresso – you choose the bean and the roast. The Robert in the name is Robert Paulig, a real expert in coffee matters, who founded the coffee house in 1987. The 'roastery' imports a selected variety of the finest green coffee from around the world and roasts the beans in small amounts to customers' tastes and requirements. It also sells coffee utensils and a selection of cakes and cookies.

Tomtebo Café
Tamminiementie 1
Tel: 9 484 511
Open: Jun-Aug 12.00-18.00; Sept, Oct & Jan-May Sat & Sun only 11.00-17.00
Closed: Nov & Dec
The centrepiece of the Folklore Centre of Tomtebo, run by the Seurasaari Foundation, is an open-air museum of some 90 years standing. The café is in the summer house (a traditional wooden construction built in 1893) of Gustaf Nyström, the renowned professor of architecture who designed this villa and, among other things, the National Library building. For years the citizens have been coming here for quiet summer walks in the park and to picnic on the nearby island, and in winter at weekends to bring their own food to barbecue at bonfire parties. The café has an exhibition of colourful folk costumes worn by Russian refugees escaping the rigours of the old communist state, and most summer evenings folk dancing is performed on a stage behind the café.

Strindberg

Pohjoisesplanadi/Norra Esplanaden 33, SF- 00100
Tel: 9 270 60 150 *Area: Parallel with Eteläesplanadi In Galleria Kämp*
Open: 09.00-01.00 (Sun 10.00-23.00)
Closed: Sun (restaurant only)
Opening on to the Esplanade on the corner of Mikongatu (Mikaelsgatan), and inside into the Galleria Kämp shopping mall, this is a very fashionable café owned by the renowned Stockman department store, busy at lunchtime with a queue at the self-service counter, and in the evenings a popular spot for a beer, glass of wine, a cocktail or an after dinner Illy coffee and liqueur.

Café Torpanranta

Munkkiniemen Ranta 2, SF- 00330
Tel: 9 484 250 *Area: North-west of centre in Munkkiemi*
Open: 10.00-21.00 (winter till 16.00)
A pretty pavilion café on the beach in a northwest suburb, with a cafeteria counter from which you choose your sandwich or pastry to enjoy with some good coffee or a glass of wine. From the large patio, decorated with flowers, you can step straight on to the beach and watch the colourful summertime activity of washing rugs on the bench tables at the nearby jetty. The rugs are left to dry on racks. This activity is particular to certain parts of Helsinki and is much enjoyed by the whole family.

Café Ursula

Ehrenströmintie3, SF-00140
Tel: 9 652 817 *Area: On Water's edge in Kaivopuisto*
Open: 09.00-24.00 (winter till 21.00)
This pretty pavilion/conservatory café is situated on the water's edge by the Kaivopuisto Brunnsparken Park, in the Embassy district south of the centre. It sells snacks, coffees and beers, and a selection of ice creams. In the park, in the summer you can play chess on a paved board with 30"-high chess pieces, or go bungee-jumping (or just watch), or hire roller blades. Otherwise, there's all the activity on the water: jet-skiers jetting, yachtsmen yachting, travellers going to distant places on giant floating hotels.

Oslo

According to legend, the recipe for beer was accidentally dropped to earth by Odin as he flew over Norway. No doubt he was distracted by the antics in Oslo – where Norwegians congregate today to celebrate his gift. The Grunnerlokka is the place for the trendiest bars until the early hours, when lively Norse hedonists decamp to the nightclubs around Karl Johans Gate. As you fall for the charms of this city, you have to question the wanderlust of Thor Heyerdahl, whose famous balsa raft can be compared with the slender Viking boats in the neighbouring Kon-Tiki Museet and Vikingskipshuset at Bygdoynes. Why ever did they want to leave?

Café Amsterdam
Universitetsgate 11, 0164 *Tram: Sentrum*
Tel: 23 35 42 45
Open: 11.30-00.30 (Fri & Sat till 02.30, Sun from 13.00)
Stained oak gives a dark, dignified look to the this lofty, spacious café, which is part of the Quality Savoy Hotel. Twenty and thirty-somethings meet here in the evenings when mainstream jazz plays; there are posters on the walls and papers to read. A wide range of draught beers, including Newcastle Brown, Hoegaarden, Leffe, Murphy's and Heineken, jostle with local brews Aass and Frydenlund. Snacky things to eat.

Arcimboldo
Wergelandsveien 17 *Metro: National Theatret*
Tel: 22 69 44 22
Open: 11.00-24.00 (Thur till 01.00, Fri & Sat till 03.00)
Closed: Sun
This is the cafeteria of the 'Artists' House' Kunstnernes Hus, a fashionable art gallery founded in 1930. Popular with showbiz and media folk, it's a great place for people-watching as well as picture-viewing, and there's a fine view across to the gardens of the Royal Palace. Daily changing menu of straightforward dishes.

Grand Café, Grand Hotel
Karl Johansgate 31, 0101 *Metro: Stortinget*
Tel: 22 42 93 90
Open: 06.00-23.00
In the main street leading from the castle into town stands the venerable and aptly named Grand Hotel, whose 280 bedrooms are the smartest in Oslo. In its renowned café a large modern painting takes the eye in the bar, but it is the painting on the far wall that is so well known. Painted in 1928 by Per Krohg, it depicts many of the habitués of the 1890s: the then owner Kristian Fritzner is surveying a scene that includes the artist Edvard Munch, the playwright Henrik Ibsen, two army officers, several journalists and many other notable patrons of the day. In the centre of the room is a mouthwatering hors d'œuvre table groaning under a wonderful choice of traditional dishes. Outside are old-style tables and chairs where the punters can watch the world go by or bury their heads in the daily paper.

Kafé Celsius
Radhusgate 19, 0158 *Tram: Aker Brugge*
Tel: 22 42 45 39
Open: 11.30-00.30 (Fri & Sat till 01.30, Sun 13.00-21.30)
Closed: Mon in winter
Celsius is housed in one of the oldest buildings in the city, dating from 1629 and once the Town Hall. It's a popular haunt of artists and is flanked by galleries, one for the work of young artists. At lunchtime and on Sunday the music is classical, while in the evening it's more Piaf and traditional café style. The lunch menu (sandwiches, salads, omelettes, pasta) runs until 14.30; the choice in the evening is similar but more elaborate, with some added fish dishes. To accompany, or to enjoy on their own, is a wide range of red and white wines from around the world.

Café Hemingway
Ovre Slottsgate 10, 0157 *Metro: Stortinget*
Tel: 22 33 06 68
Open: 11.00-01.00 (Fri & Sat till 03.00, Sun 13.00-24.00)
Photographs of Ernest Hemingway adorn the walls of this spacious, air-conditioned café, which offers the choice of standing space on the parquet floor by the bar, comfortable seating at dark pine tables, and wooden slatted seats on the pavement of the pedestrianised street. The café serves beer from a small independent Norwegian brewery, and snacks and light meals include baguettes, salads, grills, brunch and cakes, with coffee, tea and wines by the glass if you don't want beer. Rock music downstairs.

Café Luxembourg
Nedre Slottsgate 2, 0153 *Metro: Stortinget*
Tel: 23 10 73 00
Open: 15.00-24.00 (Wed & Thur till 01.00, Fri & Sat till 02.00)
Closed: Sun
A roomy café which gets many of its customers from the attached hotel, whose entrance is in the next street. (The café is not open in the morning, so the hotel 'borrows' it for breakfast.) The menu includes open sandwiches, fish soup, lasagne, burgers and mozzarella, tomato and basil salad. Teas, coffees, wines by the glass.

Theatercaféen, Hotel Continental

Stortingsgaten 24/26, 0117 *Metro: National Theatret*
Tel: 22 82 40 50
Open: 11.00-23.00 (Sun 15.00-22.00)

Part of the 150-room Hotel Continental, with its corner entrance, the Viennese-style Theatercaféen opened in 1909, a year after the National Theatre across the road, and has been in the same family ever since. The café has always attracted Oslo society and celebrity, and some 70 of their portraits hang on the walls. Some come to relax with a newspaper on one of the settees, others for animated discussion or to celebrate a success or an anniversary; some pop in for a quick drink, perhaps with an open sandwich, while others settle down to a full-blown repast of classic Norwegian dishes that ends with excellent pastries.

3 Brodre (Three Brothers)

Ovre Slottsgate 14, 0157 *Metro: Stortinget*
Tel: 23 10 06 70
Open: 11.00-01.00 (Wed-Sat till 02.00)

There are plenty of reminders here of its former life as a hat and glove shop. The ceiling has painted glass panels of branches with autumn leaves, an eye-catching feature dating from 1897. The old counters are still there, too, and the tiled floor, with cast-iron radiators standing on it, the wall paintings and the glass chandeliers could all be of the same vintage. Downstairs is a Mexican restaurant, while upstairs is a piano bar every evening except Sunday. 3 Brodre is located in the city's main shopping and entertainment area.

Stockholm

Every city has at least one asset it likes to show off about – and in Stockholm it's water. Not only does Stockholm have miles of canals and sea-front, the water inside them is so clean you can swim in it! If the rest of the city isn't quite as spotless as the water, then it's a close run thing. From the cobbled backstreets of the Old Town (Gamla Stan) to the seventeenth century Royal Castle, Stockholm is one polished capital. Here in the 'city of water', you can never go far wrong if you keep your pleasures liquid. For culture, head for Sweden's most visited museum, the Vasamuseet, where you can see the miraculously well preserved remains of the Vasa which sank on her maiden voyage in 1628. To get closer still to the water, try one of the dozens of pleasure cruises in the Stockholm archipelago. And when you're ready to go under, head for the buzzing nightlife between Kungsträdgården and Stureplan.

Engelen/Kolingen (downstairs)
Kornhamnstorg 59b (Gamla Stan) Box 7065, 103 86
Tel: 8 20 10 92 *Area: Gamla Stan*
Open: 16.00-02.00 (downstairs till 03.30)

A corner site bar on Gamla Stan (Old Stockholm), with live music every night except Monday, when it's the turn of stand-up comedians. The bar leads to a blackjack table, to a restaurant in an elegant room, and to downstairs, which is a real rabbit warren – another bar, more blackjack tables, cloakrooms etc. House wine is sold by the bottle but you only pay for what you drink. The cheerful, energetic staff, always eager to help, are used to dealing with demanding crowds. Steakhouse-style food.

Gamla Stans Bryggeri
Skeppsbrokajen, Tullhus 2, Gamla Stan *Area: Gamla Stan*
Tel: 8 20 20 65
Open: 14.00-01.00 (Fri & Sat till 03.00, Sun till 23.00)

A micro-brewery in an enormous, very well-appointed shed on the quayside known as Customs House 2. Its main output is unfiltered beer, which is therefore acceptably cloudy. Above the central bar made of substantial oak (the brewing takes place in the very centre) is a pair of roll-back roof panels. This place gets really busy at the time of the Water Festival (an event to compare with Semana Grande in Spanish cities), when a live band entertains in great style, but it's also popular in the winter when the terrace is dismantled and the action is all inside.

Café Gateau
Sturegallerian, Stureplan 2 *Area: Kungsträdgården*
Tel: 8 611 65 93
Open: 08.00-18.00 (Sat 10.00-17.00, Sun 11.00-17.00)

Café and bakery in a smart shopping mall. The bakery shop is on the ground floor and the café is up a sweeping stair in the gallery overlooking the shop and the shoppers as they move from boutique to boutique. The pastries are excellent, as is their deli-type lunch, and the coffee is Illy. Wine is also offered, and beer, both draught and bottled. You can cut your own slice of crusty twisted loaf to go with, perhaps, a bowl of gazpacho, a popular summer choice. In the winter season (October-May), when it's dark and cold outside, this place is packed and cosy and a resident piano player entertains.

Grand Hotel, Verandan

Blasieholmshamnen 8, Blasieholmen *Area: Kungsträdgården*
Tel: 8 679 35 86/717 00 20
Open: 07.00-11.00 for breakfast, 12.00-15.00 (Sat & Sun 13.00-16.00) for lunch, 18.00-22.00 for smorgasbord. Bar open 11.00-02.00 (Sun 12.00-00.30)
The 19th-century Grand, on the waterfront near the National Art Museum, is Stockholm's leading luxury hotel, and the terrace offers fine views across the water to Gamla Stan (Old Stockholm) and the Royal Palace. Verandan is renowned for its smorgasbord, and other offerings include an à la carte menu and two- or three-course fixed-price menus, all offering traditional Swedish cuisine. The surroundings of this grand hotel, designed by Frenchman Regis Cadier in 1874, are quite formal, and there is a dress code in the restaurants.

Café Kristina

Vasterlanggatan 68, Gamla Stan, S-111 29 *Area: Gamla Stan*
Tel: 8 20 80 86
Open: 11.00-22.00/23.00, Sun 13.00-22.00
On the road that runs the length of Gamla Stan, this was once Queen Kristina's session room, built in 1625 and restored internally in 1904, externally in 1947. After several varied incarnations it is now a rather grand café with a handsome panelled ceiling. The style of the food is Italian.

Mandus

Osterlangatan 7, Gamla Stan *Area: Gamla Stan*
Tel: 8 20 60 55
Open: 17.00-24.00
A small café/bar very near the Royal Palace, with a loyal local following. There are a couple of tables outside, several inside and seating at the curved bar where the patron surveys his domain. Three white and three red wines are sold by the glass, and the food is good: fish specialities, mussels, reindeer, ox fillet, goat's cheese, gravad lax, chanterelles.

Martini

Norrmalmstorg 4, 111 46 *Area: Hötorget*
Tel: 8 440 38 80
Open: 11.00-24.00 (Wed & Thur till 02.00, Fri & Sat till 03.00, Sun 13.00-23.00)
In the centre of Stockholm's downtown, where all the best shopping and entertainment are to be found, this is an Italian-style café/restaurant but with a Swedish feel and Swedish cuisine. The place to be is either on the terrace in summer, or at the large bar in the centre of the room. People of all ages come here, alone, as couples or to meet as a group, to enjoy a good glass or coffee, or to sip a cocktail. On Friday and Saturday a DJ starts spinning at 23.00.

Café Mix

Sibyllegatan 2 *Area: Östermalmstorg*
Tel 8 660 0625
Open: 11.00-16.00 (Sat 11.00-17.00)
Closed: Sun
The oldest building in this part of town, Café Mix was once the Royal Bakery, sandwiched between the Kungliga Dramatiska Teatren and the Royal Stables. It came close to being obliterated in the 1970s to create a new car park, but it was nearly all saved when its history and antiquity were pointed out; by then, the original ovens had already been destroyed. The back part

of the building is the Music Museum, where its Friends hold classical concerts in the winter season, hence the resident piano. Snacks run from jacket potatoes and crêpes to lasagne and moussaka. No smoking inside.

Mosebacke Etablissement
Mosebacke Torg 3, Sodermalm, 116 46 *Area: Slussen*
Tel: 8 55 60 98 90
Open: 17.00-01.00 (Thur-Sat till 02.00)
Located at the back of one of the oldest theatres in Stockholm, this place has a restaurant with a dance floor and stage. Breakfasts are served from the kiosk on the terrace, lunch at the grill. Saturday and Sunday brunch with live jazz. At night there's an entrance fee to go inside to listen to or dance to live music or DJs starting at 22.00 and going on until closing time. A bonus is the great views over the rooftops of Gamla Stan, across the water to the Grand Hotel, Strandvagen's grand houses, Skeppsholmen and the funfair at Djurgardsstaden.

Operabaren
Operahuset, Karl XII's Torg, 111 86 *Area: Kungsträdgården*
Tel: 8 676 58 07/08
Open: Café 11.30-03.00 (Sun from 13.00) Bar 12.00-01.00 (Sun 17.00-24.00)
A haunt of royalty and the famous and a place of several names, depending on which part you choose: the opulentissimo Operakallaren restaurant, the refined, clubby Operabaren, Café Opera (one of the city's top night spots), Bakfickan. Matsal is the main dining room, Nobis the wine cellar. The first parts opened in 1787, but the café dates from 1895, and the bar from 1904. The cafe has a spectacular ceiling painting by Vicke Andren and huge crystal chandeliers, while the rest has a contemporary look. At midnight it becomes a disco, but during the earlier parts of the day it is equally popular for lunch, tea or an early supper.

Ortagarden
Ostermalmstorg *Area: Östermalmstorg*
Tel: 8 662 1728
Open: 10.30-21.30 (Sat 11.00-20.30, Sun 12.00-20.30)
A vegetarian café in the City-owned Saluhallen market, which provides the raw materials for the seasonal menus. Ortagarden is a great favourite with users of the market, but even out of market hours it attracts a regular local clientele who come here to enjoy live piano Monday, Tuesday (and sometimes Sunday) while they sup or snack. Coffee is the traditional filter variety.

Café Riche
Birger Jarlsgatan 4, 114 14 *Area: Östermalmstorg*
Tel: 8 679 68 40
Open: 11.00-03.00, bar from 17.00
The bar counter at Café Riche is an elaborate zinc-topped affair, where tapas-style snacks are sold – naturally, the head of a bull graces the wall. The Veranda, or terrace, has high-backed wicker basket chairs, and the restaurant, which offers a full à la carte menu, is partly in a glassed-in area of the terrace and partly inside. The staff give the bar a real Latin American feel, assisted by the music and the cocktails to complement the jamon. This place really hops at night – and that could easily mean dancing on the bar!

Stampen
Stora Nygatan 5, Gamla Stan *Area: Gamla Stan*
Tel: 8 20 57 93/86
Open: 19.00-03.00
A smoky, swinging jazz club with a good list of wines (many available by the glass), beers and spirits. Upstairs is funky, with all sorts of musical instruments and other artefacts hanging from the ceiling. Sometimes, like during the Water Festival, there is an entrance charge.

Sundbergs Konditori

Jarntorget 83, Gamla Stan, 111 29 *Area: Gamla Stan*
Tel: 8 10 67 35
Open: 08.00-19.00 (summer till 23.00)
Johan Ludwig Sundberg opened his café here in 1785, in a building that was already nearly 200 years old. Standing in a pretty little square, it is renowned for its coffees, teas and hot chocolate, and has also earned an almost legendary name for its pastries, sweets and liqueurs. The interior has retained all its period charm, notably in the 'glass' ceiling, a feature of the old houses of Gamla Stan, and in the Venetian glass chandelier. Outside, in the largely pedestrian cobbled square, is a roped-off area with cane chairs and tables, while inside is a display counter on one side and tables on the other, with a huge copper coffee urn among the cups and saucers on a table in pride of place under the chandelier. A great favourite with both locals and the tourists who flock to this part of the city.

Vau De Ville
Hamngatan 17, Norrmalm, 111 47 *Area: Kungsträdgården*
Tel: 8 611 25 22
Open: 11.30-01.00 (Fri & Sat till 02.00, Sun 13.00-01.00)
French staff provide a smiling welcome at this busy corner bar/restaurant in brasserie-style. Green chequered table cloths, globe lighting – only the zinc bar top is missing! The clientele are much as you'd find in Paris; in fact you could be forgiven for thinking you were there. And the cooking? French, naturellement.

Vette-Katten
Kungsgatan 55/Klara Norra Kyrkogatan 26, 111 22 *Area: Hötorget*
Tel 8 21 84 54/20 84 05
Open: 07.30-20.00 (Sat 09.00-17.00, Sun 12.00-17.00)
The smartest cake shop in town, established in 1928, and much expanded since. Years ago artists would come here to eat on credit, often trading their work for something to eat. Now the smart set come here for their pastries and bread (very delicious they are too, and so are the chocolates!). Originally, the only entrance was in Kungsgatan, but having expanded over the years, they now have three entrances in two streets.

Ask a Spaniard to sum up their country and you'll be met with a puzzled look. Why? Because there's no such single place as Spain, instead there are 'Las Españas' – 'the Spains'. Travelling the country, it's difficult to imagine worlds further apart than the rugged mountains of the Pyrenees and the manicured beaches of the Costa del Sol. One theme that does run through all of Spain however, is the local love of life. Out here, it seems that any excuse for a fiesta will do and festivals cross the entire spectrum– from the sublime (Holy Week in Seville) to the plain dangerous (bull-running in Pamplona). 'Nightlife' is something of a relative term in Spain as it's only in the small hours that things really take off. As the heat of the day subsides, the party temperature starts to climb – giving you plenty of time to enjoy a glass of Rioja and a plate of tapas in some of the best bars and cafés in Europe. Spain's cultural heritage, meanwhile, reads like a 'Who's Who' of the arts – and spans human history from prehistoric cave paintings in Cantabria to the ultra-modern Guggenheim museum in Bilbao. With so much on offer, your only problem is deciding which Spain to visit.

Madrid

Brilliant blue skies and soaring temperatures can make Madrid thirsty work, but with more than 17,000 cafés and bars to choose from your biggest problem is deciding how to fit everything else in. For many people Madrid is the Prado – and not surprisingly, as it's one of the greatest art galleries in the world. But it's also well worth making the effort to visit the Reina Sofia (modern) and the relatively new Thyssen-Bornemisza with its outstanding Caravaggios and Rembrandts. Lively plazas, grand tree-lined boulevards and the snaking back streets of the old quarters make Madrid a city best explored on foot. For a loftier alternative, head for the teleférico that climbs high above the tree line in Casa de Campo – a 4,500 acre former royal hunting estate.

Café de los Austrias
Plaza de Ramales *Metro: Baixa-Chiado*
Tel: 91 559 8436
Open: 09.00-02.30 (Fri & Sat 11.00-03.00, Sun 17.00-02.00)
A popular, convivial café with an attractive wooden bar, marble tables, old prints of royalty on the walls and not a trace of the nunnery that once occupied the site. There's a particularly good ambience towards midnight as everyone congregates for drinks. Good selection of gourmet coffees, drinks, tapas and pinchos (bite-size snacks).

Café Central
Plaza del Angel 10 *Bus: 6,26. Metro: Tilso de Molina or Sol*
Tel: 91 369 4143
Open: 14.00-01.30 (Fri & Sat till 03.30)
The city's best jazz venue, Central has been a café since the 1980s and before that was a mirror shop. It is located just off the bustling Puerta del Sol, hub of the city's bus system and junction of several thoroughfares. A full range of coffees, teas, drinks and snacks is available all day, and it's crowded throughout the late evening with people who come to enjoy the live jazz performed by Spanish and international musicians in a sophisticated and buzzy atmosphere.

Café del Circulo de Bellas Artes
Calle Alcalá 42 *Bus: Routes to Cibeles. Metro: Banco de España*
Tel: 91 521 6942
Open: 09.00-01.00 (Fri & Sat till 03.00)
A spacious, airy café, part of a varied and prestigious arts centre that includes exhibition halls, galleries, a cosy, hushed library, a theatre and

concert hall. It is also the scene of an annual carnival ball. Good tapas accompany the drinks. Try to get a seat by the window or out on the terrace and watch Madrid life go by. Calle Alcalá, which follows the ancient route into Madrid from the east, is the longest road in the city; in the 18th century it was known as one of the grandest in all Europe.

Café Comercial

Glorieta de Bilbao 7 *Bus: 3,21,40,147,149. Metro: Bilbao*
Tel: 91 521 5655
Open: 07.30-01.00 (Fri & Sat till 02.00, Sun from 10.00)

A treasured institution overlooking the Glorieta de Bilbao, with a lofty chandeliered ceiling, heavy wooden tables, mirrored walls and pillars. It is constantly busy with a complete cross-section of locals and visitors and has a civilised, intellectual atmosphere: earnest conversation, including the traditional tertulia, shares time with chess and draughts and the newspapers, and there's Internet access in the upstairs bar. Resident pianist Friday and Saturday evenings. Classic eats: *churros* with coffee or hot chocolate, good tapas and a three-course menu of the day.

El Espejo (restaurant)

Paseo de Recoletos 31 *Bus: Routes to Plaza de Colón*
Tel: 91 308 2347
Open: 10.00-02.00 (Fri & Sat till 03.00)

This very popular and fashionable place was created in 1978 with the look of 1900s Paris, with mirrors, bar and exquisite tiling echoing the period; it has a black-and-white tiled floor, marble-topped tables with ornate metal legs and red upholstered bentwood chairs. A variety of snacks and a large selection of drinks and speciality coffees are always available, or if you prefer choose the restaurant at the rear in the same elegant style – specialities include *merluza rellena* (stuffed hake) and *biscuit de almandres* (almond cake).

El Espejo – El Pabellon del Espejo (cafeteria)

Paseo de Recoletos 31 *Bus: Routes to Plaza de Colón. Metro: Colón*
Tel: 91 319 1122
Open: 10.00-02.00

One of the places to be and be seen in Madrid, El Pabellon, on the doorstep of El Espejo, is a beautiful glassed pavilion, complete with marble slab floor, huge chandeliers and an ornate marble-topped wooden counter with mirrors that takes the eye as you enter. Coffees, teas, beers and wines are always available, as are tapas and tostadas (Spanish canapés) from the bar. In summer it more than doubles its size with an outside park terrace.

Los Gabrieles

Calle de Echegaray 17 *Bus: Routes to Puerta del Sol. Metro: Sevilla or Sol*
Tel: 91 429 6261
Open: 12.30-02.30

The interior of this sometime biscuit shop and gypsy-run brothel is clad almost throughout in the most exquisite Andalusian glazed tiling, depicting 19th-century scenes of drinking, shopping and purveying of various goods. Food service stops at 18.00, when the place starts to take off for the night,

the bars heaving with a young, convivial, well-heeled crowd. On Tuesday nights a flamenco concert starts at 21.00.

Café Gijón

Paseo de Recoletos 21
Tel: 91 521 5425 *Bus: Routes to Cibeles. Metro: Banco de España*
Open: 07.00-01.30 (Sat till 02.00)
A bastion of Madrid's café culture since 1888, the place where the tradition of *tertulia*, the gathering of friends to discuss a certain topic, often literary, held sway. Gijón attracts a constant stream of local business people, journalists, writers, artists and visitors from all over the world. Hemingway was a regular, and Gijón remains the definitive literary café; each year it awards a prize for the best short story. Black coffee with a scoop of ice cream is a summer favourite, especially when enjoyed on the terrace. The main restaurant is downstairs (paella a speciality), but a good range of tapas and snacks is always available at the bar.

Café Manuela

San Vicente Ferrer 29 *Bus: 3,40,149. Metro: Tribunal*
Tel: 91 531 7037
Open: 16.00-02.30
Story-telling (*cuentacuentos*) and poetry nights are a highlight of Café Manuela, a lively, vibrant place with a unique atmosphere that owes a lot to its plush late-19th-century Alfonsino decor: marble floor, cream and beige walls, red divans, wooden counter and marble tables. The evenings are multi-lingual, with tales told in English and French as well as Spanish, and there are also debates (*tertulia*) on topics of art and literature. Saturday nights are given over to live traditional Spanish music. San Vicente Ferrer is known for its jewellery shops.

Nuevo Café Barbieri

Calle del Avemaria 45 *Bus: 6,26,32. Metro: Lavapiés*
Tel: 91 527 3658
Open: 15.00-02.00 (Fri & Sat till 03.00)
Rescued in the 1970s from a decline that had seemed terminal, this splendid café has some wonderful features. The room is supported by lovely 19th-century columns and these, along with the beautiful curved bar, the elegantly fading mirrored walls, the seductive lighting and the reams of voluptuous red velvet, make it easy to imagine that you are in an old-time music hall or some other equally romantic setting. Coffee is a speciality (about 20 varieties to choose from), best enjoyed with one of the sumptuous cakes on offer. An interesting and sociable young crowd gathers here, and for the solo visitor there are newspapers to read.

Café de Oriente

Plaza de Oriente 2 *Bus: 3,148. Metro: Opera*
Tel: 91 541 3974
Open: 08.00-01.30 (Fri & Sat till 02.30)
In the centre of the Plaza is an equestrian statue of King Philip IV that was designed by Velazquez and once stood in the courtyard of the Buen Retiro royal park. With the Royal Palace opposite and the Opera House just round the corner, this grand and stylish café keeps exalted company. Antiques and paintings are liberally scattered around, and there's plush red seating, with white lace antimacassars, and wooden-framed mirrors complete with coat racks. In the summer the action moves out on to the canvas-canopied

terrace. It's a popular place at any time of day, from breakfast right through to a late-night drink; tapas and pizza are served to the end, and a full restaurant menu is served down in the vaults.

Taverna del Real
Plaza Isabel II *Bus: 3. Metro: Opera*
Tel: 91 559 6922
Open: 11.00-00.30 (Fri & Sat till 01.30)
A lively little spot serving both performers and opera-goers from the Teatro Real opposite. Through the narrow entrance, the bar opens up into a larger rear room with an upstairs bar area and a downstairs plant-filled garden room. Sawdust is strewn on the marble floors, and the place is always busy with people coming for drinks and coffees. Specialities: beer, vermouth from the barrel, tapas, shellfish, rice dishes.

Café de Ruiz
Calle Ruiz 11 *Bus: 3,21,40,147,149. Metro: Bilbao*
Tel: 91 446 1232
Open: 14.00-03.00
A pleasantly old-fashioned café, comfortable and atmospheric, with an appealing interior of fin-de-siècle furnishings, lots of wood, old mirrors and lamps, tiled floor and large windows. Fruit juices, splendid milk shakes (*batidos*), coffees, hot chocolate and ice creams are available in an extensive choice, with or without alcohol, and there's ham, chorizo, cheese and paté for snacking. Debates cover astrology on Tuesday, poetry and literature on other days, newspapers to read.

Salon del Prado
Calle del Prado 4 *Bus: 6,9,26,32. Metro: Antón Martin*
Tel: 91 429 3361
Open: 14.00-02.00 (Fri & Sat till 03.00, Sun till 01.00)
An elegant, civilised café in the Huertas/Santa Ana area where a mainly young crowd gathers to enjoy a coffee (plain, Russian, Irish...) or something stronger while listening to the evening's entertainment, which could be anything from comedy to chamber music (concerts on Thursday). Canapés come free with the drinks.

La Sastrería
Hortaleza 74 *Bus: 3,40,149, Metro: Chueca or Alonso Martinez*
Tel: 91 532 0771
Open: 10.00-02.00 (Sat & Sun from 11.00, Fri & Sat till 02.30)
Once a tailor's shop, La Sastreria still retains reminders of that incarnation. Staff, dressed in a modern design based on old tailors' costumes, complete with tape-measures as lapels, are courteous and helpful, gliding around the large room for table service, or you can help yourself from the busy bar area. Coffee varieties include Irish, Turkish and Viennese. Hot food at lunchtime; sandwiches and cold snacks in the evening.

Barcelona

There's never a bad time to visit Barcelona. But find yourself caught up in the heaving bars and cafés of Las Ramblas as 'Barca' celebrates a home win – and you know you've seen it at its best. Ask most Catalans and they'll agree, but try to find out 'what's the city's number two attraction?' after football and you'll get a barrage of different answers. Gaudi's eccentric cathedral (La Sagrada Familia) is a 'must see' as are the Pablo Picasso and Joan Miró museums. Alternatively, afternoons quickly slip by wandering the jigsaw of streets in the Gothic Quarter. And in the unlikely event that this sounds too much… there's always the beach.

Café del Born Nou
Plaça Comercial 10 *Metro: Jaume I*
Tel: 93 268 3272
Open: 09.00-02.30 (Thur-Sat till 22.00)
Closed: 25 Dec, 1 Jan & Easter
Regular art exhibitions and monthly live musical evenings are among the attractions at this spacious café with high ceilings, a wooden floor and surrounds, and wide glass doors that open on to the terrace. Newspapers for solo visitors. The café stands opposite the old Born market.

Laie Libreria Café
Pau Claris 85 *Metro: Urquinaona*
Tel: 93 302 7310
Open: 09.00-01.00 (Sat from 10.00)
Closed: Sun
This art-exhibiting café on the first floor of a large bookstore serves speciality teas, infusions and exotic coffees to a young, arty and literary clientele, who enjoy a browse through the newspapers and magazines provided. Breakfast, buffet lunch, afternoon tea, à la carte dinner with a Mediterranean flavour. Live jazz nights take place between February and September, with special requests from the audience.

Mauri
Rambla Catalunya 103 *Metro: Passeig de Gràcia*
Tel: 93 215 8146
Open: 09.00-14.00 & 16.00-21.00
Mauri is located in a beautiful building dating back to 1886, at the upper end of the Rambla Catalunya, in the elegant Eixample area. It is part shop and part café, whose counter tempts with a mouthwatering array of delicious up-market snacks, including caviar and foie gras sandwiches, croquettes and pastries; coffee, tea and cold drinks are waitress-served. The shop sells all sorts of goodies including home-made chocolates. Handy for tourists visiting Gaudi's nearby Casa Milà and for shoppers visiting the design emporium Vinçon. Almost opposite is another Mauri at 102, with an original elaborate painted ceiling.

El Meson del Café
Calle Llibreteria 16 *Metro: Barri Gòthic*
Tel: 93 315 0754
Open: 07.00-23.00
Closed: Sun
This splendid little coffee shop close to the Cathedral and just off the Town Hall square retains several reminders of its 90-year history. The original coffee machine is a proud part of the decor, and other original features are wooden panels depicting street life in the Barcelona of 1900. Super

speciality coffees include one with double cream and whisky, and home-made *churros* (deep-fried pastries) sell like hot cakes. They also make their own chocolates from the purest ingredients. Staff are friendly and efficient.

Café de l'Opera
Ramblas 74 *Metro: Liceu*
Tel: 93 317 7585
Open: 08.00-02.30 (Fri & Sat till 03.00)

The best of the numerous cafés on the Rambla, this one has been favoured by such worthies as Picasso, Miró and Dali. Today's clientele revolves around shopping during the day and the Opera at night. At street level is a long marble bar with an ornate plaster ceiling and mirrors engraved with female opera figures; upstairs, green-painted wall panels, mirrors and crystal lamps take the eye. Specialities include 12 different types of coffee, 300 teas, and, of course, hot chocolate with *churros*, the perfect nightcap as well as the perfect start to the day. In warmer months the outside tables are great for people-watching.

El Paraigua
2 Pas de l'Ensenyança *Metro: Liceu*
Tel: 93 302 1131
Open: 08.30-02.00 (Sat 18.00-03.00)
Closed: Sun

A bar on two levels, tucked away through an archway off Ferran; it used to be an umbrella shop, which is what its name means. Upstairs, open for breakfast onwards, is art nouveau, while the evening basement bar, where you can sip cocktails or a whisky to classical music, has stone-vaulted ceilings in baroque style. Well worth a visit for the decor alone, but you'll also be rewarded with a warm welcome and courteous service.

El Pi Antic
Plaça Sant Josep Oriol *Metro: Liceu*
Tel: 93 301 7191
Open: 10.00-24.00

Popular with both local residents and visitors to the Gothic quarter of the city, this large double-fronted café-restaurant started life in 1571 as a small palace, other parts of which can be seen through the courtyard next door. Large stone arches span and support the traditional wooden ceiling, and the black-and-white marble floor and pink marble-topped tables create a cool atmosphere in which to take a coffee or snack in the summer. A pianist plays in the evenings on Saturday, Sunday and Bank Holidays. Specialities are paella and Catalan dishes.

Els Quatre Gats
Carrer Montsió 3-bis *Metro: Catalunya*
Tel: 93 302 4140
Open: 08.00-01.00 (Fri & Sat till 03.00, Sun 17.30-01.30)
Closed: 1st 3 weeks Aug

A Gothic Revival building designed in 1897 by Puig I Cadafalch. Picasso staged an early exhibition here, and other leading figures from the world of art, including Miró and Utrillo, made it their regular haunt; the paintings on the walls, which are reproduced on the table mats, date from the early 1900s. It's a fine place to meet for a glass of wine or one of their speciality coffees, and if you bring an appetite there's a restaurant at the back that specialises in Catalan cuisine. Piano and violin evenings.

El Tio Che
Rambla del Poble Nou 44-46 *Metro: Poblenou*
Tel: 93 309 1872
Open: 10.00-01.00 (Fri & Sat till 03.00). Winter 09.00-13.00 & 16.00-22.00 (Fri-Sun till 23.00).
Closed: Wed in winter
A family-run ice cream joint on a pedestrian street near the beach, started in 1912 by current owner Alfonso Iborra's great grandfather. *Horchatas*, made with *chufa* nuts, are a speciality – in summer some are made without sugar for diabetics – or try the *leche merengada*, milk with sugar and cinnamon, and the home-made ice creams (30-odd flavours). Tapas and *bocadillos* are also served, and at Christmas they make special *turrones* (nougat). The parlour looks lovely with its white ceramic walls, and outside there are two terraces with marble-topped tables and blue parasols.

Bilbao

Sipping a coffee in Plaza Nueva – surrounded by the historic buildings of Casco Viejo – it's difficult to believe that you're in the same city as Spain's latest cultural landmark, the Guggenheim Museum. Besides proving the single-handed saviour of Bilbao's postcard industry, the Guggenheim has also helped wash the city's industrial past downstream – putting it squarely on the tourist map. The building itself is so good, by the way, that you should leave almost as much time to admire the exterior as the world-class exhibitions it houses (art buffs should also visit the neighbouring Museo de Bellas Artes). While the tone in Bilbao is always upbeat, time your visit for August and you'll see the city erupt into the Semana Grande. Prepare for a riotous seven days of folk music, dancing, bullfighting, parades and lots and lots of sangria.

Bar Basque
3 Astarloa *Metro: Abando*
Tel: 94 424 2621
Open: 10.00-22.00
Closed: Sat & Sun
Just off the main street of Bilbao's shopping centre, this Belle Epoque-style bar has been serving shoppers, shop staff and office workers since the 1970s. Tapas are served until 16.00, after which it's drinks and nibbles only, the former including lots of speciality cocktails. Spot the brass snake that winds its way up one of the pillars, and the silk adorning the walls above the panelling.

Café Bar Bilbao
6 Plaza Berria (Plaza Nueva) *Metro: Casco Veijo*
Tel: 94 415 1671
Open: 07.00-23.00 (Fri till 24.00, Sat 09.00-24.00, Sun 09.00-14.30)
A delightful old café, one of several in an enchanting arcaded square in the old part of town. It has an all-marble horseshoe bar in one room and tables with waiter service in the other. The bar is loaded with an amazing array of tapas, among which ham croquettes, stuffed peppers, *jamon* and fried cuttlefish are specialities. The atmosphere here really buzzes and the staff dash around to keep up with the orders.

Café Boulevard
3 Paseo de Arenal *Metro: Casco Veijo*
Tel: 94 415 3128
Open: 07.30-23.30 (Fri & Sat till 02.30, Sun from 11.00)
In business since 1871, and still attracting the customers with its coffee, breakfasts and day-long hot and cold snacks. Nowadays it has a neon-lit frontage that looks a bit like a cinema and a vast, elaborately decorated interior with marble, gilt and lots of mirrors.

Café La Granja
3 Plaza Circular *Metro: Casco Veijo*
Tel: 94 423 0813
Open: 07.00-24.00 (Sat & Sun 09.00-02.30/03.00)
One of three roomy old cafés under the same management, La Granja is an easy walk from the Arenal Bridge and the old town, Casco Viejo. Its main clientele is office workers in the morning, shoppers at lunchtime and a young, lively crowd in the evening.

Café Iruña
Jardines de Albia, Berastegui 5 *Metro: Abando*
Tel: 94 423 7021
Open: 07.00-01.00 (Fri & Sat till 02.30)
July 2003 sees the centenary of Iruña, which overlooks the Albia Gardens and the monument to A Trueba. It has two striking bars, the first with revolving doors, a chandelier and a mosaic-decorated floor, the other with walls tiled in blue, white and yellow and tiled panelled tableaux advertising sherry and brandy from various producers. Here, at the long horseshoe bar, the locals swap news, sip their drinks and nibble their tapas.

Serantes

16 Licenciado de Poza *Metro: Indautxu*
Tel: 94 443 5006
Open: 07.30-00.30 (Sun 10.00-01.00)
Whether it's as snacks at the bar or part of a full meal in the upstairs restaurant, seafood is king here, with first-rate oysters, cockles, mussels, crayfish, deep-sea prawns and a local crustacean called *percebes*. The other speciality is *Jabugo* cured ham, pork and sausages, so piscivores and carnivores can both head here in confidence.

Victor Montes
8 Plaza Nueva, Casco Viejo *Metro: Casco Veijo*
Tel: 94 415 5603/7067
Open: 10.00-24.00 (Sun till 15.00)
Tapas with a difference are prepared in the kitchens of Victor Montes, a café-restaurant, delicatessen and wine merchant in the arcades of a picturesque square in the old quarter. The snacks do not rely on the usual ham and pork but feature goose, duck, salmon and even caviar, and the quality throughout is commendably high. The glass-fronted cabinets display a wonderful selection of wines and spirits as well as the tapas. Pavement tables.

La Viña

10 Calle Diputacion *Metro: Abando*
Tel: 94 415 5615
Open: 08.00-22.30
Closed: Sun
Legs of cured *jamon* hang over the bar and racks of wine bottles behind it at this popular wine bar in the shopping district. There's plenty of room to stand at the bar, and the rest of the room is set with marble-inlaid wooden tables with ornate pedestals and matching octagonal stools. Other tasty food specialities include foie gras, a refined cured ham called *Cecina*, chorizo, tuna, salmon, anchovies and cheese, which can all be enjoyed in house or bought at the shop at one end; and there's a very good *viña real* among the numerous wines available by the glass.

Seville

With the Andalucian sun spotlighting the Plaza del Triunfo, you get straight to the point of the city's historic maxim 'Qui non ha vista Sevilla, non ha vista maravilla', 'He who hasn't seen Seville hasn't known wonderment'. To one side of the square, the ornate Giralda tower watches over the largest gothic cathedral in the world; to the other sits the breath-taking Alcazar palace. No wonder, then, that Seville was chosen by so many artists as the backdrop for some of their greatest works, including Bizet's Carmen, Lord Byron's Don Juan and Rossini's operatic barber. As dusk falls, the pace of life in Spain's fourth city changes up a gear as locals celebrate another of their homegrown passions, flamenco. The cafés and bars of the Old Quarter buzz with life and one thing is guaranteed: you won't get an early night. Grab your own share of 'wonderment'.

LA ALBERIZA

6 Betis *Area: West bank of Rió Guadalquivir*
Tel: 95 433 2016
Open: 13.00-16.00 & 21.00-24.00
Closed: Mon

Sherry and ham are the co-stars at La Alberiza, a traditionally styled building with dark green-shuttered windows and high beamed ceilings. The sherry barrels are stacked solera-style around two walls of the bar, behind which is the kitchen and beyond that a formal restaurant serving excellent seafood dishes. But the main action is in the bar, where whole cheeses stand on the counter, legs of *jamon* hang from the ceiling and barrels on the flagstoned floor provide a resting place for your glass. Busy, buzzy and very atmospheric.

Bar Belmonte

24 Calle Mateos Gago *Area: North-east of Alcázar Gardens*
No telephone
Open: 08.00-00.30/01.00

A busy tapas bar, popular with the young of Seville, with some tables and chairs set out under shady trees in a narrow street in the Old Town behind the Cathedral. Beer is very popular here, but a jug of sangria is always ready in the fridge, and some of the wines and sherries are kept in blue-and-white pottery coolers on the bar counter.

Meson 5J

1 Calle Castelar *Area: East of the bullring*
Tel: 95 421 5862
Open: 07.30-24.00

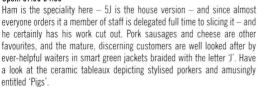

Ham is the speciality here – 5J is the house version – and since almost everyone orders it a member of staff is delegated full time to slicing it – and he certainly has his work cut out. Pork sausages and cheese are other favourites, and the mature, discerning customers are well looked after by ever-helpful waiters in smart green jackets braided with the letter 'J'. Have a look at the ceramic tableaux depicting stylised porkers and amusingly entitled 'Pigs'.

Giralda

1 Mateos Gago *Area: North-east of Alcázar Gardens*
Tel: 95 422 7435
Open: 09.00-24.00 (Sun from 10.00)

A popular bar-restaurant whose decor features blue, white and bronze tiling. A list of the day's tapas is chalked up on a blackboard, and the chalk is also used to mark up customers' orders on the well-lacquered mahogany bar top. Marble pillars support a vaulted ceiling, and there's a hum of activity as the waiters tend to chattering customers sitting at the marble-topped tables. Outside, aluminium tables and chairs are set on the pavement. If swordfish is on the menu, try it.

Bodega Santa Cruz

1 Calle Rodrigo Caro *Area: Just north of Alcázar Gardens*
No telephone
Open: 07.00-01.00

A great sawdust bar for locals and an occasional smattering of tourists. This is the place for local gossip, a drink and some good cheap tapas. It's got soul, it's got character, it's got great local atmosphere, and it's cheerful enough to put a smile on the most miserable face!

Bodegon Torre del Oro

15 Santander *Area: West of Alcázar, towards the river*
Tel: 95 421 4241
Open: 07.00-24.00/01.00

Photographs of famous bullfighters clutter the walls and professional barmen in black bow ties are always attentive in this 15th-century building two minutes from the city's bullring. The bar area is hung with tresses of garlic and haunches of *jamon*, and the height of the ceiling and the paddle fans keep the place cool in even the hottest weather. A favourite among the tapas is cod's roe and mayonnaise with a glass of fino.

TOP TIPS FOR TAPAS

Our hands-on, four point guide to understanding, finding, enjoying and paying for Spain's outstanding contribution to world cuisine...

1. UNDERSTAND THE VOCABULARY

It's a noun, *tapas*, and it's a verb, *tapear*, but more than anything it's a way of life for almost every one of Spain's 40 million inhabitants. Get to grips with *tapas* and you've got the country on a plate. Derived from the word *tapa* (lid), the dish takes its name from the custom of placing a saucer on a glass of sherry to keep off the fruit flies. Some time later, a legendary barman (in Andalucia, they say) came up with the idea of balancing a small snack on the saucer to tempt customers. *Tapas* was born, and the country never looked back. Today, *tapas* is the fuel that ignites the other four passions in Spanish life: chatting, arguing, joking and flirting.

2. RIGHT TIME, RIGHT PLACE

Tapas is traditionally eaten before lunch (1-2 p.m. or after) and again before dinner (8-9 p.m. or after). Big cities tend to do the best tapas – and to find the best bars simply head for the places where people meet and greet (universities, big squares, and railway stations). But once you've found your perfect bar, please don't get too comfy. The whole point of local 'bar-hopping' (*tapear*) is keeping on the move. If you stick to one bar and one menu all night, you've missed the point entirely.

3. FEAST FOR THE EYES

Not just one of the most mouth-watering dishes on earth, tapas is also one of the easiest to order. Traditionally laid out in hand-made pottery bowls at the bar, all you have to do is point. As long as the bar staff have understood you want a single portion (*tapas*) rather than a main dish (*raciones*), you simply wait, and enjoy what they bring you. The choice is giddying. You won't find every dish in one bar, you won't even find them all in one city – but tour Spain's bar scene and you'll discover 60 or more tapas classics. Some are served hot, others cold; some use shellfish, others use pork, beef or vegetables; some are fiery, others mild. Rest assured, within this gourmet landscape, you'll find your haven. Whether it's prawns sizzled in garlic and oil (*gambas al ajillo*), lambs kidneys in sherry sauce (*riñones al jerez*), broad beans with ham (*habas con jamón*) or fried potatoes in a hot pepper sauce (*patatas bravas*), there's a dish with your name on it.

4. PAYING UP

As always in Spanish bars, the tradition is to pay when you leave. While tapas is generally good value, it pays to keep track of things as empty plates and a biggish bill can mount up alarmingly quickly. Finally, as you head off into the night in search of your top tapas, bear a few last local customs in mind: sitting at a table usually costs 25 per cent more than eating at the bar; swanky joints will charge up to twice as much for a dish you'll find in a humbler café; and bars serving tapas on toothpicks often use them to tally the bill – so don't throw them away. *Hasta la vista!*

FIESTA FEVER

With more than 3,000 fiestas a year in Andalucia alone, nobody knows how to party quite like the Spanish. Whether it's Seville's stately Semana Santa or the sheer fun of Buñol's tomato fight, Spain's festivals all share a celebration of life. We give you the fabulous five.

FALLAS, VALENCIA, MARCH 15TH – 19TH

Guy Fawkes would have loved it. For five days in March, Valencia stages the most incendiary party in Europe as thousands of giant papier-maché caricatures go up in flames. The tradition dates back to the 18th century when carpenters spring-cleaned their workshops and made bonfires in honour of their patron, St Joseph. With the spring days growing longer, the carpenters found they didn't need the torches to light their workshops. One bright spark decided to lampoon a local politician by fashioning his *falla* into a scarecrow and setting it alight. Today, up to two million fire-starters join in the fun.

FIESTA DE SAN FERMÍN, PAMPLONA, JULY 6TH – 14TH

If Ernest Hemingway has written about it then it's a safe bet that it involves gallons of alcohol and testosterone. Pamplona has plenty of both. For the alcohol, there's San Fermín, the patron saint of wine makers and special patron of this lunatic event. For the testosterone, there's up to 3,000 fearless locals (and a good smattering of foreign backpackers) who take on six bulls over 800 metres of Pamplona's streets. The only real goal is not to get trampled, but if the bulls don't get you, the effects of the night before probably will.

SEMANA SANTA, SEVILLE, EASTER WEEK

Holy Week in Seville is without doubt one of the most overwhelming religious spectacles on the planet. In the 14th Century, the Catholic Church decided its flock needed to be reminded about The Passion and began to re-enact the events leading to Christ's crucifixion in the streets of Seville. Today's processions are organised by over 50 brotherhoods, each of which carries two Pasos (sculptural representations of Christ and the Virgin Mary) followed by up to 2,500 costumed followers. The solemn tone is marked by drumbeats and the processions climax in the early hours of Good Friday.

FIESTA DE SAN ROQUE, VILAGARCIA DE AROUSA, GALICIA, AUGUST 16TH

A decade ago, Galicia was in the middle of a drought and by August things were getting desperate. During the feast of San Roque, locals in Vilagarcia de Arousa got down on their knees to pray and offered their last precious drops of water as libations. Luckily someone was listening – and the rains began to fall. Today the fire brigade kick-starts the annual festival by drenching the town with 30 tons of water, before the population replies with buckets, basins and hosepipes.

LA TOMATINA, BUÑOL, VALENCIA, LAST WEDNESDAY IN AUGUST

Come the end of August, the population of modestly-sized Buñol trebles to 30,000; at 11a.m. sharp, trucks roll into the town square loaded with an arsenal of 125,000kg of tomatoes. And with a salvo of tomato-laden rockets exploding overhead, the world's biggest food fight begins. For the next two hours the town descends into a pulpy chaos. Unlike many of Spain's fiestas, La Tomatina isn't steeped in history – but grew from a fracas in a local restaurant in 1944.

Valencia

There's a saying that Valencianos have no time for the tragic side of life – and nowhere is this more evident than in the lively bars and cafés of Calle Caballeros. Spain's third city boasts the best nightlife on the mainland and with the completion of the futuristic City of Arts and Sciences, Valencia looks set to be catapulted to the top of the nation's tourist itinerary. Valencia's best-kept secret is Barrio El Carmen. Glossed over in most guidebooks as being the 'bohemian' quarter – El Carmen has spent the last decade quietly undergoing a renaissance and is now home to some of the city's best restaurants, cafés and art galleries. Wander the labyrinth of Moorish streets on a Friday or Saturday night – and get connected to one of the most animated nightscenes in Europe.

El Generalife
5 Calle Caballeros *Area: Barrio del Carmen*
Tel: 96 391 7899
Open: 08.00-18.00 & 20.00-01.30
Closed: Mon & Tue

Valencianos and tourists are both staunch supporters of this pleasant place in a corner of the Plaza de la Virgen with its sumptuous basilica and opposite the Palacio del Generalidad (a 15th-century palace that is the seat of local government). The café-restaurant is on two levels, with some tables in the square outside. Good menu plus daily specials.

Mare Nostrum
85 San Vicente Martir & Plaza Ajuntamiento
Open: 08.00-01.00 *Area: North west of Estación del Norte*

Two stylish, civilised grand cafés, one in a side street near the station, the other at the narrow end of Plaza Ajuntamiento. What is probably the best coffee in the whole of Valencia comes in a host of different ways to accompany pastries and sandwiches, and the hot chocolate is very good, too. Both places are spacious and well ventilated, with lofty ceilings and stacks of sacks and barrels printed with the names of coffee plantations around the world.

Cafeteria Noel
Av Marquez de Sotelo 4
Tel: 96 352 9494 *Area: West of Plaza del Ayuntamiento*
Open: 07.30-23.00 (Sun from 09.00)

In a side street off the main square, this fine old cafeteria boasts what is probably one of the longest bar counters in Spain. Customers drop by to take refreshment and enjoy one of the fine sandwiches, bocadillos or perhaps delicious chapata filled with salty anchovies drenched in rich olive oil, and for hungrier souls there is also an à la carte menu. Two coffee grinders are clearly labelled *suave* and *fuerte* (mild or strong). A second counter on the other side offers a large range of patisserie, charcuterie and wines to take home.

The UK and Ireland aren't a destination for the indecisive. Why? Because when it comes to choosing between the white coral beaches of Connemara, County Galway and the buzz of Europe's biggest carnival in London's Notting Hill, some people just can't make up their minds. One of the biggest draws in either country is undoubtedly their history – stretching back 5,000 years to the prehistoric stone circle at Stonehenge and the Celtic barrows of Ireland's West Coast. Take a walk almost anywhere in either country and you're bound to bump into a piece of the past. In some places you'll have the monument to yourself. In others (Bath, Cambridge, Oxford and Cork to name a few) you'll notice that other people have made the same plans for their summer's day outing. Which brings us to the British and the Irish themselves. Starting with the British, it's true to say that the end of the Colonial era in the 1930s helped Britain to loosen her stiff upper lip (while still maintaining her reputation for eccentricity). As millions of record buyers and TV viewers worldwide will agree, the upside of that individualistic streak shines through in the trail-blazing genius of The Beatles, Fawlty Towers, and countless others. For the Irish, the legendary charm of the local 'craic' (a mixture of humour, banter and good-natured fun) is as true today as it ever was. Add to that the new-found dynamism that's put Dublin squarely on the world economic and cultural map and you have a country that's got the best of old and new. One area where the UK and Ireland haven't been able to reinvent themselves is the weather, but with a rich collection of museums and art galleries in both capitals, time indoors is well spent. Even the region's cuisine has had an international makeover and menus in London and Dublin today keep pace with any city on earth. Add to this a booming café culture on both sides of the Irish Channel, and some of the best nightlife in the world, and these islands really are beginning to look distinctly inviting.

London

Judging by the hubbub of party-people in Soho's streets every night of the week, London is swinging today even more than in the 60s. The buzz is back. And so when Samuel Johnson wrote that "when a man is tired of London he is tired of life", we can assume he wasn't kidding. England's capital simply has a phenomenal amount to offer – and with 8,500 restaurants, 3,700 pubs, 159 theatres, and 70 cinemas it's sometimes hard to know how to plan your evening. By day London is just as busy. And with the British Museum attracting 5.5 million visitors a year, and the Tate Modern setting the pace for the global art world, you'll want to add both venues to your list of places to visit. For a bird's-eye view of London, take a flight on the British Airways London Eye where a jigsaw of architectural styles, monuments and parks paints the history of one of the world's truly great cities.

The Arches
7 Fairhazel Gardens NW6
Tel: 020 7624 1876 *Tube: Finchley Rd or West Hampstead*
Open: 12.00-23.00
This splendid little mecca for wine enthusiasts was previously an antiques and collectables shop, and the present owner Harry Gill has added to the amazing collection of bric-a-brac that bursts out of every corner and hangs from every inch of wall space. The serious, extensive and ever-changing wine list is the work of Harry, who likes to offer his customers the opportunity to try wines that could be beyond their pocket by imposing the gentlest of mark-ups. He also keeps some fine cognacs and armagnacs, a good selection of bottled and draught beers and the usual varieties of teas and coffees. There's a bar menu of snacks and light bites, and full meals can be enjoyed in the restaurant downstairs.

Blue Mountain
18 North Cross Rd SE22 *Train: East Dulwich BR*
Tel: 020 8299 6953
Open: 09.00-18.00 (Sun from 10.00)
A delightful little café in a former dairy in East Dulwich, with several rooms, each done out in a different style. There are also some tables in the garden and out on the pavement. Breakfast is served from 9 till noon, and among the favourite daytime snacks are 'melts' served in a baguette with salads. There's a notable patisserie counter, and the cappuccino is spot on. Blue Mountain is a great favourite with families: children's portions can be provided on request, and high chairs are available. There's a good selection of coffee (beans or ground) to take away – the superb Jamaican Blue Mountain is of course the star.

Bluebird Café
350 King's Rd Chelsea SW3 *Tube: Sloane Square*
Tel: 020 7559 1000
Open: Bar 12.00-23.00, Café 09.00-22.00 (Sat till 21.00, Sun till 18.00)
Sir Terence Conran's King's Road Gastrodrome way down King's Road is a combination of restaurant, café, bar, food market, flower market and kitchen shop, all housed in an art deco building that was, when built in 1923, Europe's largest motor garage. The café, with seats for 60 and as many more outside on the forecourt (but you still might queue), proposes croissants, home-made scones, biscotti and a tempting list of dishes sourced from the food market. A popular venue at all times, and great for Sunday brunch. A recent evening deal in the café centres round a cheese fondue.

Café Bohème
13 Old Compton St, Soho W1 *Tube: Leicester Sq or Piccadilly Circus*
Tel: 020 7734 0623
Open: 08.00-03.00 (Thur-Sat 24 hrs, Sun 09.00-23.30)
Intimate and usually quite loud, with something of the look and feel of a Parisian brasserie, French prints on the walls and round-the-clock service Thursday to Saturday. Drop in for anything from a coffee to a full-scale meal of classic dishes at very reasonable prices. A perennially popular place which attracts the whole spectrum of Soho characters, after-office drinkers, pre- and post-clubbers and tourists in this permanently bustling part of town. Sunday breakfast helps to revive bleary-eyed clubbers. Pavement tables get even closer to the full Soho experience.

La Brioche
238 West End Lane NW6 *Tube: West Hampstead*
Tel: 020 7431 8175
Open: 08.00-22.30 (Mon till 19.00)
Brioches, baguettes, croissants, and especially bruschette are the order of the day here. Breakfast can be simple and French with patisserie, or something more substantial like the full English or smoked salmon and scrambled eggs on bruschetta. And there are some excellent pastries, tortes and cakes, all on display in the cabinet as you come in, to enjoy with a very good Piazza d'Oro espresso. Wines by glass or bottle. On Fridays there's live music, and at the weekend it's packed, with everyone trying to get a seat.

Browns Restaurant & Bar
82-84 St Martins Lane, Covent Garden WC2 *Tube: Leicester Square*
Tel: 020 7497 5050
Open: 12.00-24.00
A handsome building housing a 320-seat restaurant and bar on the ground floor. It is open for lunch, afternoon tea, pre- and post-theatre suppers and dinner. The main menu is very diverse, full of good, wholesome classic dishes and ending with moreish puddings. To accompany here are beers and around 40 wines (a dozen available by the glass) as well as some sparklers. The building was formerly Westminster County Courts, and the upstairs courtroom, complete with the bench and judges' chairs, is an atmospheric setting for parties or functions.

Also at:
47 Maddox Crt W1 Tel: 020 7491 4565 (last food orders 22.00; closed Sun). Elaborate architecture and internal fittings in the former premises of Wells & Co, gentlemen's and military outfitters.
9 Islington Green N1 Tel: 020 7226 2555. Next to the lively antiques and collectables market.
8 Old Jewry EC2 Tel: 020 7606 6677 (last food orders 22.00). A 300-cover restaurant in the former premises of the Commonwealth Bank of Australia.
Hertsmere Rd E14 Tel: 020 7987 9777 (last food orders 21.45). Browns West India Quay is housed in a former sugar warehouse built by Napoleonic prisoners of war in the early 19th century. 200-seat restaurant, bar, outside seating.
3-5 Kew Green, Richmond Tel: 020 8948 4838 (open 12.00-11.30, Sat from 11.00, Sun till 22.30). 150-seat restaurant, outside dining area and separate bar.
201 Castelnau SW13 Tel: 020 8748 4486 (open 12.00-23.00). Restaurant with elegant alfresco eating area and Pavilion Garden Bar.

Corney & Barrow
1 Leadenhall Place EC3 *Tube: Monument*
Tel: 020 7621 9201
Open: 08.00-22.30 (Wed-Fri till 23.00)
Closed: Sat & Sun
Two of the best-known institutions meet in the City: Corney & Barrow at Lloyds of London. Beneath the New Exchange (the one with its guts on the outside), the long-established wine importers Corney & Barrow sell early morning snacks, sandwiches, hot light dishes and cakes to be washed down with excellent coffee, beers from Sweden, Germany, the UK and Japan, or something from their long wine list. Giant games, satellite sports on tv, and a spacious outdoor terrace are further attractions, and corporate barbecues can be booked on Monday, Tuesday and Wednesday. Coffee is served from 8,

lunch from 11.30 to 3, evening meals from 4 to 10.30. There are nine other branches in the City, with slight variations in opening times, plus one at 9 Cabot Square, Canary Wharf (Tel: 020 7512 0397) and one at 116 St Martin's Lane WC2 (Tel: 020 7655 9800). Half the C&Bs, including St Martin's Lane, have fitted kitchens that allow them to offer a more extensive menu.

Café in the Crypt
The Crypt of St Martin-in-the-Fields, Duncannon St WC2
Tel: 020 7839 4342 *Tube: Leicester Sq or Charing Cross*
Open: 10.00-19.30
Those in the know give thanks for this cool, civilised retreat from the hubbub of Trafalgar Square. Soft lighting and gentle classical music set a soothing tone, and the tombstone- and flagstone-covered floor and the brick arches provide a setting with a difference for the regulars and the tourists who refresh themselves with a cup of tea or a glass of wine and a snack or one of the daily-changing hot specials. Profits go towards the maintenance of the famous church above.

Chamomile
45 Englands Lane NW3 *Tube: Belsize Park or Chalk Farm*
Tel: 020 7586 4580
Open: 07.00-18.30
Specialities here are the wide range of coffees, the delicious pastries, all baked on the premises, and the all-day breakfasts. Notable among the last is the house special of scrambled free-range eggs and smoked salmon, toast and a glass of orange juice. Four pavement tables under a blue awning are popular when the weather's fine, while inside, the tables are quite close to each other, but the pale furnishings and high ceiling give a sense of space. Four reds and four whites from France and the New World in ½ bottles, and a range of healthy juices.

Café Delancey
3 Delancey St, Camden Town NW1 *Tube: Camden*
Tel: 020 7387 1985
Open: 09.00-23.30 (Sun till 22.30)
A few steps off bustling Camden High Street, Café Delancey is a long-established, long-hours local stalwart with on-the-ball staff, wooden floors, pot plants, a separate bar area and some outside tables on the pavement and in an internal courtyard. Everything on the menu is available all day, starting with coffee and croissants with the daily papers and ranging via salads, deep-fried camembert with calvados jelly and croques ('Delancey' has mozzarella, tomato and crushed olives) to hearty favourites such as eggs and bacon or sausages and onions with the Delancey signature rösti.

Euphorium Bakery Bar Restaurant
203 Upper St, Islington N1 *Tube: Angel*
Tel: 020 7704 6909
Open: café 08.00-17.00, bar 12.00-14.30 & 18.00-22.30 (Sun 09.00-15.30)
A stylish, relaxed Upper Street favourite, Euphorium is café, bar, restaurant and bakery. The café on the left displays its mouthwatering breads and patisserie, and beyond it is the bar with its zinc-topped tables, and the restaurant at the back. On fine days there are some dozen tables in the garden. Interesting wines available by bottle, half bottle and glass. Restaurant food ranges from leek and potato soup or Caesar salad to grilled snapper, chicken tagine, calves' liver and osso buco.

167

Fifth Floor Café
Harvey Nichols *Tube: Knightsbridge*
Knightsbridge SW1
Tel: 020 7235 5000
Open: 10.00-22.30 (Sun 12.00-18.00)
After a major shop for desirable designer clobber, those in need of refreshment head for the heights and this bright, chic café, which shares the floor with a restaurant, bar and food market. All the food is seasonal and fresh, and the Mediterranean-inspired menu changes constantly; the cakes, served with the popular 'Fifth Floor Tea' from 15.30 to 18.00, are home-made. A variety of coffees is available, many freshly ground on site. Outside tables on the rooftop terrace. Children are welcome, with high chairs available for tiny tots not quite ready to swap plastic spoons for plastic money. Café, bar and restaurant are all open long after shop hours, with access by express lifts from Sloane Street and Seville Street.

Gill Wing Café
300 St Paul's Rd N1 *Tube: Highbury & Islington*
Tel: 020 7226 2885
Open: 08.00-23.00
An oasis by Highbury & Islington Corner, this excellent café offers genuine French pastries, cuisine and wine. Manager Michael endows this busy junction with a certain French flair, drawing customers who come to browse through the papers over a croissant and coffee, or lunch Parisian-style with a kir or Ricard to start (but with a roast on Sunday), or enjoy a simple evening meal. Michael plays good jazz music as a background during the day, and there are regular live music events in the basement. The cream-coloured walls, the art nouveau lights and the bentwood chairs set at marble-topped tables produce a delightful ambience into which all types and ages are attracted and all are welcome.

Bar Italia
22 Frith Street W1 *Tube: Leicester Square*
Tel: 020 7437 4520
Open: 24 hours
A real Soho institution, where London meets Italy at any time of day or night for coffees, juices, smoothies, ciabatta sandwiches, hot panini specials, light meals, pastries and Serie A and Italian news from Italy on the big screen. Occupying the ground floor of the house where John Logie Baird first demonstrated television in 1926, Bar Italia has been in business since 1949, when it was opened by Abbot and Costello and Ronnie Scott. The founder was Lou Polledri, and it has been in his family ever since. Lou had a good friend in the boxer Rocky Marciano, whose picture hangs behind the bar; it was sent to Lou by Rocky's widow.

Konditor & Cook
Young Vic, 66 The Cut, Waterloo SE1 *Tube: Waterloo*

Tel: 020 7620 2700
Open: 08.30-23.00 (Sat from 10.30)
Closed: Sun
With its own bakery on the premises, this bright, lively café attached to the Young Vic theatre sells a great range of superb cakes and pastries to add to the good savoury selection. The breakfast menu, served until 11.30 (till noon on Saturday), runs from toasted brioche, croissants and *pain au chocolat* to scrambled eggs and smoked salmon and the full English fry-up.

The main modern European menu is available from noon to 20.00 and can be accompanied by coffee, tea, Belgian hot chocolate, juices and smoothies, beers, three white wines and two reds by bottle or glass, champagne by bottle or half bottle. The decor is as modern and vibrant as the food, with striking use made of natural oak, steel and concrete. The glass conservatory-style frontage is a real sun-trap in this excellent place, where the posters on the walls change with the current Young Vic productions. Well worth a trip across the river, for both food and theatre.

Le Metro

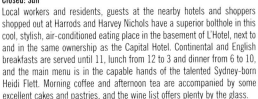

28 Basil St SW3 *Tube: Knightsbridge*
Tel: 020 7589 6286
Open: 07.30-23.00
Closed: Sun

Local workers and residents, guests at the nearby hotels and shoppers shopped out at Harrods and Harvey Nichols have a superior bolthole in this cool, stylish, air-conditioned eating place in the basement of L'Hotel, next to and in the same ownership as the Capital Hotel. Continental and English breakfasts are served until 11, lunch from 12 to 3 and dinner from 6 to 10, and the main menu is in the capable hands of the talented Sydney-born Heidi Flett. Morning coffee and afternoon tea are accompanied by some excellent cakes and pastries, and the wine list offers plenty by the glass.

Mona Lisa

417 King's Rd, Chelsea SW10 *Tube: Sloane Square*
Tel: 020 7376 5447
Open: 07.00-23.00 (Sun 09.00-17.30)

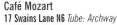

Take a trip to the World's End and this most egalitarian of cafés, where the whole front opens up and plastic-clad tables spill out on to the pavement in fine weather. The dishes on the long all-day breakfast menu are excellent fuel before a day's work or for a lunchtime pit stop, and there's a lengthy list of filled rolls and sandwiches for quick snacks or takeaways. Elsewhere on the long menu are a few other true Brit dishes, but the main thrust is Italian, with big portions of pasta (the parmesan is freshly grated at the table) and classics of the chicken valdostana and liver with butter and sage variety. Good composite salads, too, and always ask about Pepe's specials. Usually smoky, always fun, with hard-working, nearly always affable staff, Mona Lisa is one of the few places where a down-to-earth bacon buttie with brown sauce can be found sharing a table with a classy sea bass and a balsamic-dressed salad.

Café Mozart

17 Swains Lane N6 *Tube: Archway*
Tel: 020 8348 1384
Open: 09.00-22.00

Hampstead meets Vienna at this civilised Austrian café that's a favourite with local solos and families, dog-walkers and anyone who's worked up an appetite with an invigorating walk on nearby Parliament Hill. Scrumptious sachertorte, apple tart, plum tart and other Viennese pastries, cheesecake, dumplings, goulash, chicken schnitzel and salads are all good choices, and they also do an all-day cooked breakfast. Wood-panelled walls give a period feel to the interior, while outside on the broad pavement there are three rows of tables and chairs, with heaters and an awning making them an option even in cold weather (assisted perhaps by a cup of the famous Café Mozart hot chocolate).

Picasso
127 King's Rd SW3 *Tube: Sloane Square*
Tel: 020 7352 4921
Open: 08.00-23.00 (Sun till 22.30)

A popular 70-seat Italian café among the trendy clothes and shoe shops on busy King's Road, with some tables out on the pavement, packed with snackers from early in the morning till late at night. English and Continental breakfasts start the day, and over the long lunchtime tables are reserved for those who are eating. The menu offers sandwiches, pasta, risotto and daily specials, and there's always a good choice of cakes and pastries. Picasso opened in the early 1950s, the second in the Dino's Group of cafés and restaurants.

Portrait Café
National Portrait Gallery, 2 St Martin's Place WC2
Tel: 020 7312 2465 *Tube: Charing Cross, Leicester Sq*
Open: 10.00-17.30 (Sun 12.00-18.00)

A photogenic café in the National Portrait Gallery, reached down a dark stairway but surprisingly bright when you get there, thanks to a glass ceiling that gives the long, narrow room almost a conservatory feel. A display of black-and-white photographs fills the walls. The food choice runs from generously-filled sandwiches to soup, inventive salads, quiches, cakes, pastries and ices. Coffee, cold drinks, and organic wine by glass or bottle.

St John
26 St John St, Clerkenwell EC1 *Tube: Farringdon*
Tel: 020 7251 0848/4998
Open: bar 12.00-23.00 (Sat from 18.00) restaurant 12.00-15.00 & 18.00-23.00
Closed: L Sat & all Sun

A one-time smokehouse, the chimneys still intact, has been combined with a Georgian town house to become a flagship of British meat cooking, in which Fergus Henderson's menu delights and surprises and Trevor Gulliver's wine list always include some interesting bin ends available by the glass. The look of the place is bright and functional, with a concrete floor, plain white walls and industrial furniture lit by long, suspended enamelled lamps and a skylight. For snackers there's a separate section with a terrific all-day bar menu in the same vein; they have their own bakery on the premises, producing some of the finest bread in London.

Sausage & Mash Café
268 Portobello Rd W10 *Tube: Notting Hill Gate*
Tel: 020 8968 8898
Open: 11.00-22.00
Closed: Mon

Large S & M symbols in frosted glass announce this friendly little café virtually under Westway. The name says it all, for this is *the* place to come for a hearty meal of sausage and mash. The sausages come in eight varieties, including Cumberland, creole smokey, wild boar with juniper and vegetarian Glamorgan. There are three kinds of mash – regular, celeriac and green pea – and three gravies – madeira and thyme, roasted red onion and Guinness, so the combinations of S and M and G are almost endless. Other options on the menu include soup of the day, baguette sandwiches and salads, but it's bangers that lead the way. Ice creams or the home-made pud of the day to finish; coffees, teas, juices, sodas and beers to drink. Takeaway available.

Smithy's Wine Bar & Restaurant
Leeke St WC1 *Tube: King's Cross*
Tel: 020 7278 5949
Open: 11.00-23.00 (Sat till 18.30)
Closed: Sat & Sun

Tucked away discreetly down a cobbled street, this building was once a main depot of the London General Omnibus Company, dating from the days when the buses were horse-drawn and incorporating a blacksmith's workshop. It has now become a compulsory stop on any true wine-lover's tour of London. The old ramp that led to the stables climbs over the real charcoal grill, and the floor is still wood-block, grain-up, and laid in a brick pattern. Converted as recently as 1982, the bar has a great range of beers on draught and by the bottle, but the *pièce de résistance* is the astonishing wine list of over 200 wines from all over the world, listed on blackboards hanging around the bar, and nearly all available by the glass (175 or 250ml). Snacks and bigger dishes (modern British, organic where possible) are listed on another blackboard and can be ordered throughout the day. Everything comes fresh from the markets to be prepared and sold the same day. Seafood is a speciality. Live music on Monday and Tuesday.

The Troubadour
265 Old Brompton Rd SW5 *Tube: Earls Court*
Tel: 020 7370 1434
Open: 10.00-23.00

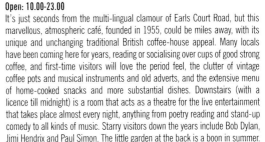

It's just seconds from the multi-lingual clamour of Earls Court Road, but this marvellous, atmospheric café, founded in 1955, could be miles away, with its unique and unchanging traditional British coffee-house appeal. Many locals have been coming here for years, reading or socialising over cups of good strong coffee, and first-time visitors will love the period feel, the clutter of vintage coffee pots and musical instruments and old adverts, and the extensive menu of home-cooked snacks and more substantial dishes. Downstairs (with a licence till midnight) is a room that acts as a theatre for the live entertainment that takes place almost every night, anything from poetry reading and stand-up comedy to all kinds of music. Starry visitors down the years include Bob Dylan, Jimi Hendrix and Paul Simon. The little garden at the back is a boon in summer.

Patisserie Valerie
105 Marylebone High St W1 *Tube: Baker St*
Tel: 020 7935 6240
Open: 07.30-18.45 (Sat from 08.00, Sun 09.00-17.45)

Patisserie Valerie has for many years been providing Londoners with a superb range of cakes, patisserie and chocolates, and breakfasts that are the perfect way to start the day. This is Patisserie Valerie at Maison Sagne, opened in the 1920s by Monsieur Sagne, a notable Swiss chocolatier and patissier. The most elegant and old-fashioned of the Pat Vals (Pats Val?), it features some splendid murals, including one of Lake Geneva.

Also at:
215 Brompton Rd SW3 Tel: 020 7823 9971
44 Old Compton St, Soho W1 Tel: 020 7437 3466
A Parisian setting on two floors.
8 Russell St, Covent Garden WC2 Tel: 020 7240 0064
250 years of history at what was previously Boswell's Coffee House. It first opened its doors in 1752 as a tea house, and it was here in 1763 that the diarist Boswell met Dr Johnson.

171

UP THE SMOKE

Spool back a couple of decades and journeys to London were routinely described as going 'up the smoke'. Sadly, the label had more to do with bad air quality than the draw of London's tobacconists. That was then. Today London has a spectrum of tobacco retailers to match any city on the planet. Join us for the ultimate walking-tour of cigar smoker's London

VINTAGE STUFF, J FOX & R LEWIS, 19 ST JAMES' STREET

Heading into St James' Street is like stepping into a time machine with the controls stuck on 'last century'. Harvie & Hudson, Fortnum & Mason… the surrounding Mayfair shop names read like a public school roll-call. Nestled into the street like a vintage bottle in a cellar, Fox & Lewis has been supplying London with tobacco for the past 214 years. The place oozes history.

Highlight of the store is the 'cigar museum' — an Aladdin's cave of smoking paraphernalia including the world's oldest box of Havanas and dusty ledgers recording the smoking habits of some legendary customers (like Sir Winston Churchill, who consumed some 200,000 cigars in his lifetime).

To enjoy the true ambience of the place, you light up an El Rey Del Mundo demi-tasse and surrender to the shop's old-world charm. Heaven.

NOUVELLE CUISINE, MONTE'S, 165 SLOANE STREET

As a rule of thumb you can tell how posh a part of London is by the ratio of cars to Black Cabs. Surfacing on Knightsbridge Road, they're nose to tail. After 200 metres of the most expensive window shopping in London, you come to the shimmering exterior of Monte's cigar shop.

A compelling mixture of old and new, Monte's blends art-deco lighting with fashionable stripped floors. "We had a slightly old fashioned image when we opened in 1995," explains the manager, "and Jamie has just livened us up". The Jamie we're referring to is culinary wunderkind and TV chef Jamie Oliver. You feel you belong here.

Towards the tail end of a peppery Hoyo de Monterrey Epicure No.2, you might also find yourself wishing you were a member of the neighbouring Monte's 'The Club' — a state-of-the-art haven for the consumption of rolled tobacco. The annual membership of £500 is the only possible snag.

TRADING PLACES, BURLINGTON BERTIE, 57 HOUNDSDITCH

By now you're getting a taste for the high-life. For the journey across town to the City, you naturally hail a cab. Minutes later, among the glass monoliths in Houndsditch, you stumble upon Burlington Bertie. Opening for business five years ago, this shop was one of the first cigar retailers to understand the City's dictum: 'time is money'. Offering a 60 minute cigar delivery service anywhere in the Square Mile, Bertie ensures you've got a stogie in your hand before the ink on your bonus cheque has dried. You could fall in love with this idea. Lighting up a thumb-sized Rafael Gonzalez, you amble back onto the street a happy human being. If there's a better city for cigar smokers than London, we'd like to know about it.

Brighton

From the map, Brighton might look like a minor seaside town, but up close this buzzing community is a magnet for clubbers, diners and hedonists right across the whole of the South of England. At times, the scene here is so lively it rivals the line-up in London. First off, of course, there's the in-built asset of the sea – and the beach, West Pier and marina exploit that natural resource to the maximum. But then with typical Brighton pizzazz, the community has gone on to build a world-class arts festival (held in the new Brighton Dome each May); a cutting-edge club scene (for some, the best in Europe); plus innovative restaurants, galleries and museums. To choose from this menu of pleasures, buy a traditional 'vanilla ice-cream with a flake' on the Pavilion Promenade – and survey one of the most cosmopolitan scenes in the country.

Barkers Café Bar
17-18 Dukes Lane *Area: In the Lanes near central Post Office*
Tel: 01273 325945
Open: 09.00-17.30 (Sun 09.30-17.00)
In an area full of interesting little shops, Barkers is a popular daytime wining and dining venue. Plants and a mural provide the decor, and the room is furnished with green tables and chairs. The aluminium versions outside are in great demand in the warmer weather, especially as the café is on a wide stretch of a pedestrian street.

Browns
3-4 Duke St *Area: On outskirts of the Lanes near central Post Office*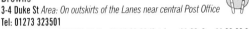
Tel: 01273 323501
Open: Restaurant 12.00-23.00 Bar 09.00-23.00 (Sat from 11.00, Sun 11.00-22.30)
Part of the very popular and successful Browns chain, this one, the original, opened in 1973 in premises previously occupied by the Halifax Building Society. The 110-seat restaurant serves an excellent selection of dishes both traditional and modern on a wide-ranging menu complemented by bottled beers and a wine list that includes many by the glass. Browns Bar two doors down, with a handsome mahogany bar, leafy plants and Edwardian-style lighting, opens for breakfast and serves a menu of baguettes, light snacks, coffees and teas throughout the day; a full range of drinks both alcoholic and soft is available.

Curve
45 Gardner St *Area: In North Laines, near Komedia Theatre*
Tel: 01273 603031
Open: 10.00-23.00 (Sun 11.00-21.00)
In what was formerly a bric-a-brac market, Curve is a cheerfully decorated bar and brasserie combined with a cabaret and theatre venue. Opened in September 1999, it is owned by the English family, who are renowned as the owners of one of the best seafood and oyster bar-restaurants in town. Spread over two floors, Curve offers a good choice of English and Continental food, a very decent wine list (two house wines available by the glass) and excellent coffee. Management and staff are Italian, always friendly and on the ball.

Ha!Ha! Bar & Canteen
Pavilion Buildings *Area/Zone: Next to Pavilion Gate*
Tel: 01273 737080
Open: 11.00-23.00 (Sun 12.00-22.30)
One of a chain of 18 spread around the country, this cheerful place opened in July 1999. Bright and spacious, with a gleaming zinc bar dominating one side, it's a very inviting spot to pause for a drink and a snack, and solos can browse through the newspapers that are laid out on a butcher's block just inside the door. There's a wide selection of wines and beers, lots of coffee and own-brand of preserves, oils, vinegars and the like: get an order form from the staff and explore the shelves.

Café Puccino's
1 Bartholomew St *Area/Zone: Opposite Brighton Town Hall*
Tel: 01273 204656
Open: 08.00-19.00 (Fri & Sat till 23.00, Sun 09.00-18.30)
Bare boards and copper-topped round tables; a sofa in the window. Puccino's offers a comfortable and relaxed atmosphere in which to enjoy a baked potato, a croque, a plate of pasta or an all-day breakfast. Three white wines and three reds are available by the glass, and there's a good choice of coffees and teas. It's a place that appeals to all ages, and for those who want to stay over Bed & Breakfast accommodation is available upstairs.

Bristol
Sipping a drink on Bristol's revitalised quayside, it's easy to forget that you're actually in the UK. Café culture is booming here and, combined with colourful street performers and the overspill from Arnolfini gallery, it all makes for a heady cocktail. Besides acting as Bristol's economic lifeline, the river Avon proved the inspiration for two of the city's greatest landmarks, the Clifton Suspension Bridge and the world's first iron-hulled steam liner, the SS Great Britain (both incidentally the handiwork of Isambard Kingdom Brunel). On land, look for Bristol's tranquil side among the Georgian streets and traditional pubs of Clifton – the perfect place to sample a pint of West Country scrumpy cider.

Boston Tea Party
75 Park St *City Centre: College Green*
Tel: 0117 929 8601
Open: 07.00-22.00 (Mon till 18.00, Sun 09.00-19.00)
Named after the infamous shindig in New England, this likeable café is located halfway up the hill from College Green. The ground floor of the shop displays all the goodies and has some tables and chairs. Inside is non-smoking, but puffers can light up in the heated, multi-level sheltered garden. They offer cooked breakfasts, but the best are on Sundays, which are very special. Popular with students, this is one of the best coffee houses in Bristol; good wines are also available (some by the glass), but no beers.

Browns
38 Queen's Rd, Clifton *Wills Memorial Building*
Tel: 0117 930 4777
Open: 11.00-23.30 (Sat from 10.00, Sun from 12.00)
Bristol's Browns occupies a very grand building modelled on the Doge's Palace in Venice that has in its time seen service as a market site, hospital, museum, art gallery and university dining rooms. Built in 1783, it was badly damaged during the Second World War; the left hand side was almost totally destroyed, and only the last window is original. Opened as Browns in 1992, it is one of the most elegant venues to relax, entertain, or be entertained,

with very friendly, attentive staff and lots to see. The long menu is always available, with hot sandwiches, salmon cakes, burgers and steak, mushroom & Guinness pie among the Browns classics. They also offer a children's menu, afternoon tea and bar snacks. Lots of bottled beers, and more than a dozen wines by the glass. Terrace for alfresco supping.

Chicago Rock Café
Unit 2 The Watershed, 1 Canon's Rd *Area: Waterfront Centre: College Green*
Tel: 0117 929 1361
Open: 11.30-01.00 (Fri & Sat till 02.00, Sun till 22.30)
There's entertainment most nights of the week at this lively place, one of 50 or so Chicago Rock Cafés around the country. It is located alongside Bordeaux Quay at the mouth of the River Frome in the centre of town. Weekend nights are party time. The food offered, all GM-free, ranges from elaborate sandwiches in various breads to snacks and main courses. Good wines and beers and excellent espresso.

Chicane Café
3 Christmas Steps, Lewins Mead *Area: City Centre, nr Hippodrome*
Tel: 0117 914922
Open: 08.00-17.00 (Sat 10.00-16.00)
Closed: Sun
Local artists display their work at this popular student meeting place with a short wine list, a few bottled beers, two on draught, good coffee, breakfasts and day-long snacks. Along Lewins Mead, where traffic now races where water once did, are some old Bristol houses, leading to Christmas Steps, which in turn lead to the University. Halfway up the steep steps is where you'll find Chicane Café.

Clifton Wine Bar
4 Richmond Terrace, Clifton *Area: Clifton: Victoria Square*
Tel: 0117 973 2069
Open: 11.00-23.00 (Sun till 22.30)
A long-established wine bar in the vaulted under-pavement of a terrace high up over the city in Clifton. At the back is a large terraced garden for the summer crowds, for this is one of the most popular venues in the area. The breakfast menu is available till 15.00 as is all their food – salads, baguettes, good-value main meals and blackboard offerings of the day. The main bar is flagstoned, with an elaborately carved bar counter. It's aimed at students, being near the Students Union, and there's a big screen for watching the big sporting events. Good wines and good coffee.

Mud Dock Café
40 The Grove *Area: Waterside nr Arnolfini*
Tel: 0117-934 9734
Open: 11.00-23.00 (Mon till 18.00)
A stylish café above a bicycle shop, overlooking the dock and with some tables outside. The decor is agreeably different (bikes hang from the ceiling) and so is the menu, with dishes like green apple and mixed leaf salad with roasted pistachios, or merguez and mash. A good range of beers and wines and happy, efficient service set the seal on one of Bristol's top spots for a relaxed meal. A mud dock is the earliest type of dry dock: in tidal quays such as this site boats would sink into the mud, exposing their hulls and allowing work to be carried out. A second Mud Dock, also a combination of bike shop and café, is in Exeter, in a converted warehouse on the quay by the River Exe.

Prom Music/Café/Bar
24 Promenade, Gloucester Rd, Bishopston *Area: by the Arches*
Tel: 0117 942 7319
Open: 11.00-23.00 (Sat from 10.00, Sun 10.00-22.30)
The all-day breakfast is a very popular order at the Prom, where other favourites include tapas, burgers and pasta. Apart from Tuesday, which is quiz night, there is live music nightly — jazz on Monday, and the other nights varying from blues to folk to rock. Split level, the bar is in the right window, the musicians on the left, and the clientele on bent ply chairs at simple tables on both levels. Outside tables.

Tantric Jazz Café Bar

39-41 St Nicholas St *Area: Hippodrome, City Centre*
Tel: 0117 940 2304
Open: 10.00-01.00 (Sun from 17.00)
Live jazz is performed nightly at Tantric Jazz, and Sunday evenings are dedicated to jam sessions. In a quiet street near the banking centre, it has quite a low ceiling but feels spacious because it's a double-fronted property. Oilcloths cover the tables in café style, and there's a Moroccan slant to the dishes listed on the blackboard. Newspapers are available on the big coffee table by the window. The evening entry price covers the music and any dish on the menu.

Taverna dell' Artista
33 King St *Area: Near Bristol Odlwick (Theatre Royal)*
Tel: 0117 929 7712
Open: 19.00-02.00 (restaurant 19.00-23.30, Fri & Sat till 24.00)
Closed: Sun & Mon
The building dates back to 1640 and is the oldest in King Street. It has a restaurant upstairs and pizzeria/café with a full on-licence to 02.00 downstairs. The café is frequented by casts of the productions at the nearby Old Vic, and their audiences — and, of course, the loyal regulars who have been coming here since it first opened 30 years ago. Always busy, it's one of the favourite meeting places in Bristol. The owners also have Trattoria da Renato across the road,

Hotel du Vin
The Sugar House, Narrow Lewins Mead *Area: City Centre: Christmas Steps*
Tel: 0117 925 5577
Open: 07.00-21.30 (Sat & Sun 08.00-22.00)
The site, on the banks of the River Frome, was the old Sugar House (until 1831) and was subsequently put to a variety of industrial uses. The entrance is through a courtyard with a fountain and smart planked teak tables and chairs. From there you move into the spacious and comfortable lounge bar with leather-bound sofas and coffee tables. There's an excellent wine list, first-class coffee and meals in the Bistro (booking essential). Breakfasts are available for non-residents from 07.00 to 09.30.

The Vintner Wine Bar
12 St Stephen's St
Tel: 0117 929 1222
Open: 11.00-23.00 (Sat from 18.00)
Closed: Sun
A long-established wine bar in the arched, bare stone vaults of Crusader House in the banking district of the city centre. Filter coffee and a good wine

list. There's a quiet garden for summer sipping in the shadow of St Stephen's Church next door.

Watershed Café

Multimedia Centre, 1 Canon's Rd *Near Millenium Square*
Tel: 0117 921 4135
Open: 09.30-23.00 (Sat from 10.30, Sun till 22.30)

A banana warehouse overlooking the old dock basin has been converted into an arts and entertainment centre on Bordeaux Quay, where the River Frome flows into the River Avon. The café has been here since the early 1980s and serves filled baguettes and full meals, wines by the glass, lots of draught and bottled beers and first-rate coffee. The company leases the whole of the upper floor and also has a cinema and a photographic gallery, where courses on film and photography are run.

Leeds

Wandering around the Victorian centre of Leeds, it's easy to lose track of time. As part of the city's recent makeover, they've done away with 'nine to five', opting instead for around-the-clock flexi-time, which means there's never a dull moment. Leeds' late-night bars, restaurants and clubs buzz with energy and it isn't surprising that they draw people from all over the North. Shopping is a favourite daylight pursuit and Leeds boasts one of only two Harvey Nichols department stores in the UK (the other is in London's Knightsbridge). For a dash of culture, it's hard to beat the City Art Gallery, which houses the finest collection of twentieth century British art outside the capital.

Art's Café

42 Call Lane *Area: Near Corn Exchange*
Tel: 0113 243 8243
Open: 11.00 (12.00 for food)-23.00 (Sun 12.00-22.30)

Art's Café, one of the first of its type in the happening Calls area, provides a cool, mellow ambience for enjoying good coffee, a decent selection of wines and day-long snacks (with a full and inventive menu in the evening). This is a corner site on split levels, with lots of wood inside and lots of glass to watch what's going on outside. Close to the Corn Exchange.

Browns Restaurant & Bar

The Light, The Headrow
Tel: 0113 243 9353
Open: 11.00-23.00 (Sun 12.00-22.30)

The 1930s premises of the Leeds Permanent Building Society were converted into a stylish member of the Browns chain that opened next to The Light leisure and entertainment complex in October 2001. Spacious, cool and comfortable, Browns offers a day-long menu of classic dishes, bar snacks, wines and beers and a choice of places to enjoy them: looking down The Headrow towards the Town Hall from tables by the splendid arched windows; alfresco on the terrace overlooking the central courtyard of The Light; sipping and chatting in the wood-panelled former manager's office.

Carpe Diem

Civic Court, Calverley St *Area: Opposite Millenium Square*
Tel: 0113 243 6264
Open: 11.00-23.00 (Fri & Sat till 01.00, Sun 12.00-24.00)

A roomy cellar bar beneath a local authority building, with another entrance down wrought-iron stairs on Great George Street. Established in 1997, and catering for the business market and as a young person's venue at the weekend, Carpe Diem serves excellent food, from sandwiches and burgers to poached salmon and sirloin steak. Sunday lunch is served all day. Major sporting events are shown on big screens, and there's entertainment most nights of the week: big-screen films on Sunday and Monday, local bands Thursday, jazz/funk on Friday; there are two pool tables. Real ales: Tetley, Pedigree, Guest of the Month; on draught: Tetley Smooth, Carlsberg, Stella, Grolsch, Guinness, Guinness Extra Cold; bottled: lots. A function room is available for free hire.

Fat Cat Café
8 South Parade *Area: Near Town Hall*
Tel: 0113 245 6288
Open: 10.00-23.00 (Sun till 17.00)
This was once a bank, and after that an insurance company office – does that explain the name? It's now a successful café whose outstanding feature is the splendid original wood panelling that was uncovered during the conversion. A late breakfast starts the day but the place is busiest at lunchtime and from early evening onwards, when it serves a full selection of snacks along with many draught beers and some 20 wines. One of several Fat Cats – the first opened in Bangor, North Wales, in 1992.

Henry's
Greek St *Area: Between Town Hall and Train Station*
Tel: 0113 245 9424
Open: 08.00-23.00 (Sat from 12.00, Sun 12.00-19.00)
A pleasant bar-café that's open for breakfast, the time for reading the mail or a newspaper; at lunchtime it's busy with snacking and chatting; the cocktail hour provides relaxation after work; and later on a full menu tempts you to make an evening of it. Sandwiches, salads and pasta are among the popular choices. Beyond the first area, which has the look of a Parisian pavement café, there's lots of stained wood (floor, bar, stools) lightened by the large ceiling light panel and a plant-filled fountain.

Café In Seine
13 Duncan Street
Tel: 0113 242 2436
Open: 12.00-23.00 (Fri & Sat till 02.00, Sun till 17.00)
A Continental-style bar offering a huge choice of coffees, pots of tea, sandwiches, soup, mussels, salads, daily specials, 3-course meals. Wines by glass or bottle, cocktails by glass or small or large pitcher. In the evening and at the weekend DJs provide the entertainment.

Milo
10-12 Call Lane
Tel: 0113 245 7101
Open: 12.00-23.30
Closed: Sun
A pop rock café at its liveliest on Friday and Saturday nights, when a DJ takes control. The Douglas fir bar has a curved plywood front, the walls are rough plaster and the ceiling is clad in stainless steel that undulates across the room. Chief offerings are Columbian coffees, lots of cocktails and snacks such as New York deli sandwiches. Small, trendy, friendly.

Norman
36 Call Lane *Area: Near Corn Exchange*
Tel: 0113 234 3988
Open: 09.00-01.00 (Sun 11.00-17.00)
Very popular, very arty and quite weird, with a design by Jam of London that includes a door made out of toast, inflatable curvy walls and doorless lavatories. Norman attracts the students and young professionals who flock to the Exchange Quarter, especially in the evenings and at weekends, when the place is bursting at the seams. Residents play house, funk and hip hop. Food includes noodles and other Japanese-style snacks, and there's an American-style pick-up service: you ring, order and then collect in small cardboard cartons. Includes a juice bar.

Quid Pro Quo
Yorkshire House, Greek St
Tel: 0113 244 8888 *Area: Between Town Hall and Train Station*
Open: 10.00-23.00
Closed: Sun
Quid Pro Quo is one of many cafés and bars that occupy the ground floors of office blocks. It's large and busy, and the area immediately in front of it has been enclosed in glass as a permanent terrace. There's a good list of wines, mostly available by the glass, to accompany the sandwiches, salads, snacks and mains such as bangers 'n' mash or Thai curry.

Soho
35 Call Lane *Area: Near Corn Exchange*
Tel: 0113 242 9009
Open: 12.00-23.00 (Fri-Sun till 22.30)
The look here is bare brick walls, a curved glass bar top with a wavy copper front, upholstered bar stools and striking coffee tables with swirls of different-coloured sand under glass panels. Snacks and more substantial meals are available in the bar and resident performers play a variety of sounds.

Manchester

Jump on the Metro to Salford Quay and you're greeted by a showcase of stunning new architecture and Victorian loft-conversions that would be unrecognisable to the 'matchstick men and matchstick cats and dogs' that Lowry painted just half a century ago. Pull up a waterside chair, order a creamy pint of Boddingtons beer and reflect on how Manchester has washed her industrial past downstream. Back in the city centre the transformation continues. Manchester has long been competing with London for the best nightlife in the country, and now the area around Rochdale canal is set to steal the UK's café crown. Arts in the city run the whole gamut from fringe theatre, at the Cornerhouse, to the sublime classical performances put on by the North's premier orchestra, the Hallé, based at the Bridgewater Hall. Add in the largest Chinatown in the UK, and the Lowrys museum (with the largest collection of 'Lowry's' in the world) and you've got all the ingredients for a great city.

Abbaye
42 Canal St *Tube: Piccadilly Gardens*
Tel: 0161-236 5566
Open: 11.30-23.00 (Thur till 01.00, Fri & Sat till 02.00, Sun till 22.30)
A Belgian-style *moules et frites* café-bar with a bar running the length of the ground floor and a restaurant above. Beer, both bottled and draught, comes in many varieties, with a special glass for each, and there's a list of about 20 wines, all available by the glass. If you don't want a full meal you can have a sandwich, a salad or some mussels in the bar.

179

Atlas
376 Deansgate, Castlefield *Area: Tube: G Mex*
Tel: 0161-834 2124
Open: 11.00-23.00 (Sun till 22.30)
A highly successful café that broke new ground in Manchester's café culture when it opened in 1983. The design is simple, airy, bright and modern, with floor-to-ceiling windows front and back and lightweight tables and chairs. It's a popular spot with media people and musicians, who come to chat and snack on soup, ciabatta sandwiches, salad or a pasta dish. The café is built in a railway arch, and a patio at the back overlooks the canal. Atlas has its own deli across the road.

Bar 38
10 Canal St *Tube: Piccadilly Gardens*
Tel: 0161-236 6005
Open: 11.00-24.00 (Thur 11.30-01.00, Fri & Sat 11.30-02.00, Sun 12.00-22.30)
A roomy brewery-owned café-bar with an impressive glass frontage on two floors. The designer decor is orange and blue – look for the fish-eye mirror on the back wall – and the floors bare timber. A feature downstairs is the communal stainless-steel hand-washing fountain. There's a straight-forward wine list and an interesting range of food. Music of all kinds.

Barça
Arches 8 & 9, Catalan Square, Castlefield *Tube: G Mex*
Tel: 0161-839 7099
Open: 09.00-01.00 (Sun 11.00-17.00)
Taking its name from the abbreviated form of Barcelona (it's in Catalan Square), this bar-restaurant in converted railway arches is *the* place for drinking and snacking in Castlefield, especially in fine weather overlooking the canal basin. The day could start with coffee in a comfortable leather armchair; later on come beers and a daily-changing bar menu served until 17.00, restaurant menu, jazz on Sunday afternoons, guest DJs some other days. In the evening, it's pitchers of Bud and jugs of cocktails. The industrial-style decor has won many architectural awards.

Lead Station
99 Beech Rd, Chorlton Green *Area: Stretford*
Tel: 0161-881 5559
Open: 11.00-23.00 (Sat from 10.00, Sun 10.00-22.30)
Once a police station, now a popular café-bar. Waitress service will bring you coffee and breakfast, a glass of wine and a snack at simple wooden café tables and chairs. Especially busy at weekends, with lots of newspaper reading plus families having a break. The terrace at the back is a summer bonus.

Manto
46 Canal St *Tube: Piccadilly Gardens*
Tel: 0161-236 2667
Open: 11.00-24.00 (Sat till 01.00, Sun till 22.30)
One of the first bars to open up the Canal Street café scene (1992), Manto continues among the leaders and expanded with a restaurant floor in 1998. There's plenty of standing room by the bar, or you can take your drink to a table on the balcony, inside or out, or to a pavement table. Snacks are served until about 22.30, lunch and dinner menus, Breakfast Club on Saturday and Sunday mornings.

Metz

3 Brazil St *Tube: Piccadilly Gardens*
Tel: 0161-237 9852
Open: 12.00-23.00 (Fri & Sat till 24.00, Sun till 22.30)
The address of this popular Bavarian-style café-bar is misleading as Metz is really on Canal Street, on the other side of the canal, with a tiny iron bridge to take you over there. Apart from a cantilevered balcony just above water level where you can sit outside, there's also a permanently moored barge with terrace tables under a removable canopy. In the main room, candles and stripped pine. With no fewer than six champagnes on the list, parties here really fizz.

Polar Bar Café

414 Wilbraham Rd, Chorlton-cum-Hardy *Bus: 16,85,87*
Tel: 0161-881 0901
Open: 11.00-23.00 (Sun till 22.30)
An elegant Edwardian cast-iron and glass canopy fronts this popular café-bar, while inside is a spacious bar and café tables scattered around it. It's particularly busy in the evening and at weekends, when the crowds gather to enjoy the draught beer, the good coffee and the appetising snacks. Organic food and fresh juices are to the fore, and the owners have acquired the next-door premises to open a deli-café.

RSVP

64 Deansgate *Tube: Piccadilly Gardens*
Tel: 0161-839 0985
Open: 08.00-23.00 (Thur, Fri & Sat till 02.00, Sun 10.00-22.30)
Once T Hayward & Co's glass and china shop, RSVP has a preservation order inside and out, and the handsome cabinet once used to display the Hayward wares now holds some of its wines. Open early for breakfast (excellent caffè latte), they also do a two-course set lunch. Lots of bottled beers, wines by the glass (two sizes) and a variety of cocktails. Weekend is party time, with dancing till dawn and free entry till 2 o'clock in the morning.

The Temple of Convenience

100 Great Bridgewater St
Tel: 0161-288 9834
Open: 11.00-23.00 (Sun 12.00-22.30)
A lapsed public loo has found a new role as a tiny, friendly little café-bar serving tea, coffee, great beers, wine and all-day snacks. Live jazz sessions take place on the second and fourth Thursday of every month, and acoustic music three Tuesdays each month. The musicians and the crowds can make as much noise as they like as there are no neighbours to inconvenience.

Via Fossa

Canal St *Tube: Piccadilly Gardens*
Tel: 0161-236 6523
Open: 11.00-24.00 (Thur till 01.00, Fri & Sat till 02.00, Sun 12.00-22.30)
An extraordinary bar on several levels floors designed by Frank Ennis and making use of Gothic pews from redundant churches in Limerick. In the bars are everything from altar screens to pulpits, scarlet brocade curtains and a row of chamber pots, and you can survey the whole scene from the gallery. Good beers, reasonable food and a guaranteed good time among a cheerful mixed crowd.

York

If York didn't quite invent history, then it was one of the very first in on the act. With a pedigree going back to AD71 (when the Romans founded the slightly less catchy 'Eboracum') York has been busy ever since. And it's been a productive two millennia. A trip to the Yorkshire Museum whets the appetite with its internationally acclaimed collection of Roman, Viking and Anglo-Saxon treasures. From there, it's on to a tour of the medieval city walls, and a trip to the living museum of Norman and Gothic architecture that's York Minster. To round it all off, head for the thoroughly modern pleasure of a cappuccino in a café on a cobbled York side street. It's been a long day, so be generous with the dusted chocolate.

Bettys Café & Tea Rooms
6-8 St Helen's Square *Area: Near Museum Gardens and central Post Office*
Tel: 0904 659142
Open: 09.00-21.00

Bettys has made a name for itself with its excellent home baking, which runs to over 400 items both sweet and savoury, and stepping into any of the branches is a truly self-indulgent experience. Speciality beverages, unusual snacks, hearty meals such as sausages and mash or haddock and chips, and cakes to die for – try one and you're sure to take some home! Relaxing, comforting, with waitresses who really know how to smile – let's face it, as the locals say, if you haven't been to Bettys you haven't been to York! There's another Bettys in York (Little Bettys in Stonegate), and branches, all very child-friendly, are in Harrogate, Ilkley and Northallerton. The Harrogate branch was the first in this splendid chain, opened in 1919 by Frederick Belmont, a Swiss confectioner.

Café Concerto
21 High Petergate *Area: Next to York Minster*
Tel: 01904 610478
Open: 10.00-22.00

One of the very best of York's many cafés and informal eating places. Just 100 yards from the Minster, Café Concerto is small, relaxed and friendly, with lots of plants in the window, and yellowing sheet music on the wall. You can enjoy an enormous cup of mocha while listening to Ella Fitzgerald and reading the newspapers provided; or choose from the excellent patés and gratins and savoury tarts, accompanied by interesting breads and salads. There's a daily 'Concerto Dauphinoise', perhaps with ham, feta, sweet cherry peppers and basil. Everything is home-made and the cakes and puddings are as great as everything else – so leave room! Reasonably priced wines are available by the glass. Definitely a place not to be missed.

Gert & Henry's
Jubbergate, The Market *Area/Zone: On main Market Square in City Centre*
Tel: 01904 621445
Open: 10.00-22.00
Closed: Sun

In a building that in parts must be 500 years old and a café-restaurant for at least the last 100, the ambience is of a cosy tea room. Teas are indeed served, along with coffees, beers, wines and full meals. The espresso is excellent, served with an amaretto biscuit. Traditional English food, substantial and very reasonably priced. The music is Ella and Broadway musicals.

Harkers Café Bar
1 St Helen's Square *Area/Zone: Next to Guild Hall and Mansion House*
Tel: 01904 672795
Open: 10.00-23.00 (Sat from 09.00)
In a spacious building in a largely pedestrianised square, Harkers serves breakfast, lunch, dinner and a pre-theatre dinner (not Saturday). Civilised refreshment in comfortable surroundings. Happy hour from 17.00 Sunday to Tuesday, 17.00-20.00 Wednesday to Friday.

Treasurer's House Tea Rooms
Minster Yard *Area/Zone: Next to Yok Minster, behind St William's College*
Tel: 01904 646757
Open: 11.00-16.30
This elegant town house was originally the home of the Treasurers of York Minster. It was restored to its original splendour by the Yorkshire industrialist Frank Green between 1897 and 1930, since when it has been in the care of the National Trust. Period rooms contain a fine collection of 17th and 18th century furniture, glass and china, and from thc medieval hall to the old kitchen there is something to interest everyone. In the basement Tea Rooms home baking is the main attraction (Yorkshire lemon tart is a favourite from the National Trust cookbook), while soup, sandwiches, a Yorkshire cheese platter and filled jacket potatoes give excellent support. Children have their own section of the menu, and high chairs can be provided. House wines and three Yorkshire fruit wines, produced in the cellars of a 19th century flax mill in the village of Glasshouses, are available by the glass or bottle. No smoking. Another National Trust Tearoom in York is at Goodramgate.

Edinburgh

It's not until you've made it to the top of the Royal Mile that Edinburgh's claim of being 'the Athens of the North' really makes sense. On a clear morning, the skyline is an impressive jumble of domes, spires and Georgian architecture waiting to be explored. But wait until Hogmanay, and it erupts in a street party and a riot of fireworks. If you can't make it for the New Year's Eve celebrations, then the International Festival in August is the next best thing, flooding the capital with world-class talent and over a million visitors. Year round, the city is dotted with enough museums and galleries to keep you busy, but make sure you don't leave without visiting the National Gallery. After a day's sightseeing, the Royal Mile and its rows of pubs begin to wake up. Whatever you do, just don't expect an early night.

Blue Moon Café
36 Broughton St/1 Barony St EH1 *Area: City centre: nr Playhouse Theatre*
Tel: 0131-557 0911
Open: 11.00-00.30 (Fri till 01.00, Sat 09.00-01.00, Sun 09.00-00.30)
A great meeting place for both local residents and visitors. The menu is wide-ranging (traditional, vegetarian, continental breakfasts, filled potatoes, focaccia sandwiches, garlic mussels, vegetable enchiladas, burgers, lasagne, Tex-Mex), and there's a decent wine list and plenty of bottled and draught beers. Particularly friendly and helpful staff. Lone visitors have plenty to read.

Browns Restaurant & Bar
131-133 George Street EH2
Tel: 0131-2254442
Open: 11.00-23.30 (from 12.00 Sunday & Bank Holidays).
Edinburgh's Browns opened in George Street in December 1998, introducing the style, the ambience and the cooking that have proved so popular in Bath,

Brighton, Bristol, Brighton, Cambridge, Oxford and several venues in London. The restaurant has seats for 200+, a private dining room and a bar overlooking the street. The well-established Browns menu – hot sandwiches, salads, pasta, classic main courses such as salmon cakes, country chicken pie and chargrilled steaks, fish and other daily specials, tempting puddings – is joined by seasonal Scottish specialities. Special opening times apply during the Edinburgh Festival in August.

City Café
19 Blair St EH1
Tel: 0131-220 0125
Open: 11.00-01.00
A favourite meeting place for the city's youth, or anyone with a love of chrome, pool (two tables), beer, coffee, burgers, smoke and music. Daylight hours see quiet visits by victims of the night before, early evening sees after-workers and tourists, then it's back to the night life. Great bar, good house red, good food – nachos, fry-ups, club sandwiches, venison burgers, vegeburgers. Menu available till 22.00. A cross between art deco and 50s in style, it has a very long bar with a laminate top and an aluminium reeded front. There are four tables out on the terrace on the steep hill.

The Elephant House
21 George IV Bridge EH1 *Area: George IV Bridge*
Tel: 0131-220 5355
Open: 07.30-22.00 (Sat & Sun 08.00-20.00)
A very popular and relaxed café serving a wide selection of teas and coffees and also offering a decent choice of beer and wine. Food is mostly pies and quiches and salads, but there are a few hot specials, plus an all-day Continental breakfast and lots of desserts. The walls are adorned with pictures of elephants, coffee information and shows of local and student artwork. There are also newspapers, chess sets and a board for small ads. Good view of the Castle from the back window of a typically lofty Edinburgh room in what was once a solicitor's office. Definitely a place to remember when in Edinburgh.

Malmaison Brasserie & Café
1 Tower Place, Leith *Area: Royal Yacht Britannia*
Tel: 0131-555 6969
Open: Brasserie 07.00-22.00 (Sat & Sun 08.00-22.30), Café/bar 10.00-22.00 (Sun till 22.30)
Part of a hotel in a Scottish Baronial building; on one side of the entrance is the brasserie, on the other the café, French in style. Food is served all day and in summer it's very pleasant to sit outside on the cobbled quayside. Inside is a central bar surrounded by intimate booths, tables and chairs, some high at bar level, some for eating at with wicker chairs, and some coffee tables with carvers and a chesterfield. Patisserie and snacks are available throughout the day in the café, and there's a good choice of wines by the glass.

Plaisir du Chocolat
251-253 Canongate EH8 8BQ
Tel: 0131 556 9524
Open: 10.00-18.00

Behind an arched balcony, lined with tubs of herbs, is this truly French chocolatière. It is so complete and so perfect it could have been transported just as it is from a little side street in Paris and reassembled in its present location. Service is helpful, polite and knowledgeable from staff who know exactly what their product is. The food itself is wonderful and is served in a setting that is at once quite formal and totally relaxed. There is an unofficial ban on the use of mobile phones inside, which helps in sustaining the feel of real calm that pervades the whole place. The teas and the cakes are of the highest quality, so it's not surprising that the little deli attached to the café does very good business. Also open for dinner Friday and Saturday.

Kaffe Politick
146 Marchmont Road EH9
Tel: 0131 446 9873
Open: 10.00-22.00

Should be listed in the Oxford English Dictionary with the definition 'endlessly fashionable and chic'. Kaffe Politick really is one of those rare places that seems to have found a perfect niche for itself and has no need to reinvent itself every so often. It is content to let the others chase the changing tastes of the market place, knowing that without even trying it will always be at the cutting edge. Fresh vegetable and fruit juices can accompany the bagels, panini, salads and moreish Belgian waffles with caramelised apple or fresh fruit and maple syrup. The café is heavy on the theme suggested by the name, done out in striking black and white, and the cushioned benches are as comfortable as anything in town.

Ryan's
2 Hope St, West End *Area: West End*
Tel: 0131-226 6669
Open: 07.30-00.45

In Edinburgh's fashionable West End, occupying a strategic corner site on ground and basement floors, Ryan's is a very popular meeting place. Outside, a host of aluminium tables and chairs crowds the pavement; there's a glassed-in terrace for taking coffee or breakfast on chillier days, while inside there's a warm welcome in spacious rooms under a faux-vaulted ceiling with soft lights and pretty flowers. Good wines, and the best pint of Guinness in town.

Valvona & Crolla Ltd
19 Elm Row EH7 *Area: City Centre, near Playhouse Theatre*
Tel: 0131-556 6066
Open: 08.00-17.00
Closed: Sun

One of the absolute must-visits on a trip to Edinburgh, Valvona & Crolla is an Italian specialist retailer, wine merchant, café, bar, baker. Through what must be the greatest Italian deli-cum-wine shop in the UK, steps lead to the café with an atrium running its length. Wonderful coffee, ten wines by the glass (or you can buy a bottle in the shop, add £3 corkage and enjoy it in the café). Super bakery. No smoking. Twice a month and throughout the Festival, it's open in the evening for dinner featuring regional Italian recipes.

Glasgow

To really get under Glasgow's skin you've got to find out a little about her past – and there's no better place to start than the People's Palace Museum. Fittingly for one of the cities which helped launch the industrial revolution, today's Glasgow is at the cutting edge of modern trends. And as you'd expect from the largest city in Scotland, there's plenty going on. After a pilgrimage round several of Charles Rennie Mackintosh's buildings (of which the Glasgow School of Art steals the show), there's no better place to relax than Pollok Park – also home to the exquisite Burrell Collection of art. Glasgow really comes into her own at night where, between the City Centre and the West End, there's a 21st century café and clubs showcasing the local fashion, design and music scenes that Glasgow is so proud of.

Austin's
61 Miller St *Metro/Tube: Buchanan Street*
Tel: 0141-221 0444
Open: 12.00-24.00
One large room divided into four areas: an eating area with wicker-style chairs set at wood and chrome tables; a lounge area with coffee tables and upholstered stools and a sofa; high tables and bar stools; and a marble-topped bar. The floor is partly herringbone timbered and partly crazy-paved in tiles and slate, while the ceiling is upheld by two giant pillars of a tree trunk with branches outstretched. Espresso coffee, wines by bottle or glass, snacks listed on a blackboard. Cheerful staff, and a happy 25+ clientele.

Babbity Bowster
16-18 Blackfriars *Metro/Tube: Buchanan Street*
Tel: 0141-552 5055
Open: 08.00-24.00
An up-market pub/café-bar/restaurant with a hotel attached, in a Robert Adam town house in the revived Merchant City district. Breakfast is served from opening time, and at noon the full menu becomes available for the rest of the day. Barbecues on the patio in summer. The name derives from a Scottish dance, as does the name of the first-floor restaurant, Schottische. Babbity means 'bob at', Bowster is a bolster. Very good wines; snacks include Italian-style panini and venison sausages & mash.

Café Gandolfi
64 Albion St *Metro/Tube: Buchanan Street*
Tel: 0141-552 6813
Open: 09.00-23.30 (Sun from 12.00)
Scrubbed oak floors, mahogany-panelled walls and chunky hand-crafted furniture are distinguishing features of this bustling café (originally a Victorian pub) in the old Merchant City district where the old fruit, cheese and furniture markets once stood. Following breakfast from 09.00 and mid-morning snacks of croissants and fruit scones, the choice widens at lunchtime with a seasonally-changing menu. There is always a wide choice of sandwiches and a good selection of cheese, and at the bar is a selection of wines available by the glass (two sizes), the whites kept in a cooler.

Café Rogano

11 Exchange Place *Metro/Tube: Buchanan Street*
Tel: 0141-248 4055
Open 12.00-23.00 (Fri & Sat till 24.00)

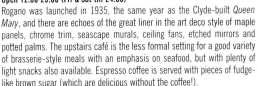

Rogano was launched in 1935, the same year as the Clyde-built *Queen Mary*, and there are echoes of the great liner in the art deco style of maple panels, chrome trim, seascape murals, ceiling fans, etched mirrors and potted palms. The upstairs café is the less formal setting for a good variety of brasserie-style meals with an emphasis on seafood, but with plenty of light snacks also available. Espresso coffee is served with pieces of fudge-like brown sugar (which are delicious without the coffee!).

Willow Tea Rooms

217 Sauchiehall St *Metro/Tube: Cowcaddens*
Tel: 0141-332 0521
Open: 09.30-16.30 (Sun from 12.00)
Closed: Some Bank Holidays

Charming, civilised tea rooms in a beautifully restored building designed in 1904 by Charles Rennie Mackintosh. The place seems made for the old-fashioned cream teas that are served all day, and there's also a fair selection of salads and savoury snacks. The founder, Miss Catherine Cranston, was an advocate of temperance, so this tea room is unlicensed. Perhaps she also believed in not getting into debt, as they don't take credit cards! At the newer Willow at 97 Buchanan Street (Tel: 0141-204 5242) you can enjoy a glass of wine with your food.

Belfast

If you're looking for a building to help unravel the history and charms of Belfast, there are several that fit the bill. Completed in 1870, Belfast Castle gives a sweeping view of things from its site on Cave Hill. Belfast City Hall, likewise (completed in 1906) has been witness to a lot of history, and is a 'must' for tourists. But if you want to get straight to the heart of this intriguing city, head for the Crown Liquor Saloon. A gem of Victoriana, it was one of the very greatest 'gin palaces', which were once the mainstay of industrial Britain. While you're there, marvel at the lovingly preserved interior, and get acquainted with Belfast's greatest asset: her people.

Café Society

3 Donegall Square East *Area/Zone: City Centre near City Hall*
Tel: 028 90 439525
Open: 08.30-21.00 (Thur-Sat till 22.00)
Closed: Sun

A chic Continental café and restaurant in the main square by the City Hall, close to the city's chief shopping district. The day starts with an excellent choice for a light breakfast accompanied by a variety of coffees and delicious hot chocolate. At lunchtime it serves light snacks, and from 17.30 a bistro meal for two is available.

Madison's

59-63 Botanic Avenue *Area/Zone: University area near Queen's University*
Tel: 028 90 330040
Open: 07.00-24.00 (Wed-Sat till 01.00)

The roomy café-bar part of a well-appointed 35-room hotel, with plenty of light coming in through the imposing glass frontage. A long bar down one side serves the open space in the centre, and beyond are tables where you can enjoy breakfast or lunch. A party atmosphere makes the place buzz in the evening.

McHugh's
29-31 Queen's Square
Tel: 028 90 247830 *Area/Zone: East City Centre*
Open: 12.00-01.00 (Sun till 24.00)

The welcome is always warm at McHugh's, which retains its 18th-century front room with a low ceiling, curved bar and carved wood around the shelves behind it. The other spaces are more modern, certainly very comfortable, but less intimate. Open late every night, with live music on Thursday, Friday and Saturday. The menu changes monthly.

Monico Bars
17 Lombard St *Area/Zone:Wine Cellar Entry, near Castle Court*
Tel: 028 90 323211
Open: 11.00-23.00
Closed: Sun

Shoppers can take a break from the hassle and bustle in the comfortable lounge and salon areas here, sipping a coffee or a beer in one of the inviting booths. Hand-drawn real ales are the speciality. At lunchtime there's a menu of the day of traditional Irish fare.

Morrisons
21 Bedford St *Area/Zone: City Centre, near Ulster Hall*
Tel: 028 90 248458
Open: 12.00-24.00 (Thur-Sat till 01.00)

Morrisons in Belfast, just like the famous sibling in Abbeyleix, is modelled on a Victorian grocer's shop. The provisions are not for sale, and the counter where food would have been sliced and weighed and served now acts as a servery for meals. Business people come here at lunchtime and after work, and in the evening all ages gather to enjoy the company and the traditional surroundings.

Vincents
78/80 Botanic Avenue
Tel: 028 90 434546 *Area/Zone: University area Queen's University*
Open: 09.00-23.00 (Sun from 10.00)

A smart modern venue with wooden-seated wrought-iron chairs set at light wooden tables, Vincents matches the mood of its setting in the cosmopolitan area south of the centre. In the morning good coffee and breakfast is served to business people or anyone wanting to relax with a newspaper, while the main choice of food ranges far and wide, from France to America and Morocco to Mexico.

Dublin

If Dublin was applying for the job of 'world city', then there'd be an awful lot of credits on the CV. Dublin does the lot. But within the skill-set of this thoroughly modern city, there are two things the capital does better than almost anywhere on earth, and those are beer and music. Wherever you go in the city, you get generous helpings of both. Whether you're in the shopping nirvana of Grafton Street, carousing with the in-crowd in Temple Bar, or searching for a little peace along the banks of the Liffey, you're never far from a tune and a pint. And when you've sipped a Guinness in a buzzing Dublin pub – and shouted over the din that it's the best beer you've ever tasted – that's when you've arrived in Ireland.

The Bridge Café Bar (Bewley)

10 Westmoreland Street *Area/Zone: City Centre near Trinity Coillege*
Tel: 1 670 8133
Open: 10.00-23.00 (Fri & Sat till 01.30, Sun from 12.00)
One of a chain of excellent, atmospheric cafés in Dublin and elsewhere in Ireland. This one features a modern interpretation of art nouveau, with a broad zinc bar top, tiled panels on the dark, polished wood counter, and behind the bar a large tiled panel of a peacock. The ceiling has three circular panels with relatively modern scenes and the fourth is a verrière of leaded coloured glass. The cafeteria, open from 07.30 till 18.00, is next door, and Bewley's also has Dublin outlets in Grafton Street and South Great George Street and a 70-bed hotel in Fleet Street. The Grafton Street Bewley's is a lovely three-storey 18th-century building with lofty ceilings and stained-glass windows.

Brogan's

75 Dame Street *Area/Zone: City Centre near Olympia Theatre*
Tel: 1 679 9570
Open: 10.30-23.00
Brogan's is a virtual museum to all things Guinness. Advertisements, toby jugs, mugs, glasses and a host of other artefacts bearing the Guinness name fill the place – and you can also get a very good glass of the real thing.

The Bruxelles

7 Harry Street *Area/Zone: City Centre near Grafton Street*
Tel: 1 677 5362
Open: 10.30-01.30 (Sat till 01.00)
Regular live jazz sessions keep things buzzing at the Bruxelles, which enjoys a prime location just off Grafton Street. The decor features an extraordinary example of early art nouveau ceramics by JB Rooke as well as etched mirrors and elegant cabinet work. Open for drinks 15 hours a day, it also offers traditional Irish food and a contemporary dinner menu.

Fitzers

51a Dawson Street *Area/Zone: City Centre off Grafton Street*
Tel: 1 677 1155
Open: 12.00-23.30
A bright, airy and very popular café-bar where eyecatching canopies on an impressive glass frontage are matched by equally striking interior decor that is softened in the evening by lamplight and candle-light. All types of beers and wines are on offer, alongside a varied modern menu that includes dishes from Japan, Italy and California, with particularly good salads and vegetarian dishes. Outside tables in summer. One of four Fitzers in Dublin: the others are in Temple Bar Square (1 679 0440), in the National Gallery Merrion Square (1 661 4496) and in the Royal Dublin Society building in Merrion Road (1 667 1301).

DUBLIN ROCKS

Ask anyone in the music business, and they'll tell you Dublin is the music capital of the world. The city rocks. Let us take you on a bricks-and-mortar tour of the soul of Dublin.

When U2 scored a global hit with their Joshua Tree album in 1987, Dublin suddenly became the world's hippest music centre. Over 15 years later, it still is. And for a country of barely three million people, Ireland has produced an avalanche of world-class entertainers: Enya, Sinéad O' Connor, Chris de Burgh, Boyzone, the Corrs, Pogues, Boomtown Rats, Cranberries, and Dubliners. At one time or another, they've all found themselves in Dublin…

BEWLEY'S ORIENTAL CAFÉ, 78 GRAFTON ST
A jewel of a coffee shop, Bewley's has been around forever and the menu helpfully lists the celebrities who have visited since the doors opened in 1927. One man they conspicuously fail to mention is local hero Bob Geldof (now Sir Bob) who sat in Bewley's to write the punk anthem '*Rat Trap*' – one of the Boomtown Rats' biggest hits.

THE DOCKERS, SIR JOHN ROGERSON'S QUAY
Out towards the less polished end of town, you can stop off for a lunchtime pint at The Dockers, U2's long-time favourite haunt. Sitting right next to the band's legendary studio, The Dockers still occasionally sees the boys heading here for a wind-down. U2, after all, are real local boys – forming the band in 1977 at a North Dublin school, and Bono naming himself after a hearing-aid shop in O'Connell St.

BAD ASS CAFÉ, CROWN ALLEY
Hard to believe, but the artist who scored a number one hit in 18 countries with 'Nothing Compares 2 U' was once a waitress in this café. Yes, none other than Sinéad O' Connor waited tables here before she was signed to Ensign Records at the tender age of 17.

O'DONOGHUE'S, 15 MERRION ROW
Wander the back-streets and you'll soon find a real Dublin treasure, O'Donoghue's. It was in the back bar of this smoky little drinking hole that folk-kings The Dubliners first met in 1962. Just a few foot-stomping years later, the band had notched up a global hit with their classic 'Seven Drunken Nights'.

MERCHANT'S ARCH, WELLINGTON QUAY
Trendy Temple Bar down by the Liffey isn't the bohemian place it was in the 70s when Thin Lizzy used to meet up here. Boys from north of the river, Lizzy drew on the hip, alternative mood of Temple Bar to develop their unique blend of rock, heavy metal and folk – delivered to audiences worldwide with typical Dublin verve.

THE GRESHAM HOTEL, O'CONNELL ST
If you make your way over the Ha'penny Bridge, you'll come across Dublin's most famous hotel, The Gresham. Already secure in the 'Rock & Roll Hall of Fame' as the only Irish venue The Beatles ever played at (the Fab Four jammed in their suite), The Gresham is also the place where folk purists The Chieftains agreed their line-up. Order a pint, and drink in the history.

Café Java
5 South Anne Street *Area/Zone: City Centre off Grafton Street*
Tel: 1 670 7239
Open: 07.45-18.00 (Sat from 09.00, Sun from 11.00)
A stylish modern café on two levels serving good coffee, sandwiches and excellent salads. It's very popular during the day and you might even have a short wait for a table (outside in summer).

La Med
22 East Essex Street *Area/Zone: Temple Bar*
Tel: 1 670 7358
Open: 11.00-23.00 (Fri & Sat till 24.00, Sun till 17.00)
Closed: Mon
Café, restaurant and jazz bar with French owners, a French feel and a French influence in the food and drinks. La Med opens on to East Essex Street in the heart of Temple Bar, Dublin's Left Bank, and runs through to the quays overlooking the Liffey.

Kaffé Moka
39 South William Street
Tel: 1 679 8475
Open: 07.30-04.00 *Area/Zone: City Centre near Stephen's Green*
A popular and very friendly coffee house on three floors, where customers can linger with a newspaper or a book from the upstairs library, or enjoy a game of chess, draughts or even snakes & ladders. You can choose your coffee from the house blend, Java, Columbia, Kenya or Costa Rica and they'll make up a bag of beans (whole or ground) for you to take away. They also have an impressive range of teas and infusions, and they make first-rate sandwiches. Regular events include poetry nights, tarot readings and live music. Another Kaffé Moka is on Lower Rathmines Road, a brisk walk or a short bus ride from the city centre.

The Old Stand
37 Exchequer Street *Area/Zone: South City Centre next to Tourist Board*
Tel: 1 677 7220
Open: 11.00-23.00
A comfortable, traditional sporting pub in the heart of town close to the tourist office. Centuries old (its licence was *renewed* in the reign of Charles II in 1659!), it serves coffee in the old-fashioned way, in a pot on a tray, or you can choose from a wide range of beers and stouts. Very good straightforward food (steaks a speciality) is served from 12.30 till 21.15 (till 20.15 on Saturday). The tourists are particularly keen on the Old Stand's Irish stew. Sister establishment, in Duke Street, is Davy Byrnes, immortalised in James Joyce's Ulysses.

The Oliver St John Gogarty
58-59 Fleet Street *Area/Zone: Temple Bar*
Tel: 1 671 1822/1595/1683
Open: 10.00-23.00 (Left Bank bar till 01.30)
Named in memory of a distinguished surgeon, poet and politician, this long established bar-restaurant, loved equally by locals and tourists, also operates as a hotel, with 30 bedrooms and 6 penthouse rooms. Live Irish music is performed every afternoon and evening in the low-beamed main bar, and the Left Bank bar stays open late every night with a DJ till 01.30. Traditional Irish cuisine is served in the 95-cover restaurant.

The Palace
21 Fleet Street *Area/Zone: Temple Bar*
Tel: 1 677 9290
Open: 10.30-23.00 (closed on Sunday between 14.00 & 16.00)
Established in 1828 and associated down the years with Irish writers including James Joyce, Brendan Behan and Patrick Kavanagh, the Palace retains its period decor and well-preserved frontage. Very friendly staff, who know all the local gossip and the history of this 'Left Bank' area of Dublin, will serve you a filter coffee or something stronger, which you can take to the comfortable parlour at the far end.

The Temple Bar
47-48 Temple Bar *Area/Zone: Temple Bar*
Tel: 1 672 5286
Open: 10.30-23.00 (Thur & Sun till 24.00, Fri & Sat till 00.30)
A long-established and well-loved café with seats for 200 and walls cluttered with prints, pictures and photographs which testify to its long standing. The place is always busy, really buzzing in the evenings and at weekends. Live Irish music on Sundays. Just sandwiches for snacks.

Thing Mote
15 Suffolk Street *Area/Zone: City Centre bottom of Grafton Street*
Tel: 1 677 8030
Open: 10.30-23.00
The name means Assembly Mount in a corruption of the language of the Norsemen who left their stamp on Dublin a thousand years ago. Mainly a bar, Thing Mote is very popular with the students from Trinity College next door, and the warmest and friendliest of Irish welcomes greets every visitor. Light eats include sandwiches, rolls and home-made soup.

Thomas Read
4 Parliament Street
Tel: 1 671 7283 *Area/Zone: City Centre opposite City Hall*
Open: 10.30-23.00 (Thur, Fri & Sat till 01.30)
Opposite the entrance to Dublin Castle, Thomas Read enjoys a prime people-watching corner site with tall windows, awnings, double doors, a lofty ceiling supported by two columns, globe lights, round tables and bentwood chairs – this could almost be a Paris pavement café. It's always busy, especially at weekends, with customers of all age joining in the fun. Excellent coffee, light snacks and a wide range of beers.

Trastevere
Unit 1, Temple Bar Square *Area/Zone: Temple Bar*
Tel: 1 670 8343
Open: 12.00-23.00 (Fri & Sat till 23.30)
A taste of Italy in Dublin. Trastevere (the name means 'across the Tiber' and is a lively district of Rome), occupying a corner site in the handsomely rebuilt square, is chic and modern, and tall windows let you watch life pass by while enjoying a drink or a snack. That life might easily include street theatre or a music procession, for this part of the city is a designated cultural area. Italian dishes share the menu with home-grown classics.